Human Rights Defenders and the Law

This book presents a comprehensive examination of the Declaration on Human Rights Defenders and provides an analysis of the level of its reflection in regional human rights systems.

The work explores the development of the role of the individual in human rights protection since the 1998 United Nations Declaration on Human Rights Defenders. It locates the nature, activities and need for protection of human rights defenders within the current international legal framework and outlines the place and scope for a specific right to promote and protect human rights. It traces the origins of the right and the main international instruments that define it, both at national and international level. Finally, it considers the impact that the right to defend human rights can have on constitutional and international law.

The book will be a valuable resource for academics and researchers working in the areas of International Human Rights Law and Constitutional Law.

Núria Saura-Freixes is an independent jurist and researcher based in Brussels. She has worked as a Lecturer in Constitutional Law and Freedom of Expression at the Autonomous University of Barcelona, and has been a Visiting Scholar at the Max Planck Institute for Comparative Public Law and International Law, as well as at other relevant centres of research.

Routledge Research in Constitutional Law

This series features thought-provoking and original scholarship on constitutional law and theory. Books explore key topics, themes and questions in the field with a particular emphasis on comparative studies. Where relevant, titles will engage with political and social theory, philosophy and history in order to offer a rounded analysis of constitutions and constitutional law. Series Editor: David Marrani

Available titles in this series include:

Diversity of Law in the United Arab Emirates
Privacy, Security and the Legal System
Kristin Kamøy

Sovereignty, Civic Participation, and Constitutional Law
The People versus the Nation in Belgium
Edited by Brecht Deseure, Raf Geenens and Stefan Sottiaux

Law and the Philosophy of Language
The Ordinariness of Law
Pascal Richard

Human Rights Defenders and the Law
A Constitutional and International Legal Approach
Núria Saura-Freixes

Law, Localism and the Constitution
A Comparative Perspective
John Stanton

For more information about this series, please visit:
www.routledge.com/Routledge-Research-in-Constitutional-Law/book-series/CONSTLAW

Human Rights Defenders and the Law

A Constitutional and International Legal Approach

Núria Saura-Freixes

LONDON AND NEW YORK

First published 2023
by Routledge
4 Park Square, Milton Park, Abingdon, Oxon OX14 4RN

and by Routledge
605 Third Avenue, New York, NY 10158

Routledge is an imprint of the Taylor & Francis Group, an informa business

© 2023 Núria Saura-Freixes

The right of Núria Saura-Freixes to be identified as author of this work has been asserted in accordance with sections 77 and 78 of the Copyright, Designs and Patents Act 1988.

All rights reserved. No part of this book may be reprinted or reproduced or utilised in any form or by any electronic, mechanical, or other means, now known or hereafter invented, including photocopying and recording, or in any information storage or retrieval system, without permission in writing from the publishers.

Trademark notice: Product or corporate names may be trademarks or registered trademarks, and are used only for identification and explanation without intent to infringe.

British Library Cataloguing-in-Publication Data
A catalogue record for this book is available from the British Library

Library of Congress Cataloging-in-Publication Data
A catalog record has been requested for this book

ISBN: 978-0-367-20899-8 (hbk)
ISBN: 978-1-032-42870-3 (pbk)
ISBN: 978-0-429-26401-6 (ebk)

DOI: 10.4324/9780429264016

Typeset in Galliard
by Taylor & Francis Books

Contents

Acknowledgements		vi
List of acronyms		vii
1	Human rights defenders and the UN legal framework: Synergies on multilevel and global constitutionalism	1
2	The UN Special Procedure on the situation of human rights defenders: A multilevel and global framework and the paradigm on human condition	24
3	Human rights defenders and the right to promote and protect human rights	49
4	Human rights defenders: Concept, subject, limits, and challenges	71
5	Human rights defenders: The intellectual dimension of individuals and collectives	96
6	The right to promote and protect human rights	126
7	Instrumental rights for the promotion and protection of human rights	147
8	Human rights defenders: The European multilevel framework	179
9	Human rights defenders and the European Union	199
	Index	221

Acknowledgements

This book was written from my research stays as Postdoc Visiting Scholar of the Max Planck Institute for Comparative Public Law and International Law in Heidelberg. I would like to thank you for the discussion, the debates, and readings at the library that contributed to write my book. In particular, I would like to thank the other guests with whom I spent hours talking on contemporary law issues.

While writing this book, I attended the PhD Kolloquium in the Goethe University Frankfurt, where I could profit of the philosophical discussing that widened my perspectives. Thank you too for this opportunity.

Thanks to Professor Dr. Yolanda Gómez for her support as thesis director of my previous PhD thesis, Professor Dr David Marrani for his theoretical comments during my research, and Professor Dr Elina Steinerte for her support, as well as to the research stays at the University of London IALS Library, Institute of Law Jersey, and at the School of Law, University of Essex.

Finally, I would like to mention María Aragón and Derek JG Williams, for their readings, comments, and linguistic support.

List of acronyms

AAC	Academic Assistance Council
ACHPR	African Commission on Human and Peoples' Rights
ACHR	American Convention on Human Rights
AFSJ	Area on freedom, security and justice
ASEAN	Association of Southeast Asian Nations
AU	African Union
CARA	Council for Assisting Refugee Academics
CERD	Committee on Elimination of Racial Discrimination
CEPAL	Comisión Económica para América Latina y el Caribe
CJEU	Court of Justice of the European Union
COE	Council of Europe
CPR	Civil and Political rights
CSCE	Conference on Security and Cooperation in Europe
CSFP	Common Security and Foreign Policy
DHRD	Declaration on human rights defenders
ECLAC	Economic Commission for Latin America and the Caribbean
EEEAS	European External Action Service
EU	European Union
EP	European Parliament
ECFR	European Charter of Fundamental Rights
ECHR	European Convention of Human Rights
ECtHR	European Court of Human Rights
ECtSR	European Committee of Social Rights
EIDHR	European Instrument Democracy and Human Rights
ECOSOC	Economic and Social Council
ESCR	Economic, social, and cultural rights
ETUC	European Trade Union Confederation
FRA	Fundamental Rights Agency of the European Union
GANHRI	Global Alliance of National Human Rights Institutions
GlobCon	Global Constitutionalism
HRC	Human Rights Council
HRDs	Human rights defenders
IACHR	Inter-American Court of Human Rights

viii *List of acronyms*

ICJ	International Commission of Jurists
ICC	International Criminal Court
ICCPR	International Covenant Civil and Political Rights
ICESCR	International Covenant on Economic, Social and Cultural Rights
IHL	International Humanitarian Law
INGOs	International Non-Governmental Organizations
LGBT	Lesbian, gay, bisexual and transgender
NGOs	Non-Governmental Organizations
NHRI	National institutions on human rights
NPM	National Preventive Mechanisms
NMT	Nuremberg Military Tribunals
OIE	International Organisation of Employers
OAS	Organization of American States
OAU	Organization of African Unity
ODIHR	Office for Democratic Institutions and Human Rights
OHCHR	Office of the High Commissioner for Human Rights
OPCAT	Optional Protocol to the Convention against Torture and Other Cruel, Inhuman or Degrading Treatment or Punishment
OSCE	Organization for Security and Co-operation in Europe
SPT	Subcommittee on Prevention of Torture and other Cruel, Inhuman or Degrading Treatment
SR on human rights defenders	Special Rapporteur on the situation of human rights defenders
RTLM	Radio-Télévision Libre des Mille Collines
TEU	Treaty on European Union
TFEU	Treaty on the Functioning of the European Union
UK	United Kingdom
UN	United Nations
UNGA	United Nations General Assembly
UNESCO	United Nations Educational, Scientific and Cultural Organization
UDHR	Universal Declaration of Human Rights
UNECE	United Nations Economic Commission for Europe
UNEP	United Nations Environment Programme
UNESCO	United Nations Educational, Scientific and Cultural Organization
US	United States of America

1 Human rights defenders and the UN legal framework

Synergies on multilevel and global constitutionalism

The paradigm of the state-nation is being broken by globalization, new actors are emerging, as well as new synergies between international and constitutional law. Hence, the classic paradigm of multilateral international law is experiencing tension as a result of these new trends in global constitutionalism (Lang et al., 2017). But I mainly utilize a multilevel analysis of the human rights defenders' legal framework considering the human rights defenders' regime at different levels: the United Nations, the Council of Europe (particularly the case law of the European Court of Human Rights), the Inter-American system of Human Rights, the African Union, and finally, the European Union system of human rights defenders (from now on, HRDs) *ad intra* and *ad extra*. Consequent to this multilevel analysis there are conclusions on human rights defenders that are closer to the changing paradigm of law, related not only to the multilevel system but also to global constitutionalism. But let us first frame global and multilevel constitutionalism. According to Peters, the concept of global constitutionalism can be described as follows:

> Global constitutionalism comprises different strands of thought most of which read (or reconstruct) some features of the status quo of global law and governance as "constitutional" and even "constitutionalist" (positive analysis) and which also seek to provide arguments for their further development in a specific direction (normative analysis). (Peters, 2015, p. 1)

Constitutionalism consists of key concepts, such as the "rule of law, a separation of powers, fundamental rights protection, democracy, and solidarity, together with institutions and mechanisms securing and implementing these principles" (Peters, 2015, p. 1). Hence, these parameters are not only necessary to individuals, but from an Aristotelian or Arendtian perspective, to the relationships among individuals and the state. If the previous paradigm of the individual's relationship with the state was built under a statist framework of citizenship and even nationality, globalization is gradually eroding that framework.

The framework of the state-nation is not valid enough to be transferred to supranational or international experiences of constitutionalism. After globalization, the nation cannot be the unique source of legitimacy for the state.

DOI: 10.4324/9780429264016-1

The Arendt's theory (1951) on "the right to have rights" is built under the Aristotelian influence. But "the right to have rights" is twofold: there is a right to have rights stemming from the human condition, and this universal right requires a framework for the exercise of these rights that is not necessarily from the state. The right to have rights is an open door, even a horizon, but it is only possible if the exercise of these rights does not depend on citizenship and sovereignty. It must instead depend on the human condition and constitutional jurisdiction, since the constitutional function is carried out by the state, or by other international actors that can provide global or regional answers to global or regional troubles.

Enlarging constitutionalism also enlarges citizenship to the global community of rights. Habermas, according to Peters (2015), recalls the Kantian concept of "cosmopolitan status", in order "to demand an international transformation of international law into a law of and for the global citizen" (Habermas 2006, cit. in Peters 2015, p. 14). This cosmopolitan status is closer to the status of human rights defenders' than it is to the citizen status.

Peters reminds us that these parameters in global constitutionalism are necessary "to inspire strategies for the improvement of the legitimacy of an international legal order and institutions without asking for a world state" (Peters, 2015, p. 1). Constitutionalism is more considered a public function of legitimacy in international global order, than a statist parameter overlapping with international law. However, in the case of human rights defenders it would be daring to affirm that a global constitution is currently enforced, because there is only a "protoconstitution" (Habermas, 2006, p. 141) extending from the United Nations Charter and the human rights treaty obligations of each state as parameters for consistency in domestic law. This is a process of constitutional control, that in this case, is a horizon of constitutionality. However, who could control the consistency of domestic law with the UN Charter and human rights treaties? To give the function of constitutional control only to individuals is risky, it could leave the door open to arbitrary decisions. Hence, here, a *jurisdiction* is required, but not only with the state. This is also controversial. The answer could be found in the need for a function of constitutional control enabled in international jurisdiction, but with better knowledge of the constitutional background than in some recent European and international court decisions.

It is particularly interesting that human rights defenders possess the dual designation both as passive and active subjects of human rights in international and constitutional law. Individuals are recognized not merely as holders of human rights, but as key stakeholders to promote and protect human rights. This recognition of the right to promote and protect human rights exists, not only from the ethical perspective, but from a legal perspective as well. This is why this book is built using a multilevel legal method of analysis, and it concludes with a theoretical perspective related to global constitutionalism. Multilevel constitutionalism is still a valid method of analysis to identify trends and synergies between international and constitutional law:

> A related concept is that of "multilevel constitutionalism" (Cottier and Hertig 2003, pp. 299–301). Here, the idea is that all layers of governance should be

considered, as a whole, as one overall constitutional system, and that constitutionalism should focus on how the constitutional functions can be secured. (Peters, 2015, p. 2)

The human rights defenders' framework emerged after the creation of the Special Representative role in the United Nations in 2000, leading to an irradiation effect, thus giving birth to a multilevel system of protection (Bennet et al., 2016).

But there is still a divergence between multilevel constitutionalism and multilevel governance (Marrani, 2012, p. 34). Some of the latest EU trends are unfortunate examples:

> The problem of a global space—the European Union (EU) and European integration being one example—is therefore fundamental to the problem of multilevel governance, of pluralism, and particularly, of legal pluralism; hence, the consideration given here to the point of interconnection. The first observation that can be made is that one individual may come to understand our world in a different way to another individual. To be more specific, one individual may perceive the world as a series of nation-states while others may not. (Marrani, 2012, p. 34)

Self-identity and personhood, however, are not exactly the same. Self-identification as human rights defenders is not the main issue with regard to their personhood. The right to promote and to protect human rights is a universal right, and it is the action of exercise, that builds personhood, but this does not occur automatically.

According to Policastro, the emergence of human rights defenders is parallel to the breakdown of the state-nation: "The transformations that are occurring to the world political order are leading to the fact that the nation state is no more the basic and undisputed subject of political relations" (Policastro, 2004, p. 9).

Human rights defenders assume the promotion and protection of human rights if the state is inactive. Due to the displacement of the state paradigm, the individual paradigm has become more prevalent. Individuals are increasingly recognized as new subjects of international law (Peters, 2016). This also has consequences for constitutional law, particularly in the case of human rights defenders. But, as Gavara de Cara reminds us, it does not mean to imply and to attribute positive obligations to individuals, or to consider individuals a substitute for public action. To attribute positive obligations to individuals is to call into question the legitimacy of the state public authorities (Gavara de Cara, 2007, pp. 277–278), and even the framework of international treaties.

In the domain of international law, there has been since 1998 a strong development of different legal levels converging on human rights defenders. Bennet reminds us that the adoption of the 1998 Declaration on human rights defenders "marked a 'milestone' in the development of a multilevel, multi-actor international protection regime for the rights of human rights defenders" (Bennet et al., 2015, p. 883).

The established multilevel system has not been analyzed enough with respect to a global perspective, and there are situations of overlap with other legal systems, such as the right to asylum (Jones, 2015). Both systems, asylum and human rights defenders, come from the breakdown of the state-nation obligations on human rights; what Jones considers the "shared recognition of the failure of states to fulfil their human rights obligations" (Jones, 2015, p. 947). The international community is failing to protect human rights defenders (Jones, 2015) despite the proliferation of normative levels. There are many human rights defenders who lack domestic remedies to face the risks, threats, and dangers their actions of human rights have produced (Jones, 2015). They require an international level of protection, like asylum or protection for human rights defenders. The coexistence of these twofold levels of protection for defenders is not very well-known, and most defenders are not aware of them (Jones, 2015). Consequently, there are cases in which human rights defenders are at risk that being not dealt through the asylum with system:

> Very little attention has been paid to the intersection of the protection of human rights defenders with other regimes of protection, including the international refugee regime. The isolation of the two regimes is mutually constructed: the refugee regime seldom acknowledges the nature and situation of human rights defenders and actors in the protection regime for human rights defenders at risk have been reticent to acknowledge refugee protection as an avenue of protection. (Jones, 2015, p. 938)

In my opinion, this twofold regime is not incompatible because dangerous situations exist that demand an urgent relocation of the human rights defenders who are at risk. In this case, the human rights defenders can give an urgent answer; the refugee system is a long-term answer. Jones considers the difficulty of obtaining a visa to be the main obstacle for relocation for defenders. This is an issue that the asylum system can solve (Jones, 2015). Hence, it would be better to have a global approach to avoid unnecessary overlap of legal systems and a better knowledge of them. For instance, in the case of the European Union, there can be many different legal levels of overlap for defenders on third countries at risk: such as the international system of asylum, the EU asylum system, the UN defenders' protection, the EU system of defenders' protection set in the European Union External Action, and the national and local initiatives on defenders. It would be better for the EU to have a global perspective on defenders' that is closer to a constitutional approach, or to develop a system of coexistence between different legal systems and levels, like the clause for the most elevated standard of protection.

EU citizenship is an attempt to create a common legal framework that is not merely based on the nationality of a particular state. However, EU citizenship and the EU system of fundamental rights are interconnected, while the framework of the EU system of rights is broader. In the EU this leads to a conception of fundamental rights protection in a multilevel legal framework (Freixes, 2015).

Globalization has reinforced international law, bilateral and multilateral, European integration, and it has also resulted in processes of reallocating competences in infra-state bodies. Consequently, when studying the impact of policies has on citizens, it is necessary to consider not only the classical legal framework of the nation-state (Saura-Freixes, 2015). It is necessary to bear in mind the other legal levels, depending on the international and regional dimensions of the issue, and on the legal integration resulting from these processes (Saura-Freixes, 2015, p. 35). Theoretically, it is necessary to point out the trend and consider that all the main rules regulating these relationships are fulfilling a constitutional function (Peters, 2015), even though they are not a formal constitution.

From this perspective, multilevel constitutionalism leads to an analysis of the connections between legal systems that cannot be forgotten. For instance, the Treaty on European Union refers to the 1951 Geneva Refugee Convention for the determination of their rights (Saura-Freixes, 2015, p. 36). This connection, as Marrani (2012) indicates, is also present in the doubled movement from transnational and international rights to national ones. This movement is notably explicit in the constitutionalisation of environmental rights through the enshrinement of the Charter for the Environment adopted in 2004 by the French National Assembly in the Constitution of the French Fifth Republic in 2005 (Marrani, 2015).

In summary, it leads to a legal debate, as Gómez Sánchez states, where there is a divergence with the state monopoly as the unique constitutional space (Gómez Sánchez, 2020, p. 46). In this multilevel legal framework, there are international and supranational organizations that are sources of law, but individuals are also subjects of rights and duties, not mere objects of international law. This change in the notion of the individual in international law concerns a functional constitutional dimension of the contemporary international law of human rights.

Furthermore, Dupuy points out that state sovereignty has evolved so that today it is not only a goal but a medium (Dupuy, 2004, p. 751). This change in the philosophy of international law has changed the logic of the constitutional state. According to Dupuy, the relationship between those governing and those being governed has evolved toward the respect of ruled rights, not only as citizens, but also as human beings (Dupuy, 2004, p. 751). This change can be considered a trend due to the changing paradigm of the Second World War, which was based on human dignity, with the paradigm after globalization, which is based on the human condition, with the result of this humanism in law theorized by Peters too (2016, 2019).

After globalization, the international civil society is going further than states. According to Dupuy, NGOs and transnational movements of action and opinion would not only be a social reality, but a "politic myth", potentially rallying people (Dupuy, 2004), thus, creating a challenge to the state and international community.

Human rights defenders have an axiological value that is not based in constituent power, nor the right to self-determination, nor the will of people, but the will of the human condition to strive for the protection and promotion of human rights, whether the human being decides to exercise it or not. The action of the human being is what constitutes the human condition and personhood according to the 1998 Declaration on human rights defenders.

Human beings need to exercise their instrumental rights to promote and protect human rights because they have a need to develop their life according to their will, not to the will of the state or other abstract entities, such as people or nations, after globalization. Individuals as human beings possess the right to exercise or not to exercise these rights under universal personhood, which is based on the human condition. This is related to the "The right to have rights" theorized by Arendt (1951), and behind it there is the Aristotelian conception of the human being as an individual that is a political, non-ideological-being. Hence, to become individuals, human beings need law. This old conception, developed by Arendt, is not then only European; the individual is not an isolated being anymore.

This thought is far from the privatization of law. But it could be a danger for us not to consider the public category from Aristotle's Politics: *zoón politikón*. The need for law is the need of the individual, and of the other individuals: the social need to become a human being. This need is political, as it is the individual's nature. This conception is present in Arendt too. It leads to a political and legal subject coincident with the human condition. Universal personhood is based on the human condition. But the right to strive for the promotion and protection of human rights and the individual status of "human rights defender" is based on the exercise of this right (according to the criteria and regime from the Declaration on human rights defenders). Finally, the conception of the "political animal" is not to be confused with the "ideological" side of politics, or even for Arendt in *The Human Condition*, the mere "social animal" (Arendt, 2018) The place of human being is the *polis*. What is forgotten during the decades that follow, secondary to the term politics is the Aristotelian aphorism, the first term: "animal". Currently it makes sense to remember it: the human condition is natural, threatened by nature but at the same time dependent on it. It is necessary to consider that the human being is not an isolated being that is only interrelated with other human beings, but also with the other "beings". Only if it is interrelated with the other beings and not isolated from them, then the human being can preserve its human condition, even under climate change and other threats such as pandemics.

This threefold binomial convergence in human rights defenders is composed of individual exercise of rights, status by human condition, and universal personhood. It does not mean the subordination of the individual to the community, or the necessary imposition of a western paradigm. This flexibility in the exercise of rights becomes necessary when the particularities are present in any human being exercising rights, not considered an abstract being. But then, in this global world if the focus is only on the rights' exercise, it can, paradoxically, be a way toward freedom and equality, or a dangerous path to inequality and oppression. In this it is useful to remember the outrageous constitutional doctrine in the United States (US) that justified racial discrimination in the term "Separate but equal" (*Plessy v. Fergusson*, 1896, US Supreme Court).

Regional human rights systems exist in all the world, such as the Inter-American and the African system of human rights, with, maybe, the exception of the Asian regions, which are complicated by the position of China and other actors. However, the distinction between economic, social, and cultural rights (ESCR), and civil and political rights (CPR) is still problematic. What can become more or less complicated, in all the areas of the world, is "how" to exercise both rights: CPR and ESCR.

The right to promote and to protect human rights depends on those mainly responsible for complying with the rights: the state. The state paradigm is broken due to globalization. The relationship between the individual and state supports human rights defenders as a legal subject. The right to freedom of expression is considered an individual right with a social function, both in the European Convention on Human Rights (ECHR), (*Soulas et autres v. France,* 10 July 2008), and in the Inter-American system. In the African Union's system, the duties set in the African Charter do not literally point to the hierarchy or sacrifice of an individual for a community, as is sometimes posited, but according to Diagne (2009), in their correlative interaction: "The question that now must be posed: Must an African philosophy of what it means to be human and, as such, to have rights be caught up in a communitarian approach? The response is clear: Absolutely not" (Diagne, 2009, p. 12). In order to clarify this concept, Diagne provides the following example: even in the oldest document on human rights existing in Africa, The Manden Charter, the individual is never subordinate to the community, but is reciprocally part of it, thus the individual's will is recognized. According to UNESCO, The Manden Charter is one of the first constitutions in the world, and it is part of the UNESCO Intangible Cultural Heritage, which has been transmitted through the ages. This charter was adopted in Mali in the 13th century, its provisions were based on the will of individuals and social peace. Its approach is closer to the twenty-first century paradigm of rights based on the human condition:

> The hunters declare
> That every life is a life; It is true that some have come into existence before others,
> But no life is older [or more worthy of respect] than another,
> And no life is superior to another.
> ....
> Consequently, the Hunters declare:
> From now on everyone shall enjoy self-determination,
> Everyone shall be free in their actions,
> Everyone shall dispose of the fruits of their labor.
>
> This is the Oath of the Manden for the rest of the world to hear (Mandé Charter, 622) (Neocosmos, 2016).

This conception of reciprocal, individual, free will as a social need (and not subordinate) to other individuals was also apparent in the social movements of anti-apartheid. Mandela used the traditional "Ubuntu" philosophy, in which the individual socially interacts reciprocally in solidarity with the other individuals. "Ubuntu" is being usually summarized as "I am because you are" (Ngomane and Tutu, 2020).

The Declaration on human rights defenders (1998) acknowledges this important work of individuals, groups, and associations in its Preamble:

> Acknowledging the important role of international cooperation for, and the valuable work of individuals, groups and associations in contributing to, the effective elimination of all violations of human rights and fundamental freedoms of peoples and individuals, including in relation to mass, flagrant or systematic violations such as those resulting from apartheid, all forms of racial discrimination, colonialism, foreign domination or occupation, aggression or threats to national sovereignty, national unity or territorial integrity and from the refusal to recognize the right of peoples to self-determination and the right of every people to exercise full sovereignty over its wealth and natural resources. (Declaration on human rights defenders, 1998)

These notions are at the heart of the Declaration on human rights defenders. They are the result of lengthy years of debates and discussion in the "United Nations Working Group on a Draft declaration on the right and responsibility of individuals, groups and organs of society to promote and protect universally recognized human rights and fundamental freedoms".

The UN Working Group on the draft of a declaration for human rights defenders (1985–1998)

The Declaration on the Right and Responsibility of Individuals, Groups, and Organs of Society to Promote and Protect Universally Recognized Human Rights and Fundamental Freedoms, otherwise known as the "Declaration on human rights defenders" (DHRD), was established by the UN General Assembly in 1998 after years of debates to achieve a consensus in the UN Working Group to draft a Declaration on human rights defenders.

According to Hodgson, on 6 March 1984, the former UN Human Rights Commission on Human Rights decided to create an open-ended Working Group to draft the Declaration on human rights defenders (Hodgson, 2003). The Declaration, often referred to as the "Declaration on human rights defenders" (DHRD), was written over a 13-year period which began in 1984 when the UN Commission decided to establish this open-ended working group to draft an instrument on human rights defenders (UN Secretary General, 2000, para. 3). The original decision to create a UN Working Group to draft the Declaration on human rights defenders occurred in the Commission on Human Rights Decision 1984/116, from 16 March 1984.

There was a precedent of the DHRD 1998 in the previous "United Nations Sub-Commission on the Prevention of Discrimination and Protection of Minorities". The Sub-Commission authorized one of their members, Erica-Irene Daes, to study the duties of the individual and the community, according to art. 29 of the UDHR. After finishing the study in 1980, Erica-Irene Daes, Special Rapporteur, being the author of this study, recommended the UN General Assembly to "prepare and adopt a declaration on the principles governing the responsibilities of the individual in connection with the promotion and observance of human rights" (United Nations, Department of Public Information, 1984, p. 218).

In 1982, Erica-Irene Daes was ordered to create of a "draft body of principles of the right and responsibility of individuals, groups and organs of society to promote and protect universally recognized human rights and fundamental freedoms". In 1983, the Sub-Commission received this "draft body of principles" and it indicated that a final report should follow in 1984. One year later, in 1985, this Working Group was created by the Commission on Human Rights by Decision 1985/112, 14 March 1985 (UNCHR, 2001). They had their first session from 27th to 30th January, and later from 7 to 12 March 1986. However, they could not foresee how long it would take to arrive at the necessary consensus about the Declaration on human rights defenders, which did not happen until 1998.

During the 13-year interim, tension emerged in the working group about the relationship between the individual and the state. The tension was due to the world's division into two blocs. There was a division between civil and political rights, which were closer to the Western Bloc, and economic, social, and cultural rights closer to the Soviet Bloc (McChesney and Rodley, 1992, pp. 49–55). Due to this clear division, the UN Working Group was under constant pressure during Cold War. This tension was present in the setting of the two different Covenants in 1966, instead of a unique global treaty on human rights. But in 1993, during the World Conference on Human Rights, 14 to 25 June 1993, Vienna, Austria, it was possible to set human rights as interrelated and interdependent in law:

a   Individuals are holders of human rights and "is the duty of States, regardless of their political, economic and cultural systems, to promote and protect all human rights and fundamental freedoms" (Vienna Declaration and Programme of Action, 1993).
b   Human rights are interdependent, indivisible and interrelated (Vienna Declaration and Programme of Action 1993, para. 5).
c   Democracy and human rights are interdependent (Vienna Declaration and Programme of Action 1993, para. 8).
d   Constitutionalization of the Charter of United Nations, other instruments of human rights, and International Law, with special relevance of International Humanitarian Law. (Vienna Declaration and Programme of Action, 1993)

Once the Cold War ended, the Declaration on human rights defenders was set up. The criteria for becoming a human rights defender were granting the interdependence, indivisibility, and interrelationship between civil, political, economic, social, and cultural rights. This was at least a positive conclusion following the trends in international law that emanated from international politics in the Cold War. The DHRD was built with the following twofold system: the duty to promote and protect human rights is the responsibility of the state, and the responsibility is on individuals. This individual's responsibility does not mean that individuals have the legal duty to promote and protect human rights. This is still a constitutional function for states, and a right for individuals. Then, they can choose if they will exercise this right or not. Hence, the theory on Compensatory Constitutionalism, theorized by Peters (2015, 2017) applies, unfortunately, to human rights defenders. Compensatory Constitutionalism emerges after the breakdown of the state-constitutional paradigm. This breakdown is dangerous for democracy, the rule of law, and fundamental rights. But if the state cannot behave and undertake their constitutional function, someone must do it. However, individuals as human rights defenders are not the answer. I agree with this position in order to compensate for the lack of constitutional enforcement; but Compensatory Constitutionalism cannot secure the weight of the constitutional function in the state, only in individuals.

When individuals must promote and protect human rights, not according to their will but only for necessity, troubles arise. When the state is not able, does not want to protect and promote human rights, or is the main responsible of human rights violations, in such cases, individuals must cope with the strong responsibility to protect and to strive for human rights, being thus, an obligation or a need for survival.

The UN Working Group on the Declaration of human rights defenders was open to all the members of the UN Commission on human rights. Even the other states could participate as observers. This was the case with Canada, who took a leading role during the first steps of the discussion. There were also other actors, such as international NGOs, who played a crucial role to ensure that human rights promotion was not "undermined in the final stages of negotiation by governments wishing to limit severely the work of human rights defenders" (Wiseberg, 2003, pp. 354–355). NGOs had a critical role in the debates that took place in the UN Working Group, and in the formation of the Declaration on human rights defenders:

> By regularly attending the meetings of the working group, NGOs had the chance and the duty to prove their interest in the ongoing proceedings. And indeed, although NGOs officially attended the meetings of the working group only as observers, certain NGOs have been active participants. The main NGO input, especially during the first couple of years, came from long-established international NGOs, such as the International League for Human Rights, the International Commission of Jurists and Amnesty International.
> (Schwitter Marsiaj, 2004, p. 5)

In 1992, the UN Working Group to draft the Declaration on human rights defenders had their first reading. However, it was necessary to wait until 1998 to be set up. There was tension in this early stage of debate between states who wanted to improve human rights for human rights defenders, and those who wanted to introduce more duties for individuals and groups. In this scenario, the most reluctant states were China, India, Cuba, and the Philippines (Wiseberg, 1991, p. 5).

The mandate of this UN Working Group was not to introduce or to create new human rights, but to define and reinforce the most relevant human rights for the protection of human rights defenders (UN, 13 March 1986). This is why the Declaration on human rights defenders later established the primary right to promote and protect human rights. Under the umbrella of this capital right there are several instrumental human rights necessary to exercise it. These include the right to freedom of expression, the right to access and communicate with international bodies, the right to protest, and the right for protection. It is important to point out that the right to promote and protect human rights is valid in the DHRD for: universally recognized human rights and fundamental freedoms. This framework differs slightly for other rights. The legal framework set by the DHRD has a subtle difference in the instance of emergent rights. Emergent rights do not fall under the umbrella of the right to promote and protect human rights, but under another right that is equally instrumental: "The right to develop and discuss new human rights ideas" (article 7 DHRD). The DHRD outlines this right in article 7: "Everyone has the right, individually and in association with others, to develop and discuss new human rights ideas and principles and to advocate their acceptance".

In summary, the initial tension inside the UN Working Group was solved by establishing human rights such as freedom of association and freedom of expression, while setting new, specific human rights for defenders, like the right to access funding (art. 13), the right to protest (art. 5, art. 6), or the right to access and communicate with international bodies (art. 5.c, art. 9.4). These human rights, both new and established, are built as instrumental legal guarantees to the main right to promote and protect human rights. This is the position followed by the UN Comment regarding the Declaration on human rights defenders (UN SRHRD, 2011).

According to Nigel Rodley, the observer from the Amnesty International Delegation, NGOs agreed with this position (1992). The main activity of the UN Working Group "was not to seek to set forth new rights but to elaborate existing rights which states are already obliged to implement" (McChesney and Rodley, 1992, p. 50). Finally, 50 years after the Declaration on human rights, the General Assembly of the United Nations approved by consensus the Declaration on the Right and Responsibility of Individuals, Groups and Organs of Society to Promote and Protect Universally Recognized Human Rights and Fundamental Freedoms. This occurred in 1998, and again, this was the 50th anniversary of the Human Rights Declaration, and a huge step forward for the recognition of individuals' roles in the protection and promotion of human rights.

The main right of the DHRD is enshrined in article 1. It is worthwhile to point out the use of the term "to strive" in this article: "Everyone has the right, individually and in association with others, to promote and to strive for the protection and realization of human rights and fundamental freedoms at the national and international levels". The original configuration of this right has an intrinsic meaning that later seems to be forgotten during further analysis. The meaning of the term "to strive" is "to try very hard to do something or to make something happen, especially for a long time or against difficulties" (Cambridge Dictionary, 2020).

This is the origin of human rights defenders. It is neither a comfortable position inside the system of human rights, nor a comfort zone in state or international organizations. Hence, it is necessary to remind its historical origins: striving for human rights against totalitarianism in the East, dictatorship in Latin America, claiming civil rights and peace in the US, anti-apartheid in South Africa, rights against late colonialism in Africa, movements from dissenters in Europe against communist authoritarianism and the evolution to Eurocommunism, military dictatorship in Greece, Spain, and Portugal, or the redefinition of women's rights and gender. Asia suffered through Tiananmen Square in China (1989) and their further long silence. The Association of Southeast Asian Nations (ASEAN) adhered to human rights principles after the Vienna Conference of 1993. However, Asia is a regional system of human rights that did not develop a particular system for human rights defenders at the international legal level without any Rapporteurship or specific policy. This is different from other regional systems, but it does not mean that there are not human rights defenders in Asia. There are. The way they promote and protect human rights is worthwhile to mention. They mostly respect the principles and criteria set up by the United Nations Declaration on human rights defenders: non-violence, interdependence and universality of human rights, and claims for recognized human rights.

Hence, this is the original context for the adoption of the UN Declaration on human rights defenders from 1985 to 1998. Nevertheless, the most remarkable precedent of human rights defenders is East Dissent. This is why the Helsinki Final Act (1975), Chapter VII, and particularly the right to know and the right to act for human rights are at the origin of the Declaration on human rights defenders, from a legal and historic perspective. The Helsinki Final Act in Chapter VII states that "they confirm the right of the individual to know and act upon his rights and duties in this field" (McChesney and Rodley, 1992). Hence, this is a right mainly built on the individual, and this is also present in the UN Declaration 1998. The individual is the main subject, and groups are considered subjects as a collective expression of individuals. However, recognizing individual action in human rights does not imply or mean the privatization of human rights.

In 1992, McChesney and Rodley wrote the key article: "Human Rights Defenders: Drafting a Declaration", which was published in the International Commission of Jurists Review. The year is relevant because it is when the UN Working Group first read the draft document in January of 1992. They pointed out the Helsinki Act, Chapter VII, for its usefulness "in support of political dissidents" and the failed attempt in the 1980s to create a Declaration on the Right to Know and Act which was mainly supported by Canada and Norway. McChesney represented the International Commission of Jurists at the working group sessions in 1991 and 1992. Nigel Rodley has represented Amnesty International in the working group since 1990. They both point out the real tension inside the Working Group between those who wanted to reinforce human rights for defenders and those who wanted to reinforce duties and restrictions (McChesney and Rodley, 1992). As for these authors, the most sensitive aspects during the working group debates hinged on the influence of the Soviet Union Bloc who tried to obstruct progress in the debate (McChesney and Rodley, 1992). They particularly remark upon the following trends and difficulties: imposition of duties, cultural or predominant ideologies, subjection to all activities to national legislation and administrative measures, reluctance to accept NGOs cooperation and monitoring in violations of human rights, limitations on foreign funding, and the responsibilities of individuals that must be public, particularly, regarding non-state actors (McChesney and Rodley, 1992).

The adoption of the Declaration on human rights defenders (1998) is a further step in the process of the individualization of international law, as theorized by Peters (2016). The *locus* of this declaration gives recognition to individuals regarding the right to promote and protect human rights. The recognition to individuals goes to further the prevalence of the principle of human dignity against the principle of sovereignty in the framework of the individualization of international law conceptualized by Peters' theory. According to this author, the constitutional paradigm is useful in analyzing the changing paradigm of legal persons in international law (Peters, 2016).

However, the constitutional and international system of fundamental and human rights still remains based on the constitutional and international state-based legal framework created after the Second World War. Contemporary globalization challenges this system of the protection of rights. The emergence of human rights defenders is evidence of the erosion of the state due to globalization. But at the same time, it is a strong challenge to constitutional and international law, particularly because it opens the door to the preeminence of the human condition paradigm over sovereignty.

The 1998 United Nations Declaration on human rights defenders

On 9 December 1998, the Declaration on the Right and Responsibility of Individuals, Groups and Organs of Society to Promote and Protect Universally Recognized Human Rights and Fundamental Freedoms was approved. This Declaration does not have the binding effect of a treaty, but it is part of the UN trend of "plural deliberation" according to Gómez Sánchez (2006, p. 273). Even if a Declaration has no binding effect, it has legal effectiveness. The Vienna Convention on the Law of Treaties (23 May 1969) defines what a treaty is in article 2, but article 3 states that even if international agreements are not treaties, they shall not affect "the legal force" of them. In the case of a Declaration, it is necessary to note the difference between "legal force" and "internal effectiveness" (Gómez Sánchez, 2006, p. 284).

Because of its non-binding nature, a Declaration allows for other types of agreements, and it is suitable in order to achieve a consensus on relevant principles. According to Hodgson (Hodgson, 2003, p. 87): "In United Nations practice, a 'declaration' is a formal and solemn instrument, suitable for rare occasions when principles of great and lasting importance are being enunciated, such as the Declaration of Human Rights (E_CN.4_L.610-EN, 1962, p. 4)".

The UN declarations are an expression of international commitment, although they are non-binding, they are always a legal instrument expectative of compliance. This shows the commitment of a state as an international person within the international community (Gómez Sánchez, 2006).

The Declaration on human rights defenders has built a new paradigm in the international and constitutional legal framework, where the principle of sovereignty has been displaced by the principle of the human condition, even going beyond human dignity as an axiological basis. The tension between these two principles, sovereignty and human dignity, was a constant issue during the 13 years of debate within the working group to draft the DHRD. But these debates hatched the human condition paradigm of the right to promote and protect human rights: it is a universal right, and it is the individual's will to exercise it, according to the criteria set up in the declaration. After the disappearance of the two Blocs, the fall of the Berlin Wall, and the disintegration of the Soviet Union, it was possible to draft the declaration and find consensus on these controversial aspects.

Article 1 of the Declaration on human rights defenders recognizes the right of individuals to collectively and separately promote and strive for human rights. Individuals are a part of this new framework for human rights created by the 1998 declaration. Often, when thinking of human rights defenders as new legal persons in international and constitutional law, they are only considered as such because of their external actions of promotion and protection of human rights. This does not give due attention to dissent and the intellectual promotion and protection of human rights.

Contemporary global society suffers from a gap between citizens and human beings (Arendt, 1951) as legal persons (Goldoni and McCorkindale, 2012). However, individuals as legal persons could be an answer to the erosion of the paradigm nation-state. Individuals must not be substitutes for public action. The sad example of human rights defenders shows us this in the case of "failed states" (Owen, 2001) or dictatorial states, where defending human rights is not a right, but a dangerous commitment undertaken by individuals against the state. It is worthwhile to point out that promoting or protecting human rights is a right but not a duty, because the main responsibility of human rights remains with the states or international organizations. Hence, if it is not a duty, then it is better to use the term responsibility, or even intellectual commitment, when referring to human rights exercised by individuals as human rights defenders.

This introduces the paradox that arose from the Second World War framework on human rights when the state is, or can be, both guarantor and violator of human rights. However, according to article 2 of the Declaration on human rights defenders, the main responsibility to promote and protect human rights remains with states, and by default, with international organizations. In certain contexts, individuals assume public action in defence of human rights. They take risks, and even suffer threats that could make them fear for their lives. Often, physical protection of human rights defenders is confused with legal recognition of their actions and rights. The right to be protected and the right to promote and protect human rights are not the same. In fact, the first is instrumental to the former. My thesis is that human rights defenders are new legal persons, and it is necessary to recognize the intellectual component of their actions to strive and to promote human rights, not only their external actions. The individual intellectual promotion and protection of human rights is in the core content of the right to promote and protect human rights. Without taking into account the twofold nature of this new legal person, the comprehension and legal protection of human rights defenders under international and constitutional law would be incomplete.

The Declaration on human rights defenders establishes a catalogue of instrumental rights to the right to promote and protect human rights. It is necessary not to confuse the main right of the 1998 DHRD with other instrumental rights. All them are necessary, but they do not have exactly the same structure and content. In this catalogue, the instrumental rights recognized in the declaration are:

a   The right to be protected (arts. 2, 9, 12)
b   The right to freedom of assembly (arts. 5.a, art. 12)
c   The right to freedom of association (arts. 5.b)
d   The right to access and communicate with international bodies (art. 5.c, 9.4)
e   The right to freedom of opinion and expression (art. 6)
f   The right to protest (art. 5.a)
g   The right to develop and discuss new human rights ideas (art. 7)
h   The right to an effective remedy (art. 9)
i   The right to access funding (art. 13).

What is relevant under the 1998 Declaration framework is that these rights are set as legal guarantees with an instrumental character to the main right to promote and protect human rights. "The Declaration reaffirms rights that are instrumental to the defense of human rights, [...]. Implementing the Declaration is a precondition for the creation of an environment that enables human rights defenders to carry out their work" (UN SRHRD, 2011, p. 5).

It is worthwhile to mention that promotion and protection of human rights is a right, but it is not a duty for individuals. According to article 2 of the Declaration on human rights defenders, the state still has the responsibility to protect, promote, and implement all human rights and fundamental freedoms.

But the real goal of the declaration is not to identify a catalogue of duties and responsibilities. The Declaration on human rights defenders seeks to set an international right to defend human rights by striving for, protecting, or promoting human rights. Hence, the Special Rapporteur on the situation of human rights defenders, Margaret Sekaggya (2008), considered one of the key messages to be: "The Declaration on human rights defenders is an international instrument for the protection of the right to defend human rights". In 2008, ten years after the DHRD, there was a joint warning on human rights defenders launched by the SR on the situation of human rights defenders with five other UN and regional mechanisms: Reine Alapini-Gansou, the Special Rapporteur on human rights defenders of the African Commission on Human and Peoples' Rights; Mr.

Thomas Hammarberg, the Commissioner for Human Rights of the Council of Europe; Ambassador Janez Lenarčič, Director of the OSCE Office for Democratic Institutions and Human Rights (ODIHR); and Dr. Santiago A. Canton, the Executive Secretary of the Inter-American Commission on Human Rights. They clearly outlined that the exercise of the right is what defines human rights defenders: "Human rights defenders are those who, individually or together with others, act to promote and protect human rights. It is their activities in the defense of human rights that makes them human rights defenders" (Sekaggya et al., 2008).

The 1998 DHRD, even if it was adopted in the international sphere, would be considered an insertion in the process of global constitutionalism:

> Global constitutionalization refers to the continuing, but not linear, process of the gradual emergence and deliberate creation of constitutionalist elements in the international legal order by political and judicial actors, bolstered by an academic discourse in which these elements are identified and further developed. (Peters, 2009, pp. 397–398)

According to Peters' theory, it is worthwhile then to keep in mind the constitutional implications of the Declaration on human rights defenders as an international instrument that uses a constitutional paradigm for analysis.

Even if the DHRD is an international instrument, there are constitutional implications due to its influence on national law. Despite this, the constitutional implications are rarely considered. Yet: "Each State shall adopt such legislative, administrative and other steps as may be necessary to ensure that the rights and freedoms referred to in the present Declaration are effectively guaranteed" (art. 2 DHRD). This national implementation of domestic law was also relevant to the SR, in whose report human rights defenders were a part of the 2008 message: "National laws, including, in particular, legislation regulating the activities of civil society organizations, should uphold the principles of the Declaration" (UN SRHRD, 9 December 2008).

However, there is not yet enough development and knowledge about the Declaration on human rights defenders at the constitutional and national levels, despite the fact that it has an irradiation effect allowing for international protection of defenders. There is a lack of consideration of national law and there are not enough legislative, administrative, and other measures. But there have been some interesting multi-level developments, i.e., from the Spanish temporary reception program under the Human Rights Office and the Ministry of Foreign Affairs and Cooperation. In Spain, there are other actions at the regional and local level in Catalonia, Aragon, Madrid, Barcelona, Asturias, Basque Country, and Valencian Community. They are a part of these programs for the temporary protection of human rights defenders including multilevel systems for temporary relocation at the regional and local level.

Other national implementation measures have been pointed out by Bennet, Ingleton, Nah, and Savage (2015, 2016), such as the Swiss guidelines for the protection of human rights defenders, that were set in December 2013 for diplomatic Swiss guidance (Leissing, 2014). The United Kingdom adopted the First

National Action Plan to implement UN Guiding Principles on Business and Human Rights with implications for the protection of defenders; in the African system, Côte d'Ivoire adopted the Law on the Protection and Promotion of Human Rights Defenders (Bennet et al., 2015, p. 3). Recently, Costa Rica also decided to create the center Shelter city for temporary protection of human rights defenders coming from El Salvador, Guatemala, Honduras and Nicaragua, with the support of The Netherlands and Fundación Acceso (Sheltercity, 2022).

Another initiative to mention is the adoption of the Model National Law on the Recognition and Protection of Human Rights Defenders' (2016), endorsed by 28 experts on human rights defenders. It is intended to assist the implementation of the Declaration on human rights defenders (International Service for Human Rights, 2022).

Bennet et al. (2015, 2016) remark on a multilevel legal framework but from a point of view focused mainly on the protection of human rights defenders. This is slightly different from our approach, more focused on its theoretical aspects and implications: first, human rights defenders' protection derives from the international human rights regime. Second, they consider that human rights defenders' framework is "goal driven-its aim is to protect and support defenders who operate in their own contexts in the face of threats and risks" (Bennet et al., 2015). Third, the regime on human rights defenders comes from a human security paradigm: "the regime adopts a human security paradigm, with individuals, groups and communities as subjects of security rather than states" (Bennet et al., 2015, p. 2). This explanation of human rights framework focuses on the protection of human rights defenders. But, as in the case of threatened journalists, hidden behind the threats to human rights defenders, the non-compliance or violation of human rights, is due to the weakening of the state parallel to globalization, and the lack of enough constitutionalization at the international level. Also, under the recognition of human rights defenders, I think not only of the external action of defending, but to include another aspect often forgotten in terms of international protection: the intellectual action inherent to human rights defenders. At the international regional level, according to Bennet et al. (2015), there is a development of a multilevel system of protection for human rights defenders. However, this system is built under the paradigm of human security and it often forgets the paradigm of the human condition.

The turning point for this changing paradigm was the Declaration of the United Nations on human rights defenders. Later, each regional and supranational system of human rights had their own particularities on human rights defenders. Let us examine the evolution and theoretical characteristics of this multilevel human rights framework in the United Nations, the Council of Europe, the Inter-American system, the African Union, and the EU system on human rights defenders.

References

Arendt, H. (1951). *The Origins of Totalitarianism*. New York: Brace, Harcourt.
Arendt, H. (2018). *The Human Condition*. Chicago & London: The University of Chicago Press.

Aristotle (1944). *Aristotle in 23 Volumes*, Vol. 21, translated by H. Rackham. London: Heinemann & Cambridge, MA: Harvard University Press. Retrieved 26 May, 2022, from: www.perseus.tufts.edu/hopper/text?doc=Perseus:abo:tlg,0086,035:1:1253a

Bennett, K., Ingleton, D., Nah, A. M., and Savage, J. (2015). "Critical perspectives on the security and protection of human rights defenders". *International Journal of Human Rights*, 19(7), 883–895. Retrieved 26 May, 2022, from: https://doi.org/10.1080/13642987.2015.1075301.

Bennet, K., Ingleton, D., Nah, M. A., and Savage, J. (2016). *Critical Perspectives on the Security and Protection of Human Rights Defenders*. Oxon & New York: Routledge.

Cambridge Dictionary (2020). Cambridge University Press. Retrieved May 14, 2022, from: https://dictionary.cambridge.org/es/.

Gavara de Cara, J. C. (2007). "La vinculación positiva de los poderes públicos a los derechos fundamentales". *Teoría y Realidad Constitucional*, 20, 277–320.

Cottier, M. and Hertig, M. (2003). "The prospects of 21st constitutionalism". *Max Planck UNYB*, 7, 261–328.

Diagne, S. B. (2009). "Individual, community and human rights". *Transition*, 101, 8–15.

Dupuy, P.-M. (2004). "Dynamique des droits de l'homme et société civile international". In *Libertés, justice, tolerance. Mélanges en honneur au doyen Gerard Cohen-Jonathan*. Bruxelles: Bruylant.

Freixes Sanjuan, T. (2005). "Derechos Fundamentales en La Unión Europea. Evolución y prospectiva: La construcción de un espacio Jurídico europeo de los derechos fundamentales". *Revista Derecho Constitucional Europeo*, 4, 43–86.

Goldoni, M. and McCorkindale, C. (Eds). (2012). *Hannah Arendt and the Law*. Oxford: Hart.

Gómez Sánchez, Y. (2006). "Los principios de autonomía igualdad y no discriminación en la Declaración Universal sobre Bioética y Derechos Humanos". In H. Gros Espiell & Y. Gómez Sánchez (Eds), *La Declaración Universal sobre Bioética de la UNESCO*. Madrid: Editorial Comares.

Gómez Sánchez, Y. (2020). *Constitucionalismo multinivel. Derechos Fundamentales*. Madrid: Sanz y Torres.

WZB Berlin Social Science Center (2022) *Global Constitutionalism Journal*. Retrieved June 4, 2022, from: www.wzb.eu/en/research/completed-research-programs/center-for-global-constitutionalism/global-constitutionalism-journal.

Habermas, J. (2006). "Does the constitutionalization of international law still have a chance?" In C. Cronin (Ed.), *The Divided West*. Cambridge: Polity Press.

Hodgson, D. (2003). *Individual Duty within a Human Rights Discourse*. Surrey: Ashgate.

Jones, M. (2015). "Protecting human rights defenders at risk: Asylum and temporary international relocation". *International Journal of Human Rights*, 19(7), 935–960. Retrieved June 4, 2022, from: https://doi.org/10.1080/13642987.2015.1075304.

Lang, E. and Wiener, A. (2017). *Handbook on Global Constitutionalism*. Cheltenham: Edward Elgar Publishing.

Leissing, A. (2014) *Implementation of the Swiss Guidelines on the Protection of Human Rights Defenders*. Bern: SwissPeace. Retrieved 26 May, 2022, from: www.swisspeace.ch/fileadmin/user_upload/Media/Publications/Essentials/Essential_3_2014_Human_Rights_Defenders.pdf.

Less, S., Schaller-Soltau, V., Schmidt, A., Oez, E., and Peters, A. (2017). *Global Constitutionalism: The Social Dimension*. Retrieved June 4, 2022, from: https://ssrn.

com/abstract=3083578Electroniccopyavailableat: https://ssrn.com/abstract=3083578 Electroniccopyavailableat: https://ssrn.com/abstract=3083578 https://ssrn.com/abstract=3083578.

Marrani, D. (2009). "Human rights and environmental protection: The pressure of the charter for the environment on the French administrative courts". *Sustainable Development Law & Policy*, Fall, 52–57.

Marrani, D. (2012). "'Mission Impossible': Interconnecting the common law legal culture and civil law legal systems in the European integration". In T. Freixes, J. C. Remotti, D. Marrani, J. Bombin, and L. Vanin-Verna (Eds), *La gouvernance multi-level. Penser l'enchevêtrement* (pp. 33–55). Bruxelles, Fernelmont: E.M.E.

Marrani, D. (2015). "Reinforcing environmental rights: The French charter for the environment". *Revista Europea de Derechos Fundamentales*, 25, 383–400.

Schwitter Marsiaj, C. (2004). *The Role of International NGOS in the Global Governance of Human Rights. Challenging the Democratic Deficit*. Zurich: Schultess.

McChesney, A. and Rodley, N. (1992). "Human rights defenders. Drafting a declaration". *International Commission of Jurists Review*, 48.

Neocosmos, M. (2016). *Thinking Freedom in Africa: Towards a Theory of Emancipatory Politics*. Wits University Press.

Ngomane, M. & Tutu, D. (2020). *Ubuntu. Lecciones de sabiduría africana para vivir mejor*. Grijalbo.

Owen, N. (2001). *Human Rights, Human Wrongs. The Oxford Amnesty Lectures 2001*, N. Owen (Ed.). Oxford: Oxford University Press.

Peters, A. (2006). "Compensatory constitutionalism: The function and potential of fundamental international norms and structures". *Leiden Journal of International Law*, 19(3), 579–610.

Peters, A. (2009). "The merits of global constitutionalism. Introduction: The meaning of global constitutionalism". *Indiana Journal of Global Legal Studies*, 16, 2.

Peters, A. (2015). "Global constitutionalism". In M. Gibbons (Ed.), *The Encyclopedia of Political Thought*. John Wiley and Sons. Retrieved 26 May, 2022, from: www.mpil.de/files/pdf5/Peters_Global_Constitutionalism__Encyclopedia_of_Political_Thought_20151.pdf.

Peters, A. (2015, April 7). "Constitutional fragments – On the interaction of constitutionalization and fragmentation in international law". Centre for Global Constitutionalism, University of St. Andrews, Working Paper No. 2 (2015). Retrieved 26 May, 2022, from: https://ssrn.com/abstract=2591370 or http://dx.doi.org/10.2139/ssrn.2591370.

Peters, A. (2016). *Beyond Human Rights: The Legal Status of the Individual in International Law*. Cambridge: Cambridge University Press.

Peters, A. (2019). *Humanisme, constitutionalisme, universalisme. Etude de droit international et comparé*. Paris: Editions Pedone.

Policastro, P. (2004). "On the reconstruction of the legal strength of the constitution in a world in transition. Multilevel constitutionalism towards multilevel democracy". In *Challenges of Multi-Level Constitutionalism: IVR 21st World Congress, Lund, Sweden, 12–18 August 2003: Law and Policy in Search of Balance*. Krakow: Polpress.

Saura-Freixes, N. (2015). *Libertad de expresión y derecho a promover y proteger los derechos humanos*. Barcelona: J. M. Bosch Editor.

Saura-Freixes, N. (2016). *Human rights defenders. El derecho a promover y proteger los derechos humanos*. Madrid: UNED.

Wiseberg, L. (2003). "The role of non-governmental organizations (NGOs) in the protection and enforcement of human rights". In J. Symonides (Ed.), *Human Rights: Protection, Monitoring, Enforcement*. London: Routledge.

Documents

Treaties

African Charter on Human and Peoples' Rights (adopted 27 June 1981, *entered into force 21 October 1986) CAB/LEG/67/3 rev*. 5, 21 I.L.M. 58 (1982) (African Charter)

American Convention on Human Rights (adopted 22 November, 1969, entered into force 18 July 1978) 1144 UNTS.123; OASTS. No. 36 ("Pact of San Jose, Costa Rica", ACHR)

Charter of the United Nations, (adopted 24 October 1945) 1 UNTS XVI

Consolidated Version of the Treaty on European Union [2012] OJ C 326/13 (TEU)

Convention relating to the Status of Refugees (adopted 28 July 1951, entered into force 22 April 1954) 189 UNTS 137

Convention for the Protection of Human Rights and Fundamental Freedoms, as amended, (adopted 4 November 1950, *entered into force 3 September 1953) ETS No*. 005 (ECHR)

International Covenant on Civil and Political Rights (adopted 16 December 1966, entered into force 23 March 1976) 999 UNTS 171 (ICCPR)

International Covenant on Economic, Social and Cultural Rights (adopted16 December 1966, entered into force 3 January 1976) 993 UNTS 3 (ICESCR)

Protocol no.11 to the Convention for the Protection of Human Rights and Fundamental Freedoms Restructuring the Control Machinery Established Thereby (adopted 11 May 1994, entered into force 1 November 1998) ETS No.155

Rome Statute of the International Criminal Court (adopted 17 July 1998, entered into force 1 July 2002) 2187 UNTS 3

Vienna Convention on the Law of Treaties (adopted 23 May 1969, entered into force 27 January 1980) 1155 UNTS 331

UN

Universal Declaration of Human Rights, UNGA Res. 217A (III) (10 December 1948)

Declaration on the Right and Responsibility of Individuals, Groups and Organs of Society to Promote and Protect UniversallyRecognized HumanRights and Fundamental Freedoms, UNGA A/RES/53/144 (8 March 1999)

UNGA "*Human rights defenders: note by the Secretary-General. Report of the Special Rapporteur on the situation of human rights defenders*" (2008) UN Doc A/63/288. Retrieved 26 May, 2022, from: https://documents-dds-ny.un.org/doc/UNDOC/GEN/N08/461/09/PDF/N0846109.pdf?OpenElement

UNGA "*Human rights defenders: note by the Secretary-General. Report of the Special Rapporteur on the situation of human rights defenders*" (2011) UN Doc A/66/203. Retrieved May 2022, from: https://documents-dds-ny.un.org/doc/UNDOC/GEN/N11/435/29/PDF/N1143529.pdf?OpenElement

UNCHR Decision 1984/116 (16 March 1984)

UNCHR Decision 1985/112 (1985) UN Doc E/CN.4/1985/66

UNCHR Report on the 40th session, 6 February—16 March 1984. *UN Doc E/CN.4/1984/77 (1984)*. Retrieved 26 May, 2022, from: https://digitallibrary.un.org/record/66414

UNCHR "*Drafting of a declaration on the right and responsibility of individuals, groups and organs of society to promote and protect universally recognized human rights and fundamental freedoms. Report of the Working Group*" (27 February 1992) UN Doc E/CN.4/1992/53. Retrieved 26 May, 2022, from: https://digitallibrary.un.org/record/225903?ln=es

UNCHR "*Report of the Working Group on a Draft Declaration on the Right and Responsibility of Individuals, Groups and Organs of Society to Promote and Protect Universally Recognized Human Rights and Fundamental Freedoms*". (13 March 1986) UN Doc E/CN.4/1986/40. Retrieved 3 June, 2022, from: https://digitallibrary.un.org/record/196062?ln=ru

UNCHR "*Draft report of the Working Group on a draft Declaration on the Right and Responsibility of Individuals, Groups and Organs of Society to Promote and Protect Universally Recognized Human Rights and Fundamental Freedoms*". (3 February 1986) UN Doc E/CN.4/1986/WG.6/WP.5. Retrieved 26 May, 2022, from: https://digitallibrary.un.org/record/196051?ln=es

UNCHR "*Report submitted by Ms. Hina Jilani, Special Representative of the Secretary-General on human rights defenders in accordance with Commission resolution 2000/61*" (2001) UN Doc E/CN.4/2001/94. Retrieved 3 June, 2022, from: https://digitallibrary.un.org/record/450010?ln=es

Sekaggya, M. *United Nations Special Rapporteur on the situation of human rights defenders*; Alapini-Gansou R., Special Rapporteur on human rights defenders of the African Commission on Human and Peoples' Rights; Hammarberg, T. Commissioner for Human Rights of the Council of Europe; Janez

Lenarcic, Director of the OSCE Office for Democratic Institutions and Human Rights; and Santiago A.Canton, the Executive Secretary of the Inter-American Commission on Human Rights. "*Joint Statement. Ten years on, human rights defenders continue to pay a high price*" (9 December 2008). Retrieved 26 May, 2022, from: www.osce.org/files/f/documents/4/d/35561.pdf

United Nations. (1984). *The United Nations and Human Rights*. New York: Department of Public Information

World Conference on Human Rights in Vienna. Vienna Declaration and Programme of Action (25 June 1993). *Retrieved 3 June*, 2022, from: www.ohchr.org/sites/default/files/vienna.pdf

OSCE

OSCE "*Conference on Security and Co-operation in Europe (CSCE): Final Act of Helsinki*" (CSCE Helsinki 1 August 1975). Retrieved 26 May, 2022, from: www.osce.org/es/mc/39506

COE

Soulas et autres v.France, App no 15948/03 (ECtHR, 10 July 2008)

EU

Council of the EU (Foreign Affairs). Ensuring protection. European Union Guidelines on human rights defenders [2008]. Retrieved June 4, 2022, from: www.eeas.europa.eu/sites/default/files/eu_guidelines_hrd_en.pdf

France

France Constitution of October 4, 1958. *Retrieved 26 May*, 2022 from: www.con seil-constitutionnel.fr/sites/default/files/as/root/bank_mm/anglais/constiution_anglais_ oct2009.pdf

Loi constitutionnelle n° 2005–205 du 1er mars 2005 relative à la Charte de l'environnement, JORF n° 0051 March 2005

Mali

"Manden Charter, proclaimed in Kurukan Fuga, Mali. Inscribed in 2009 *(4.COM) on the Representative List of the Intangible Cultural Heritage of Humanity*". Retrieved 26 May, 2022, from: https://ich.unesco.org/en/RL/manden-charter-proclaimed-in-kurukan-fuga-00290

Spain

Giza eskubideen defendatzaileak aldi batez Euskal Autonomia Erkidegoan babesteko Programa / Programa Vasco de ProtecciónTemporal para Defensores y Defensoras de los Derechos Humanos (Secretaría General de DerechosHumanos, Convivencia y Cooperación del Gobierno Vasco y CEAR-Euskadi). Retrieved 3 June, 2022, from: www.euskadi.eus/contenidos/informacion/documentos_paz_convivencia/eu_def/adjuntos/Programa-defensores-eus.pdf

Programa Català de Protecció a defensors i defensores dels Drets Humans / Programa Catalán de Protección a Defensores y Defensoras de DerechosHumanos (Generalitat de Catalunya i Comissió Catalana d'Ajuda al Refugiat). Retrieved 3 June, 2022, from: http://cooperaciocatalana.gencat.cat/ca/que-fem/eixos/defensores-drets-humans/pcpddh/

Programa Valenciano de ProtecciónIntegral y de Acogida de Defensores y Defensoras de DerechosHumanos (Concejalía de Cooperación al Desarrollo y Migración del Ayuntamiento de Valencia y CEAR-País Valencià). Retrieved 3 June, 2022, from: www.cearpv.org/que-fem/projectes/projectes-dincidencia-i-sensibilitzacio/programa-de-proteccion-integral-y-de-acogida-de-defensores-y-defensoras-de-derechos-humanos/

Programa de AcogidaTemporal a Personas Defensoras de DerechosHumanos. Plan Estratégico de DerechosHumanos del Ayuntamiento de Madrid. Retrieved 3 June, 2022 from: www.madridprotege.org/

Programa de Acogida a Personas Defensoras de DerechosHumanos en Aragón. Retrieved 3 June, 2022, from: www.aragonprotege.org/#:~:text=El%20Programa%20de%20Acogida%20a,personas%20defensoras%20y%2C%20por%20otro%2C

Programa Asturiano de atención a las víctimas de violencia en Colombia. Retrieved 3 June, 2022, from: https://pav-asturcolombia.org/

Switzerland

Conféderation Suisse. (2019) *Lignes directrices de la Suisse sur les défenseuses et défenseurs des droits de l'homme*. Bern: Département federal des affaires étrangeres

UK

Secretary of State for Foreign and Commonwealth Affairs by Command of Her Majesty. "*Good Business Implementing the UN Guiding Principles on Business and Human Rights*". Cm 8695. (September 2013). Retrieved 3 June, 2022, from: https://assets.publishing.service.gov.uk/government/uploads/system/uploads/attachment_data/file/236901/BHR_Action_Plan_-_final_online_version_1_.pdf

US

Plessy v. Ferguson, 163 US 537 (1896)

NGOs and others

International Service for Human Rights. "*Model law for the recognition and protection of human rights defenders*". Geneva: 2016. Retrieved 26 May, 2022, from: https://academy.ishr.ch/upload/resources_and_tools/ishr_Model_Law_for_the_recognition_and_protection_of_human_rights_defenders_en.pdf

Sheltercity. Available at: https://sheltercity.org/increasing-the-security-protection-of-human-rights-defenders-in-central-america/

2 The UN Special Procedure on the situation of human rights defenders

A multilevel and global framework and the paradigm on human condition

In the system of the United Nations there has been a universal participation of states, but the presence of non-state actors has increased. For Alvarez, the participation of NGOs in law-making, and the presence of other non-state actors, led to their empowerment and the creation of an international civil society (Alvarez, 2006, p. 154). However, the origin of the United Nations is as a multilateral organization that is mainly based on states. Hence, international and regional organizations, with a statist origin, are acting collectively with individuals, NGOs, or groups, such as non-state actors.

In this three-cornered framework, the United Nations opted to have several answers to the crisis of multi-lateral treaties' guarantees when states do not want to accept or adopt it. The Special Procedures or thematic mechanisms of the United Nations, disconnected with any treaty, have a crucial role in this.

In the system of the United Nations, Wapner (2007) reminds us that there has always been tension between the statist nature of the organization and the aspiration to represent something larger than states, a *demos*. Its foundation under this kind of fragmented constitutional constituent power appears in the Preamble of the Charter: "We the peoples of the United Nations" (Wapner, 2007, p. 254).

The development of instruments for the protection of human rights that do not depend on the agreement of states is a trend that is second nature to the UN as an organization. It tries to bind human rights to the human condition more than to state agreement. This tension is still present, and maybe it is impossible solve.

The Special Procedures of the United Nations are, on the one hand, a symptom of the paralysis of the statist trend, and on the other, a necessary but not always effective complementary system of protection for human rights that are not dependent on state agreement. In 2021, the United Nations had 45 thematic mandates (OHCHR, 2022). However, to arrive at these mandates (one of them being the Special Rapporteur on the situation of human rights defenders) has been a long and hard path, with a special turning point from the Commission on Human Rights to the United Nations Human Rights Council in 2006.

The origins go back to 1946, when the Commission on Human Rights was created as a subsidiary body of the ECOSOC. However, as Shaw (2008) reminds us, for 20 years the Commission on Human Rights claimed that it had no power

DOI: 10.4324/9780429264016-2

to take action in response to complaints of human rights violations (Shaw, 2008, p. 304).

Beginning in the 1960s, even under this policy of non-intervention, the UN General Assembly created a small number of special committees to conduct better research on the situation in Africa:

> The Sub-Committee on the Situation in Angola, the Special Committee on the Situation with regard to the Implementation of the Declaration on the Granting of Independence to Colonial Countries and Peoples (1961), the Special Committee on Territories under Portuguese Administration and the Special Committee on the Policies of the Apartheid of the Government of South Africa (1962). (Gutter, 2006, p. 53)

All these committees, according to Gutter, could receive information from individuals, but they could not answer them individually. They only wanted to have better management and knowledge of the situation in aforementioned territories (Gutter, 2006, p. 53).

In 1967, the first steps for UN action in response to human rights complaints took place, leading to an evolution. They listened, not only to states as makers of rules, but also to individuals as recipients of them. According to Domínguez Redondo, the adoption of the ECOSOC Resolution 1235 led to a change "which constituted the legal basis for the establishment of future Special Procedures" (Limon and Power, 2014, p. 5), and the end of the doctrine "No Power to Act" 1946–1966 (Limon and Power, 2014, p. 4). All the member states, and all the entities, including NGOs with the status of "observer" could denounce a state for violations of human rights in the annual sessions of the Commission on Human Rights (Domínguez Redondo, 2005, p. 50).

In March 1966, under Resolution 1102 (XL), the ECOSOC invited the Commission on Human Rights to consider violations of human rights, including racial discrimination and apartheid "in all countries" (Gutter, 2006, p. 55). In 1970, it created the Procedure 1503, with a confidential nature, for cases of "a consistent pattern of gross and reliably attested violations of human rights" (Shaw, 2008, p. 305).

But to arrive at the creation of thematic mechanisms, such as Special Procedures, first some urgent actions were necessary to cope with violations of human rights in specific countries. In 1975, the Ad Hoc Working Group to Inquire into the Situation of Human Rights in Chile was created *ad hoc* by the Commission on Human Rights (Gutter, 2006, p. 66). But in 1980, a thematic mechanism was adopted with the Working Group on Enforced or Involuntary Disappearances. Of course, all the people knew that Argentina was concerned. In 1982, an individual body was created: the Special Rapporteur on extrajudicial, summary or arbitrary executions. These two mandates have been renewed in 2020 (OHCHR 2022).

In 2006, there was a turning point in the non-conventional system of human rights in the UN, with the disappearance of the Commission on Human Rights and the creation of the Human Rights Council. Steiner, Alston, and Goodman sum up the different methods used prior to 2006, under this classification:

> (1) confidential consideration of a situation under the 1503 procedure (2) public debate under the 1235 procedure, which might have led to the appointment of a Special rapporteur, a Special Representative of the Secretary General, or some other designated individuals or group to investigate a situation; (3) the designation of one or more experts to consider all aspects, including violations, of a specific theme; and (4) the appointment of an expert to report on the situation in a given country under the rubric of providing technical advice. (Steiner et al., 2008, p. 746)

The United Nations Human Rights Council was created under Resolution 60/251, on 15 March 2006 by the General Assembly. In 2006, the Human Rights Council had its first session. In 2007, it adopted the *Institution-building package* HRC 5/1. Special Procedures were regulated under this new framework as well as under the new system of Universal Periodic Review.

Under Resolution 60/251 the Human Rights Council assumed the thematic mechanisms that previously existed in the Commission of Human Rights (HRC, 2006, para. 6). Hence, it was necessary to assure that "Equal attention should be paid to all human rights", meaning civil and political rights, as well as social, economic, and cultural rights (HRC, 2007, para. 58). Under this framework, it was convenient to identify the gaps in these areas of human rights, and to choose the most effective thematic mechanism. Perhaps this is the reason there was a change to the thematic mechanism in 2008 in the domain of human rights defenders.

In 2000, the Commission on Human Rights required the Secretary General of the United Nations to create a thematic mechanism for human rights defenders. Hence, in August 2000 it appointed a Special Representative of the Secretary General on the situation of human rights defenders, instead of a Special Rapporteur (E/CN.4/RES/2000/61, para.3). Hina Jilani was from Pakistan, and she was the Special Representative of the Secretary General on human rights defenders from 2000 to 2008. In 2008, after two renewed mandates, it was decided to create a Special Rapporteur on the situation of human rights defenders and Ms. Margaret Sekaggya, from Uganda, was the mandate holder 2008–2014 (OHCHR 2022).

Michel Forst, from France, held later the Special Procedure on human rights defenders. In 2014, the Human Rights Council decided to continue with this mandate and appointed Michel Forst as the new Special Rapporteur on the situation of human rights defenders (2014–2020). Currently, the new elected for the position is Mary Lawlor, from Ireland. Candidates were able to submit their applications for the post until 17 October 2019. 142 organizations set up criteria to have brought into consideration (ISHR, 2019). The official criteria were established in the Human Rights Council Resolution 5/1, and by Resolution 5/2, in the Code of Conduct for Special Procedures and Mandate-holders of the

Human Rights Council, on 18 June 2007. In 2019, it was published the New Research Guide on the Special Procedures (OHCHR Library, 2020). On 1 May 2020, Mary Lawlor, founder and director of Front Line Defenders (2001–2016) and Director of the Irish Section of Amnesty International (1988 to 2000) was appointed as the Special Rapporteur on the situation of human rights defenders (OHCHR, 2022).

The UN Special Procedure on the situation of human rights defenders

In 1998, the Declaration on human rights defenders was adopted. The declaration set a framework for instrumental rights and the right to promote and protect human rights. However, this declaration did not have any mechanism for institutional guarantee. After two years of enforcement, the Secretary General published a report on the 13 February 2000, on the Implementation of the Declaration on the Right and Responsibility of Individuals, Groups, and Organs of Society to Promote and Protect Universally Recognized Human Rights and Fundamental Freedoms (E/CN.4/2000/95). In this report, there is a compilation of several opinions by state-based actors such as governments, specialized bodies, and intergovernmental organizations, as well as other non-state actors such as international NGOs. It is worthwhile to remember the role the European Union played in creating the new thematic mechanism on human rights defenders:

> The EU considered that the Commission on Human Rights at its fifty-sixth session should create or request the Secretary-General to establish a new mechanism: a special rapporteur or special representative of the Secretary-General on human rights defenders. (UN Secretary General, E/CN.4/2000/95, 13 January 2000 para. 11)

It was a turning point in the development of the multilevel framework on human rights defenders (Bennet et al., 2016) and the EU encouraged the international community to commit to the Declaration of human rights defenders "to make it a document that really made a difference for the many known and unknown heroes whose contribution to the promotion and protection of human rights worldwide remains indispensable" (UN Secretary General, E/CN.4/2000/95, 13 January 2000 para. 11). Amnesty International considered human rights defenders to be at risk in many parts of the world. Consequently, Amnesty International "urged the Commission to appoint a special rapporteur with a mandate to monitor, document and intervene on behalf of human rights defenders under threat" (UN Secretary General, E/CN.4/2000/95, 13 January 2000, para. 15). Other international NGOs expressed their commitment in a similar manner.

After this petition from both state and non-state actors, the commission asked the Secretary General to appoint, for a period of three years, a Special Representative to "report on the situation of human rights defenders in all parts of the world and on possible means to enhance their protection" (Report of the Secretary-General, 13

January 2000, E/CN.4/2000/95). This Special Representative on the situation of human rights defenders had the following responsibilities:

a   To seek, receive, examine and respond to information on the situation and the rights of anyone, acting individually or in association with others, to promote and protect human rights and fundamental freedoms;
b   To establish cooperation and conduct dialogue with Governments and other interested actors on the promotion and effective implementation of the Declaration;
c   To recommend effective strategies better to protect human rights defenders and follow up on these recommendations. (E/CN.4/2000/95, 13 January 2000, para. 3)

Hence, under this newly appointed mechanism there was a preoccupation with the risks suffered by human rights defenders around the world. Consequently, the Secretary General made a call for the commitment of states to cooperate with this new mechanism, and submit two annual reports per year, one to the General Assembly and one to the Commission on Human Rights (UN Secretary General, E/CN.4/2000/95, 13 January 2000, paras. 4–6).

The importance of an international institutional guarantee is often forgotten because of theoretical and social complaints about efficacy. But the OSCE Guidelines on the protection of human rights defenders reminds us that international guarantees work when national guarantees fail, and it can be the last resort for the promotion and protection of human rights: "Information submitted to international bodies, in particular human rights mechanisms, is sometimes the only way for someone from outside of a country to learn about the human rights situation in that country" (OSCE, 2014, para. 265).

Under this mandate, from 2000 to 2008, Hina Jilani, as Special Representative of the Secretary General on the situation of human rights defenders, submitted 36 reports to the Commission on Human Rights: seven were sent to the General Assembly, and eight were to the UN Human Rights Council. She made 12 visits to several countries too, including: Angola, Brazil, Colombia, Guatemala, Indonesia, Israel and occupied Palestinian territories, Kyrgyzstan, Macedonia, Nigeria, Serbia and Kosovo, Thailand, and Turkey. In 2001 she set the first Report of the Special Representative on the situation of human rights defenders (E/CN.4/2001/94). The framework of action in this mandate is always the Declaration on human rights defenders. Hence, according to the first report by the Special Representative on human rights defenders, the scope of the mandate is:

> The Declaration forms the foundation for determining and developing the scope of the mandate, and for any action or initiatives undertaken by the Special Representative. In the application of the mandate to human rights defenders, the Special Representative will draw, in particular, upon article 12 read with the fourth paragraph of the preamble to the Declaration, and will be guided by the Charter of the United Nations and the Universal Declaration of

Human Rights. The United Nations international human rights instruments will constitute a more precise legal background against which the Special Representative will consider her mandate. (E/CN.4/2001/94, para. 13)

Another crucial question under this framework is the relationship between domestic and international law. These highlight the complex nature in the processes of constitutionalization in international law, in the case of international courts, "the question about the constitutional role of international courts should therefore be decided in accordance with the domestic constitution, whether directly through relevant provisions or indirectly through recognition by the national judiciary" (von Bogdandy and Venzke, 2014, p. 133). But according to this author, it is accepted as a constitutional role in the case of the Court of Justice of the European Union "by all the legislatures and the highest courts of all EU Member States" (von Bogdandy and Venzke, 2014, p. 133).

The EU framework is unique because of a specific constitutional supranational multilevel legal system with a constitutional function under a particular court, as for, the CJEU. But, in other systems it can be considered a constitutional role under the European Convention on Human Rights and the Inter-American system of human rights:

> the attribution of a constitutional role is persuasive only for the European Court of Human Rights and the Inter-American Court of Human Rights. Both treaty systems are anchored in many constitutions precisely with the intent of protecting essential constitutional principles, in particular fundamental rights, through an institution outside the domestic order. (von Bogdandy and Venzke, 2014, p. 133)

However, in other regional systems, such as von Bogdandy and Venzke consider, there are not enough indicators of a clear constitutional role (von Bogdandy and Venzke, 2014, p. 133).

Thus, in the case of the Special Procedures of the United Nations, and more specifically in the case of the Special Procedure on human rights defenders, two challenging questions emerge:

a   Even if they have no judiciary power, they can be relevant, in constitutional or internal matters in the domain of human rights.
b   Even if they have no judiciary power, they are also considered a *duplication of fora* in terms of international courts, for instance, under the admissibility rule set in art. 35.2. b European Convention of Human Rights: "The Court shall not deal with any application submitted under article 34 that: (…) is substantially the same as a matter that has already been examined by the Court or has already been submitted to another procedure of international investigation or settlement and contains no relevant new information".

Let us analyze these two questions in the case of the Special Rapporteur on human rights defenders. Pons Ràfols et al. (2009) remind us that the unconventional mechanisms of the United Nations are necessary to answer to the deficits on the normative system as a necessary counterpart (Pons Rafols et al., 2009). At the basis of these systems are the Charter of the United Nations, but as for Eide and Alfredsson: "The UDHR forms the basis of implementation mechanisms at the UN level. This is the case with regard to the communications and investigative procedures in the human rights field" (Eide and Alfredsson, 1992, p. 7).

Hence, the principle of the human condition supersedes the principle of sovereignty. But in this case it is the axiological basis for creating a system that does not depend on the state's agreement. There is a relevant difference between jurisdictional guarantees, like the ECtHR, and institutional guarantees, (Gómez Sánchez, 2020), as in other international mechanisms, such as the UN thematic mechanisms.

The Special Rapporteur on the situation of human rights defenders: constitutional function and duplication of procedures

The Special Rapporteur on the situation of human rights defenders is an unconventional mechanism and an institutional guarantee of the Declaration on human rights defenders. It is not a judiciary guarantee. However, in the international regional court's regime there is the rule of non-admissibility if the same case is submitted to a Special Procedure and to an international regional court, due to the prohibition of double international *fora*, or duplication of procedures, the prohibition wants to avoid conflicts of jurisdiction. This rule regarding the non-duplication of procedure is also present in the system of the United Nations, where, according to Pizarro Sotomayor: "the only UN Human Rights Treaty Body enabled to receive individual complaints, whose constitutive instrument does not require expressly the no duplication of procedures, is the Committee on Elimination of Racial Discrimination (CERD)" (Pizarro Sotomayor, 2009, p. 3). It could be necessary to think about the nature and the extent of all these institutional UN guarantees and their differences with judicial *fora*, like the European Court of Human Rights, or the Inter-American system of Human Rights. In all the regional systems of human rights with international courts or near judiciary bodies, there is an admissibility clause on complaints that forbid the duplication of procedures. For Pizarro Sotomayor, this is a way to avoid a kind of "forum shopping" (Pizarro Sotomayor, 2009, p. 9). However, from my point of view, it is not clear that a Special Rapporteur can be considered an actual duplication of international procedure. Let us analyze why, after comparing this admissibility clause, in the different systems of human rights. We will begin considering this admissibility clause under the framework of the European Convention on Human Rights (article 35.2 ECHR):

> The Court shall not deal with any application submitted under article 34 that: (b) is substantially the same as a matter that has already been examined by the Court or has already been submitted to another procedure of international investigation or settlement and contains no relevant new information.

In the American Convention on Human Rights (1969), there is a similar clause. However, as explained below, we find a different conception of what is meant by "another procedure" in the admissibility decisions of the two human rights regional systems. Despite that, the admissibility clause is quite similar in the two systems. In art. 46.1.c of the American Convention on Human Rights, the term used is "another international proceeding":

> Admission by the Commission of a petition or communication lodged in accordance with Articles 44 or 45 shall be subject to the following requirements: [...] c) that the subject of the petition or communication is not pending in another international proceeding for settlement.

In the African system of human rights, art. 56.7 of the African Charter on Human and People's Rights, the Banjul Charter (1981) has a similar clause regarding the conditions of admissibility in the African Commission on Human Rights. But this clause is not so explicit in the way it refers to international procedure:

> Communications relating to Human and Peoples' rights referred to in Article 55 received by the Commission, shall be considered if they: [...] 7. Do not deal with cases which have been settled by those States involved in accordance with the principles of the Charter of the United Nations, or the Charter of the Organization of African Unity or the provisions of the present Charter.

Finally, the conventional system of the United Nations has an admissibility clause to avoid the duplication of international procedures: "All of the international human rights treaties have a 'duplication' provision that requires the supervisory body to declare a petition inadmissible if it is "substantially the same as one previously studied" by it or by another international organization" (Cerna, 2011, p. 508). So, the Human Rights Committee has an admissibility clause forbidding duplication of procedures according to article 5 of the Optional Protocol to the International Covenant on Civil and Political Rights (1966):

1 The Committee shall not consider any communication from an individual unless it has ascertained that:
2 The same matter is not being examined under another procedure of international investigation or settlement;

In this case the regulation is clearer, but there is also a complex reference to the nature of the forbidden procedure that must execute the "international investigation or settlement". I doubt and wonder if a UN thematic mechanism, such as the Special Rapporteur on human rights defenders, can be considered a duplication procedure. The Special Procedures' function is not at all judiciary, nor of a settlement; it is officially defined as an institution for "constructive dialogue". Under the framework of the United Nations Special Procedures there can be the following Special Procedures as thematic mechanisms:

- Special Rapporteurs
- Independent Experts
- Special Representatives
- Working Groups. (OHCHR, 2022)

They are not a binding procedure. They cannot even be considered a decision-making or settlement procedure. But they have influence on states arising from a threefold framework based on their different functions: "reporting and fact finding", "standard-setting" (Subedi, 2011), and "constructive dialogue". Because the Special Procedures' actions on human rights are not concluded by a decision, they have no binding effect. The UN Special Procedures do not undertake any of the functions related before judiciary or settlement. It is true that they undertake investigation, but under a framework of communication, constructive dialogue, or even public naming and shaming. Their goal is not to arrive at a definitive decision, but to understand the public and the government's knowledge of a particular human rights case, or global trend. This is why the Special Procedures can act on human rights even without the agreement of states, because they do not have a decision-making or binding nature. Here, it is a trend of the human condition paradigm over the sovereignty paradigm that comes from the universal dimension of human rights and human dignity extending beyond the borders and limits of sovereign states. But it is just a partial solution to avoid the lack of agreement of states reluctant to be controlled. They do not have enough legitimacy in terms to arrive at judiciary decisions. They do not undertake a judicial procedure with procedures because it is outside of their mandate and function. Consequently, they are well-named "Special Procedures" with characteristics similar to ombudsmen and national human rights institutions, rather than to courts or tribunals. Therefore, they are both necessary and can coexist; they have institutional, and judiciary guarantees, but institutional guarantees are no substitute for the need to create stronger international judiciary guarantees. The Manual of Operations of the Special Procedures of the Human Rights Council defines it clearly:

> Thematic Special Procedures are mandated by the HRC to investigate the situation of human rights in all parts of the world, irrespective of whether a particular government is a party to any of the relevant human rights treaties. This requires them to take the measures necessary to monitor and respond quickly to allegations of human rights violations against individuals or groups, either globally or in a specific country or territory, and to report on their activities. (UN OHCHR, August 2008, para. 4)

Consequently, their functions are different from judiciary, decision-making, or settlement. Their principal functions are as follows, to:

- analyze the relevant thematic issue or country situation, including undertaking on-site missions;
- advise on the measures which should be taken by the government(s) concerned and other relevant actors;

- alert United Nations organs and agencies, in particular, the HRC, and the international community in general to the need to address specific situations and issues. In this regard they have a role in providing "early warning" and encouraging preventive measures;
- advocate on behalf of the victims of violations through measures such as requesting urgent action by relevant states and calling upon governments to respond to specific allegations of human rights violations and provide redress;
- activate and mobilize the international and national communities, and the HRC to address particular human rights issues, and to encourage cooperation among governments, civil society, and inter-governmental organizations;
- follow-up to recommendations. (UN OHCHR, August 2008, para. 5)

Their functions on human rights are guided not by a final decision, but Special Rapporteurs deal with the individual's communications on human rights violations in the form of allegation letters and urgent appeals sent to the relevant state governments by means of diplomatic channels. These communications are guided by the intention of trying to engage into "constructive dialogue": "The aim of the communications procedure is to ensure constructive dialogue with governments in order to promote respect for human rights" (UN OHCHR, August 2008). In summary, these communications are not at all a judgement or final decision:

> Communications do not imply any kind of value judgment on the part of the Special Procedure concerned and are thus not per se accusatory. They are not intended as a substitute for judicial or other proceedings at the national level. Their main purpose is to obtain clarification in response to allegations of violations and to promote measures designed to protect human rights. (OHCHR, August 2008, para. 30)

From my perspective, a Special Procedure carries out a constitutional function as an institutional guarantee at the international level. This is absolutely necessary, but it is different from a judiciary function or power. Under the case law and practices of regional systems of human rights, there are different positions concerning the prohibition of duplication procedures and Special Procedures. Let us analyze what happens in the two main regional systems where there can be a constitutional role in international judgements: the European Court of Human Rights and the Inter-American Court and Commission on Human Rights.

According to the Code of Conduct for Special Procedures of the United Nations (A/HRC/5/21 7 August 2007, A/HRC/5/21), the foremost of the General Principles of conduct for mandate-holders is independence. This is not prerogative, but a requisite and a necessary principle that shall guide their actions. Under their mandate they shall:

> Act in an independent capacity, and exercise their functions in accordance with their mandate, through a professional, impartial assessment of facts based on internationally recognized human rights standards, and free from any kind

of extraneous influence, incitement, pressure, threat or interference, either direct or indirect, on the part of any party, whether stakeholder or not, for any reason whatsoever, the notion of independence being linked to the status of mandate-holders, and to their freedom to assess the human rights questions that they are called upon to examine under their mandate. (A/HRC/5/21, 7 August 2007, art.3.a)

This is why the mandate holders must keep out personal political opinions from influencing their mission, and perform objective assessments of human rights situations: "Bear in mind the need to ensure that their personal political opinions are without prejudice to the execution of their mission, and base their conclusions and recommendations on objective assessments of human rights situations" (A/HRC/5/21, 7 August 2007, article 12.a).

The Special Procedure on the situation of human rights defenders: allegation letters, urgent appeals, and country visits

The main difference between a thematic mandate, such as the Special Rapporteur on human rights defenders, and a country mandate—referred to the human rights situation in a specific country—is that:

"In the case of country mandate holders, they report on the situation of human rights or allegations of human rights violation in a given country. In the case of thematic mandate holders, they report about the global situation of a particular phenomenon, right, or freedom, whether collective or individual". (Subedi, 2011, p. 203)

Under this framework, and according to the 2007 Code of Conduct (articles 9, 10, 11), Special Procedures have three specific sets of actions when undertaking the complaint procedure:

a   Allegation letters
b   Urgent appeals
c   Country visit

Allegation letters and urgent appeals relate to violations of human rights that come to their attention within the mandates. Individuals or groups of individuals, including NGOs, can send a communication to the Special Procedures to report a violation of human rights. The main difference between Allegation letters and urgent appeals is that in Allegation letters the communication is related to a violation that has already occurred. Allegation letters must fulfill the following criteria:

a   The communication should not be manifestly unfounded or politically motivated;
b   The communication should contain a factual description of the alleged violations of human rights;

c   The language in the communication should not be abusive;
d   The communication should be submitted by a person or a group of persons claiming to be
e   victim of violations or by any person or group of persons, including non-governmental organizations, acting in good faith in accordance with principles of human rights, and free from politically motivated stands or contrary to, the provisions of the Charter of the United Nations, and claiming to have direct or reliable knowledge of those violations substantiated by clear information;
f   The communication should not be exclusively based on reports disseminated by mass media. (A/HRC/5/21, 7 August 2007, article 9)

The Special Procedure for dealing with communication sends a letter to the concerned state "identifying the facts of the allegation, applicable international human rights norms and standards, the concerns and questions of the mandate-holder(s), and a request for follow-up action" (UN OHCHR, 2022). Mainly, these communications are used to cope with individual cases, but they can also be used to deal with general patterns and trends of human rights violations that could affect a particular group or community. Communications can refer to a violation of human rights emerging from the content of a draft, legislation, policy, or practice that is not absolutely compatible with "international human rights standards" (UN OHRC, 2022).

Urgent appeals come from an urgent request for action, due to ongoing violations of human rights, or they can happen suddenly, involving high risks such as threats or even the loss of life:

> Mandate-holders may resort to urgent appeals in cases where the alleged violations are time-sensitive in terms of involving loss of life, life-threatening situations or either imminent or ongoing damage of a very grave nature to victims that cannot be addressed in a timely manner by the procedure under article 9 of the present Code. (A/HRC/5/21, 7 August 2007, article 10)

Even if it is a non-binding method, these measures are only the last resort within contexts where it is not possible to submit a specific international complaint. According to reports on the mandates regarding the situation of human rights defenders, both the former Special Representative and the Special Rapporteurs, specify that threats to human rights defenders can come from state actors and non-state actors. Consequently, this international procedure can serve as a guarantee of a life threatened by the state. This is why it is important to raise awareness that all these communications will be published in reports. Sometimes it would be better to have more measures of protection for complainants, as well as systems for keeping their complaints anonymous. Communications can lead to different systems of physical protection for individuals, but they are not guaranteed, and even the UN used to have a disclaimer of responsibility on their website. Therefore, from my perspective, it is in some cases necessary to ask for an anonymous identification due to the further publication of the names in the report, or even in the allegation letters, being usually identified in the urgent appeals to the concerned state.

Human rights defenders are just the tip of the iceberg of a much bigger problem that comes from global weaknesses and the erosion of the constitutional state-based paradigm and fundamental rights. The lack of international protection for human rights without the adequate development of an international constitutional function is at the origin of this state breakdown. In domestic law, the problem arises from the lack of attention paid to internal mechanisms of referral in international law for the strong protection of fundamental rights. Consequently, in some contexts, individuals inevitably undertake a public constitutional function, and assume the consequences for the destruction of the public sphere. This sacrifice cannot become compulsory because individuals have a right, not a duty, nor a legal responsibility to protect or promote human rights. This appertains to the public institutional domain, in constitutional or international law, carried out by states, institutions, and international organizations. But if the states do not perform their function for the protection of fundamental rights, and international organizations do not assume enough international responsibility, individuals carry too strong a burden on their shoulders: they risk losing their life. No one should be forced by circumstances to carry on their shoulders the weight of public action in order to protect and promote human rights. This is an undue privatization of the constitutional and international function. The consequences are higher for individuals' lives: those who live under threats, loss of life, family, labour, or miss the public protection.

On the one hand, human rights defenders go further than mere protection and promotion in terms of the normal framework of claims, complaints, protests, or intellectual work on human rights. They must assume, even with their life, positive obligations that states do not undertake because they cannot or they do not want to. This is particularly true in failed states, conflicts, or in situations with not enough guarantees of rights. This is the main paradox. The state must accept the responsibility to protect and promote human rights. But the state can be the great absent or the main responsible for violating human rights. In the absence of public and constitutional action at the national, regional, or international level, individuals risk their lives. They must even protect, with their own life, the lives of other individuals or communities. In this case, we must ask if the state has lost its *raison d'être*, and the reason for their monopoly on violence. However, the state must persist doing a constitutional function, because it has the power to protect fundamental rights by public means. The right to promote or protect human rights does not mean, however, that it legitimizes any kind of violence from individual action to protect and promote human rights. The right of resistance has a different constitutional regime that is outside the framework of this essay. Even international humanitarian law sets the individual conditions for the status of protection in times of war for the civil population. That is, not getting involved in the use of violence. But the Geneva Conventions do not recognize individuals as members of the civil population when they use violence. Instead, they acquire the status of a combatant. To conclude, self-defence could be allowed, but then, it must fall under the umbrella of criminal law, international criminal law, or even international humanitarian law criteria, but not under the status of human rights defenders. The use of legitimate violence is outside of the scope of the declaration.

The last of the methods used by Special Rapporteurs, including the Special Rapporteur on human rights defenders is the country visit. On country visits, what is most relevant is that the Special Procedures "ensure that their visit is conducted with the consent, or at the invitation, of the State concerned" (A/HRC/5/21, 7 August 2007, 11.a.). Hence, the country visit is possible only if the concerned state accepts it prior. In this case, they would prepare the visit with the permanent mission of the state accredited in the United Nations Office at Geneva.

The question arises then: even if executing a constitutional function, is it possible to have any constitutional control in the conduct of Special Procedures?

First, in what this could be a theoretical answer, the absence of concentrated constitutional control in international procedures is due to its non-binding nature. But even it is not binding, it sometimes acts as a last resort for the protection of human rights. Now it is more necessary than ever that the thematic mechanisms do not carry out their mandate under political considerations. They are under the UN Charter and this would be against the human dignity paradigm that remains behind their power to act in human rights, even without the state agreement.

The Special Procedure on the situation of human rights defenders is working really hard to protect defenders' rights, but even the United Nations admits that they cannot assure their physical protection when defenders submit an individual communication to the Special Rapporteur.

It is worthwhile to point out that the protection of the right to promote and protect human rights is not only related to the right of (physical) protection of human rights defenders. It is absolutely necessary to protect the instrumental rights of the declaration such as the right of association, assembly, to communicate with international bodies, etc. The Special Procedure on the situation of human rights defenders clearly assumes a constitutional function in the protection of defenders' instrumental rights. But it cannot assume a "police" or "bodyguard" function because it goes beyond their mandate. Then, other constitutional guarantees need to be set up or to reset in states, with a multilevel perspective at the international and even the regional level. The commitment of the Special Procedures on their own independence is a *sine qua non* criterion to develop their mandate. It is important to remember that there is not any clear system of constitutional control for the conduct of Special Procedures. Hence, this would be another step in the constitutionalization of international law, that is still likely to be considered contrary to the interests of some states. In this case, the principle of human dignity is at the axiological basis for the Special Procedures under the Charter of the United Nations, but it can get in conflict with the principle of sovereignty of the state. Behind the thematic mechanisms, and more in the case of the Special Rapporteur on human rights defenders remains this unsolved paradox, especially after globalization.

From an internal constitutional perspective, it is difficult to find clauses of relationship between the UN Special Procedures and the states' constitution. This lack of reference points to lesser dialogue between Special Procedures and national courts. But there are always certain confusions in public opinion and the press that are not really aware of the functions of the UN Special Procedures. Journalists often confuse the thematic mechanisms with judiciary control.

The UN Special Procedure on the situation of human rights defenders' multilevel legal framework

In 2000, following the first thematic mechanism on human rights defenders, as a Special Representative of the Secretary General, there was a strong desire to enter into dialogue and cooperate with other regional systems of human rights. To this end, Hina Jilani, the Special Representative of the Secretary General on the situation of human rights defenders, declared:

> The Special Representative will seek to establish a working relationship with regional intergovernmental human rights mechanisms, including those under the Organization of American States, the Council of Europe, the Organization for Security and Cooperation in Europe (OSCE) and the Organization of African Unity, and to exchange information with their secretariats and experts on situations involving human rights defenders. (E/CN.4/2001/94, 26 January 2001, para. 37)

This initial will seem to aim for cooperation in order to develop regional strategies for better protections of human rights defenders. But under this mandate, Hina Jilani thought it was her task to explore the possibility of initiating other regional protection measures in compliance with her mandate. This led to the development of a real multilevel legal framework (Bennet et al., 2016) for the protection of human rights defenders. It used both universal and regional measures, leading to the adoption of national, regional, and local measures for human rights defenders. This multilevel system on human rights defenders is almost never studied in academia, particularly from a constitutional perspective.

Bennett, Ingleton, Nah, and Savage remind us that setting the UN Declaration on human rights defenders in 1998 "marked a milestone in the development of a multilevel, multi-actor international protection regime for the rights of human rights defenders" (Bennet et al., 2016, p. 1). Later, there was development in the regional systems of human rights for specific frameworks in support of human rights defenders. They were different in each system, according to their characteristics.

In 2002, the Organization of American States (OAS) created the "Unit for the protection of human rights defenders". This new body for defenders arose from a previous recommendation in 1998. It was established after the adoption of the UN Declaration on human rights defenders. In 1999, it crucially adopted Resolution 1671, entitled "Human Rights Defenders in the Americas: Support for the Individuals, Groups, and Organizations of Civil Society Working to Promote and Protect Human Rights in the Americas" (OAS Rapporteurship on Human Rights

Defenders, 2022). The role of the OAS Unit on human rights defenders focused on the coordination of the Executive Secretariat's activities in the region. The OAS unit was specifically created "to follow the situation of human rights defenders throughout the region" (OAS Rapporteurship on Human Rights Defenders, 2022).

In March 2011, the Inter-American Commission of Human Rights decided to create the Rapporteurship on Human Rights Defenders to substitute the former unit for the protection of human rights defenders (OAS Rapporteurship on Human Rights Defenders, 2022). The Rapporteurship on human rights defenders was created because of the number of petitions received. There was the will to give more visibility to the role of human rights defenders, and how they contribute to the rule of law and democracy (OAS Rapporteurship on Human Rights Defenders, 2022). The OAS Rapporteurship on Human Rights Defenders has these main functions:

- To provide support to the Inter-American Commission in the analysis of petitions presented concerning defenders and defenders rights;
- To ask concerned states to adopt precautionary and provisional measures to prevent irreparable harm against defenders;
- To prepare specialized studies on the situation of human rights defenders in order to develop better standards and to provide guidance to states.
- To carry out visits to states, with prior consent of the state concerned, to learn more about the situation of defenders in these states and the region;
- To undertake promotional activities, such as seminars, workshops, conferences... on human rights defenders. (OAS Rapporteurship on human rights defenders and Justice operators, 2022)

In 2004, the African Commission on Human and Peoples' Rights established the Special Rapporteur on human rights defenders, in the African Union, that holds these main functions:

1. seek, receive, examine and act upon information on the situation of human rights defenders in Africa;
2. submit reports at every ordinary session of the African Commission;
3. cooperate and engage in dialogue with Member States, National Human Rights Institutions, relevant intergovernmental bodies, international and regional mechanisms of protection of human rights defenders and other stakeholders;
4. develop and recommend effective strategies to better protect human rights defenders and follow up on his/her recommendations; and
5. raise awareness and promote the implementation of the UN Declaration on Human Rights Defenders in Africa. (African Commission on Human and People's Rights, Resolution 69, 2004)

Under the framework of the Council of Europe, there is not a thematic body on human rights defenders, such as the Rapporteurship in the universal system of the United Nations and in the regional systems of Africa and the Americas. However, the Council of Europe has a consistent system for defenders, with a twofold perspective: the judiciary case law of the European Court of Human Rights and the institutional guarantee by the COE Commissioner for human rights. This is relevant because the defenders' protection is carried out mainly by the protection of defenders' rights. It does not focus only on the physical protection of the subject of rights, this is a better perspective but also it is possible for the characteristics of the European area. This is worthwhile to think about, despite the violent dangers and threats toward defenders rising in the area. It reminds us that defenders are often under threat because they are the voice for protecting others' human rights. When a defender is silent, it also silences the voices of millions of individuals and the individual human rights that accompany them. In this case, the protection of defenders' rights does not exist by institutional guarantee, but mainly through judiciary control and the European Court of Human Rights case law. At the institutional level, protection is carried out by the Commissioner on human rights who give "support for the work of human rights defenders, their protection and the development of an enabling environment for their activities" because it lies at the Commissioner mandate (COE Commissioner of Human Rights, 2022).

In this case, we can observe how international institutional guarantees of defenders' rights and the judiciary protection of their rights are not opposite but complementary. Thus, we could ask why it is considered inadmissible to make a complaint to the European Court of Human Rights, and to submit it at the same time to the UN Special Rapporteur, and to the ECHR. In the event of different solutions, they are not comparable, having the ECtHR a binding case law. The functions of the Special Rapporteurs, or Rapporteurships, must never be used as a hidden "judiciary control" because the Rapporteurships do not have enough individual guarantees, and it is not their function; in fact, it exceeds their mandate. Hence, why not open the door for a multilevel solution between the UN Special Procedures and the ECtHR?

This would be conditional to the commitment of Special Procedures on independence. It is not comparable to the compulsory judiciary commitment to impartiality, which is stronger. Special Procedures and regional case law cannot be compared.

The European Union merits particular attention because there is a dimension, *ad intra,* on human rights defenders lead by an area of justice, security and freedom within the framework of the Charter of Fundamental Rights. The dimension *ad extra* of this system is with an external policy on human rights defenders undertaken mainly by the European External Action System, after the Treaty of Lisbon.

The UN human rights defenders' global framework and the human condition as paradigm of international and constitutional law

The legal framework of the Declaration on Human Rights Defenders follows the trend of individualization in international law, as well as the proliferation of new sources for rights' guarantees in the multilevel legal framework of the global world. As indicated by Rovira Viñas, nowadays, the main guarantees of the rule of law, political pluralism, and the division of powers remain insufficient due to globalization. There is a crisis regarding the efficiency of the traditional mechanisms of fundamental rights guarantees (Rovira Viñas, 2013, p. 20). At the core of this system the paradigm of human condition is protected universally under the UN thematic mechanisms and the regional human rights systems for human rights defenders, being at the axiological basis of this new active subject of law, not defined by personhood but by the exercise of rights. The right to promote and protect human rights is part of a global constitutionalism trend, as theorized before by Peters and Kumm, based on the synergies among these different legal levels.

Consequently, human rights law today emerges from different levels of law and at the same time is humanized. The humanization of international law is a cornerstone of Peters' Theory, particularly in *Beyond Human Rights* (2016). It is a change in international law that directly affects constitutional law too. According to J. H. Lee, this humanization of international law influenced other fields of international law, such as international humanitarian law (Lee, 2015). This author points out that there is a need of humanization in international law and "the aim, subject, and object of the contemporary international law should be expanded and transformed" (Lee, 2015, pp. 28–29). Lee contends that in order to change the classical paradigm of international law, which is defined by the self-interest of states, it is necessary to turn to individuals, human rights, and humanity: "To achieve that goal, the state-centered international community must be changed into the individual-centered international community where human rights and humanity are regarded highly and preciously" (Lee, 2015, pp. 28–29). For these reasons, this humanization trend in the subject of international law is also leading to changes in the constitutional paradigm.

In this sense, when considering the possible internationalization of constitutional law, Chang and Yeh have outlined several trends and forces in the process toward a progressive internationalization of constitutional law (Chang and Yeh, 2012). Two of them are central in this analysis: the incorporation of international human rights into domestic constitutions and the emergence of global rights-based discourse (Chang and Yeh, 2012, pp. 1166, 1184).

This change in the paradigm of international law according to humanization is clear. Nowadays, according to Peters, the individual is an actor of Law (Peters, 2016), almost a subject of law capable of enforcing it with his or her own activities through the protection and promotion of human rights. This change in the paradigm of international law leads to a change of the constitutional paradigm. It almost constitutes a recognition of the people's constituent power inherent to individuals, but not only based on citizenship. Nevertheless, the notion of citizenship today is not just committed to a citizenship engaged with citizenship rights, bound to a nation-state, but with human rights in a global world.

Consequently, the notion of a citizen as a subject of constitutional law is evolving toward a broader concept of citizenry with the convergence of different legal orders, but with essential rights inherent to human dignity: human rights, not only under a passive personhood but under an active exercise of the right to promote and protect human rights. The paradigm of human dignity set after the Second World War breaks down in this process. The state is not the only actor for the protection of human rights defenders, neither the only actor of promotion and protection of human rights, because the right to promote and protect human rights is recognized to everyone, individually or in association with others, at the national and international levels. Consequently, the progressive legal recognition of this humanization is based in the human condition paradigm, and the trend converges in the concept of human rights defenders.

The Declaration on human rights defenders emerged in the international arena in parallel to the process of internationalization and humanization in human rights. In this process, the state is not and cannot be the only one responsible for protecting human rights, but it is still and must be mainly responsible because its own legitimacy can depend on this, as set in article 1 of the Declaration on human rights defenders.

Fundamental rights established in constitutions are confluent with the multilevel legal framework of protection for human rights. The Declaration on Human Rights Defenders tries to guarantee human rights defenders' rights not only at internal or international level, but also in a multilevel legal framework that is necessary in a global world with referrals between the two legal systems. In this multilevel legal framework, the human being is not only in need of protection as an object of law. According to the Declaration on human rights defenders, the human being, individually or in association with others, is entitled as a subject to the right to promote and to strive for the protection and promotion of human rights. Thus, an emerging new subject of law both for international and constitutional law that merits to be considered and analyzed.

However, the construction of a multilevel legal system must not be understood as the construction of a homogeneous legal system. On the contrary, as Tenorio Sánchez also noted (Tenorio Sánchez, 2014, p. 92), the connection between international law and constitutional law should warrant respect for the idiosyncrasies of individuals, leaving the specific implementation of human rights to the lower levels of the legal system.

The social function represented by the right to promote and protect human rights originates in the individual exercise of this right. As an individual exercise, it also corresponds to an individual identity that inevitably varies from one individual to other. Defining a right on the basis of activity and the subject might make it possible to overcome the paradoxes of citizen's rights. The exercise of a specific right defines the legal subject, not vice versa. This individual exercise must be peaceful and respectful of the universal character of human rights. Universality is not the same as uniformity. An abstract universal entitlement is perfectly compatible with a differentiated application in individual cases that respects the inherent diversity of contemporary societies. Therefore, in addition to generic recognition at the universal level in the DHRD, there must be an individual application by each state according to its internal legal system, and that must respect the international legal framework and include referrals to it, while still implementing its own regulations. The architecture of the Declaration on human rights defenders reflects this delicate balance.

The main focus of the declaration is on the action, not on an abstract subject. It is the action that builds the subject, and due to the action of the subject, the promotion and protection of human rights is carried out. Thus, there is a "performative" aspect inherent to the right to promote and protect human rights; this is the possibility of enabling a right by means of individual and collective action. Due to the exercise of the right, human rights protection and promotion are achieved. Consequently, the protection of human rights is a result of individual and collective action.

Another characteristic of the right to promote and protect human rights is that promotion and protection is achieved by different means. Thus, performance is achieved through an action that cannot be specifically connected with a discourse on human rights activism and by actors that become human rights defenders due to their activities, not due to ideology or mere words. For instance, a doctor working on cases of sexual violence against women can protect and promote the human rights of women through their action in anonymous cases, even without the doctor's awareness of their role as a human rights defender. Doctor Denis Mukwege was the winner of the European Parliament Sakharov Prize 2014.

> Mukwege is an internationally recognised expert in the repair of pathological and psychosocial damage caused by sexual violence. The hospital he directs in Panzi offers psychological and physical care and women are also helped to develop new skills to earn a living, as their communities have rejected many of them. Girls are helped to go back to school and legal aid is offered to those seeking legal redress. (European Parliament Sakharov Prize, 2014)

The most important contribution to this international legal framework and its influence on constitutional law is the legal recognition of individual activities that promote, protect, and strive for human rights. This activity can be undertaken individually or in a collective manner. The right to promote and to protect human rights is then the core right of the Declaration on human rights defenders, but it is worthwhile to explore several instrumental rights set by the DHRD.

References

Alvarez, J. E. (2006). *International Organizations as Law Makers*. Oxford: Oxford University Press.
Bennet, K., Ingleton, D., Nah, M. A., and Savage, J. (2016). *Critical Perspectives on the Security and Protection of Human Rights Defenders*. Oxon & New York: Routledge.
Cerna, C. (2011). "Introductory remarks by Christina Cerna". *Proceedings of the Annual Meeting (American Society of International Law)*, 105, 507–509.
Chang, W. H. and Yeh, J. R. (2012). "Internationalization of constitutional law". In M. Rosenfeld & A. Sajó (Eds), *The Oxford Handbook of Comparative Constitutional Law*. Oxford: Oxford University Press.
Dominguez Redondo, E. (2005). *Los procedimientos públicos especiales de la Comisión de Derechos Humanos de Naciones Unidas*. Valencia: Tirant Lo Blanch.
Eide, A. and Alfredsson, G. (1992). "Introduction". In A. Eide et al. *The Universal Declaration of Human Rights: A Commentary*. Oslo: Scandinavian University Press.

Gómez Sánchez, Y. (2018). *Derechos Fundamentales*. Pamplona: Aranzadi.
Gómez Sánchez, Y. (2020). *Constitucionalismo multinivel. Derechos Fundamentales*. Madrid: Sanz y Torres.
Gutter, J. (2006). *Thematic Procedures of the United Nations Commission on Human Rights and International Law: In search of a sense of community*. Antwerpen: Intersentia.
Lee, J. H. (2015). "International legal perspective on the future of international humanitarian law action". *HUFS Global Law Review*, 7(1).
Limon, M. and Power, H. (2014). *History of the United Nations Special Procedures Mechanism*. Universal Rights Group.
Peters, A. (2009). "The Merits of Global Constitutionalism Introduction: The Meaning of Global Constitutionalism". *Indiana Journal of Global Legal Studies*, 16.
Peters, A. (2016). *Beyond Human Rights: The Legal Status of the Individual in International Law*. Cambridge: Cambridge University Press.
Pizarro Sotomayor, A. (2009). "The rule of the duplication of procedures in the regional systems of human rights". *Revista Panameña de Política*, 8.
Pons Ràfols, X., Saura Estapà, J., and Guillen Lanzarote, A. (2009). *Nous Instruments Internacionals de Protecció dels Drets Humans. El Consell de Drets Humans i l'Examen Periòdic Universal*. Barcelona: Generalitat de Catalunya. Departament d'Interior, Relacions Institucionals i Participació, Oficina de Promoció de la Pau i els Drets Humans.
Rovira Viñas, A. (2013). "Gobernanza y Derechos Humanos". In A. Rovira Viñas (Ed.), *Gobernanza Democrática*. Madrid: Marcial Pons.
Saura-Freixes, N. (2016). *Human Rights Defenders. El derecho a promover y proteger los derechos humanos*. Madrid: UNED.
Shaw, M. N. (2008). *International Law*. Cambridge: Cambridge University Press.
Steiner, H., Alston, P., and Goodman, R. (2008). *International Human Rights in Context*. Oxford: Oxford University Press.
Subedi, S. P. (2011). "Protection of human rights through the mechanism of the Special Procedures". *Human Rights Quarterly*, 33(1).
Tenorio Sánchez, P. J. (2014). *La libertad de expresión. Su posición preferente en un entorno multicultural*. Madrid: Walter Kluwers.
von Bogdandy, A. and Venzke, I. (2014). *In Whose Name? A Public Law Theory of International Adjudication*. Oxford: Oxford University Press.
Wapner, P. (2007). "Civil society". In T. G. Weiss and S. Daws (Eds), *The Oxford Handbook on the United Nations*. Oxford: Oxford University Press.

Documents

Treaties

African Charter on Human and Peoples' Rights (adopted 27 June 1981, *entered into force 21 October 1986) CAB/LEG/67/3 rev.* 5, 21 I.L.M. 58 (1982) (African Charter)
American Convention on Human Rights (adopted 22 November, 1969, entered into force 18 July 1978) 1144 UNTS.123; OASTS. No. 36 ("Pact of San Jose, Costa Rica", ACHR)
Charter of the United Nations, (adopted 24 October 1945) 1 UNTS XVI
Consolidated Version of the Treaty on European Union [2012] OJ C 326/13
Convention for the Protection of Human Rights and Fundamental Freedoms, as amended, (adopted 4 November 1950, *entered into force 3 September 1953) ETS No.* 005 (ECHR)

International Covenant on Civil and Political Rights (adopted 16 December 1966, entered into force 23 March 1976) 999 UNTS 171 (ICCPR)

International Covenant on Economic, Social and Cultural Rights (adopted 16 December 1966, entered into force 3 January 1976) 993 UNTS 3 (ICESCR)

Optional Protocol to the International Covenant on Civil and Political Rights. (adopted 16 December 1966, entered into force 23 March 1976) 999 UNTS 17

Geneva Convention for the amelioration of the condition of the wounded and sick in armed forces in the field (adopted 12 August 1949, entered into force 21 October 1950) 75 UNTS 31 (First Geneva Convention)

Geneva Convention on Wounded, Sick and Shipwrecked of Armed Forces at Sea (adopted 12 August 1949, entered into force 21 October 1950) 75 UNTS 85 (Second Geneva Convention)

Geneva Convention Relative to the Treatment of Prisoners of War (adopted 12 August 1949, entered into force 21 October 1950) 75 UNTS 135 (Third Geneva Convention)

Geneva Convention Relative to the Protection of Civilian Persons in Time of War (adopted 12 August 1949, entered into force 21 October 1950) 75 UNTS 287 (Fourth Geneva Convention)

International Convention on the Elimination of All Forms of Racial Discrimination (adopted 21 December 1965, entered into force 4 January 1969) 660 UNTS 195

United Nations

Universal Declaration of Human Rights (10 December 1948) *UNGA Res.* 217A (III) (10 December 1948)

Declaration on the Right and Responsibility of Individuals, Groups and Organs of Society to Promote and Protect UniversallyRecognized HumanRights and Fundamental Freedoms UNGA A/RES/53/144 (8 March 1999)

UNGA "*Protection of human rights in Chile: note/by the Secretary-General*" (7 October 1975) UN Doc A/10285. Retrieved 3 June, 2022, from: https://digitallibrary.un.org/record/659226?ln=es

UNGA "*Human Rights Council*" (3 April 2006) UN Doc A/RES/60/251. Retrieved 3 June, 2022, from: www2.ohchr.org/english/bodies/hrcouncil/docs/a.res.60.251_en.pdf

UNCHR "Study of reported violations of human rights in Chile, with particular reference to torture and other cruel, inhuman or degrading treatment or punishment (resolution 8 (XXVII) of the Sub-Commission on Prevention of Discrimination and Protection of Minorities and General Assembly resolution 3219 *(XXIX)*)" (31 January 1975) UN Doc E/CN.4/1166. Retrieved 3 June, 2022, from: https://digitallibrary.un.org/record/677782?ln=es

UNCHR "*Question of missing and disappeared persons*". (29 February 1980). Resolution 20 (XXXVI) Retrieved 27 May, 2022, from: www.ohchr.org/sites/default/files/Documents/Issues/Disappearances/E-CN.4-RES-1980-20_XXXVI.pdf

UNCHR Res 2000/61. *(2000) Human rights defenders,* (27 April 2000) UN Doc E/CN.4/RES/2000/61. Retrieved 27 May, 2022, from: www.refworld.org/docid/3b00f21bc.html

UNCHR "*Implementation of the Declaration on the Right and Responsibility of Individuals, Groups and Organs of Society to Promote and Protect Universally Recognized Human Rights and Fundamental Freedoms: report of the Secretary-General*" (13 January 2000)

UN Doc E/CN.4/2000/95. Retrieved 3 June 2022, from: https://digitallibrary.un.org/record/407306

UNCHR "*Report submitted by Ms. Hina Jilani, Special Representative of the Secretary-General on human rights defenders in accordance with Commission resolution 2000/61*" (2001) UN Doc E/CN.4/2001/94. Retrieved 3 June, 2022, from: https://digitallibrary.un.org/record/450010?ln=es

ECOSOC "*Measures for the speedy implementation of the United Nations Declaration on the Elimination of All Forms of Racial Discrimination*" (4 March 1966) UN Doc E/RES/1102(XL). Retrieved 3 June, 2022, from: https://digitallibrary.un.org/record/214191

ECOSOC "*Question of the violation of human rights and fundamental freedoms, including policies of racial discrimination and segregation and of apartheid, in all countries, with particular reference to colonial and other dependent countries and territories*" (6 June 1967) UN Doc E/RES/1235(XLII). Retrieved 3 June, 2022, from: https://digitallibrary.un.org/record/214657

ECOSOC "*Procedure for dealing with communications relating to violations of human rights and fundamental freedoms*" (27 May 1970) UN Doc E/RES/1503(XLVIII). Retrieved 3 June, 2022, from: https://digitallibrary.un.org/record/214705

HRC "*Resolution adopted by the Human Rights Council on 23 March 2017 34/5. Mandate of the Special Rapporteur on the situation of human rights defenders*" (3 April 2007) UN Doc A/HRC/RES/34/5. Retrieved 27 May, 2022, from: https://digitallibrary.un.org/record/1290080?ln=es

HRC "Institution-building of the United Nations Human Rights Council. (18 June 2007) UN Doc A/HRC/RES/5/1. Retrieved 3 June, 2022, from: https://digitallibrary.un.org/record/603041?ln=es

HRC "*Code of Conduct for Special Procedures Mandate-holders of the Human Rights Council*" (7 August 2007) UN Doc A/HRC/5/21. Retrieved 27 May, 2022, from: https://digitallibrary.un.org/record/603044?ln=es

HRC "*Human Rights Council Resolution 7/8. Mandate of the Special Rapporteur on the situation of human rights defenders*" (27 March 2008). Retrieved 3 June, 2022, from: https://ap.ohchr.org/documents/E/HRC/resolutions/A_HRC_RES_7_8.pdf

HRC "*Resolution adopted by the Human Rights Council 16/5. Mandate of the Special Rapporteur on the situation of human rights defenders*" (8 April 2011) UN Doc A/HRC/RES/16/5. Retrieved 3 June, 2022, from: https://digitallibrary.un.org/record/701210?ln=es

HRC "*Resolution adopted by the Human Rights Council 25/18. Mandate of the Special Rapporteur on the situation of human rights defenders*" (11 April 2014) UN Doc A/HRC/RES/25/18. Retrieved 27 May, 2022, from: https://digitallibrary.un.org/record/768970?ln=es

HRC "*Extension of mandates and mandated activities: decision / adopted by the Human Rights Council on 13 March 2020*" (16 March 2020) UN Doc A/HRC/DEC/43/115 (16 March 2020). Retrieved 27 May, 2022, from: https://digitallibrary.un.org/record/3857022?ln=es

HRC "*Mandate of the Special Rapporteur on the Situation of Human Rights Defenders: resolution / adopted by the Human Rights Council on 22 June 2020*" (6 July 2020) UN Doc A/HRC/RES/43/16. Retrieved 3 June, 2022, from: https://digitallibrary.un.org/record/3874886?ln=es

HRC "*Enforced or involuntary disappearances: resolution / adopted by the Human Rights Council on 6 October 2020*" (8 October 2020) UN Doc A/HRC/RES/45/3. Retrieved 3 June, 2022, from: https://digitallibrary.un.org/record/3888386

OHCHR "Manual of Operations of the Special Procedures of the Human Rights Council (August 2008). Retrieved 3 June, 2022, from: https://digitallibrary.un.org/record/3954073

OHCHR (2022). *"Communication report and search"*. Retrieved 27 May, 2022, from: https://spcommreports.ohchr.org/

OHCHR (2022). *"Special Rapporteur on the situation of human rights defenders"*. Retrieved May 28, 2022, from: www.ohchr.org/en/special-procedures/sr-human-rights-defenders#:~:text=Ms.,of%20Business%20and%20Human%20Rights

OHCHR (2022). *"Special Rapporteur on extrajudicial, summary or arbitrary executions"*. Retrieved 27 May, from: www.ohchr.org/en/special-procedures/sr-executions#:~:text=The%20Special%20Rapporteur%20on%20extrajudicial,HRC%20resolution%2044%2F05

OHCHR *(2022)*. *"Thematic Mandates"*. Retrieved 27 May, 2022, from: https://spinternet.ohchr.org/ViewAllCountryMandates.aspx?Type=TM&lang=en

OHCHR (2022). *"The UN Working Group on Enforced or Involuntary Disappearances"*. Retrieved 27 May, 2022: www.ohchr.org/en/special-procedures/wg-disappearances

OHCHR (2022). *"What are Communications?"* Retrieved 27 May, 2022, from: www.ohchr.org/en/special-procedures-human-rights-council/what-are-communications

United NationsResearch Guides (2022). "Human Rights Timeline: Special Procedures", *United Nations library & archives Geneva*. Retrieved 27 May, 2022, from: https://libraryresources.unog.ch/hrtimeline/specialprocedures

AU

ACHPR 69 Resolution on the Protection of Human Rights Defenders In Africa – (4 June 2004) *ACHPR/Res.69(XXXV)03*. Retrieved 27 May, from: www.achpr.org/sessions/resolutions?id=74

COE

Commissioner for Human Rights. (2022). *"Human rights defenders"*. Retrieved 27 May, 2022, from: www.coe.int/en/web/commissioner/human-rights-defenders

European Union

European Parliament (21 October 2014). *"Dennis Mukwege: Winner of Sakharov Prize 2014"*. Retrieved 27 May, 2022, from: www.europarl.europa.eu/news/en/headlines/eu-affairs/20141016STO74202/denis-mukwege-winner-of-sakharov-prize-2014

OAS

Human rights defenders in the Americas: support for the individuals, groups, and organizations of civil society working to promote and protect human rights in the Americas (4 June 2022) *AG/RES*. 1842 (XXXII-O/02). Retrieved 27 May, 2022, from: www.oas.org/xxxiiga/english/docs_en/docs_items/agres1842_02.htm

OAS (2022). *"Rapporteurship on Human Rights Defenders and Justice Operators"*. Retrieved May 27 from: www.oas.org/en/iachr/jsForm/?File=/en/iachr/r/DDDH/default.asp

OSCE

ODIHR (2014). *Guidelines on human rights defenders.* Warsaw: OSCE Office for Democratic Institutions and Human Rights (ODIHR). Retrieved 27 May, 2022, from: www.osce.org/files/f/documents/c/1/119633.pdf

NGOs and other sources

Front Line Defenders (2022). Retrieved May 27 from: www.frontlinedefenders.org/es
International Service for Human Rights (8 September 2019). "*Special Procedures | What skills do we need in the next UN expert on human rights defenders?*" Retrieved 27 May, 2022, from: https://ishr.ch/latest-updates/special-procedures-what-skills-do-we-need-next-un-expert-human-rights-defenders-rapporteur/

3 Human rights defenders and the right to promote and protect human rights

During the last decades, human rights protection has evolved into a twofold system: the internationalization of human rights protection and the individualization of international law (Peters, 2016). These two phenomena changed the paradigm of the sovereign state in international law. In 1998, following the codification of human rights with an international system of guarantees, three elements merged to form a cornerstone of international law where the individual has a new role. It is necessary to highlight the adoption of the Rome Statute that created an International Criminal Court; the new European Court of Human Rights giving to individuals an international guarantee of human rights to submit directly an application, and the adoption of the *United Nations Declaration on the Right and Responsibility of Individuals, Groups and Organs of Society to Promote and Protect Universally Recognized Human Rights and Fundamental Freedoms*, better known as the *Declaration on Human Rights Defenders* (DHRD).

A synergy can be found between the internationalization of human rights and the individualization of international law (Peters, 2016). Carrillo Salcedo (1999) and Gómez Sanchez (2020) think this synergy stems from the acknowledgement of human dignity, recognized in the "Preamble" of the United Nations Charter. Gavara de Cara (2011) employs a constitutional perspective and considers the principle of human dignity inherent to being human. Hence, it is a quality leading to the concept of non-instrumentalization, which is present in the German constitutional formulation (Gavara de Cara, 2011, pp. 99–100). This interpretation of human dignity prevents the instrumentalization or materialization of individuals; the human being is an end in itself. After globalization, this first paradigm, which is based on human dignity, evolves toward a wider, global conception of the human condition. This is consistent with Arendt's theory on the right to have rights (1951), which refers to the Aristotelian concept in *Politics,* Book I. *Zoon politikón* is an expression from the ancient Greek philosopher which is hard to translate. The term *zoé* means bare life, for both humans and animals. Humans require social and individual language to become human, and not merely bare life. Society is thus essential to human being. Agamben (2003) reflects on this thought, going further in his work, *Homo Sacer,* due to the implications on politics of the term *politikón*, when considered as power. This is why several translations of the term *zoé* are possible and not contradictory. In Aristotle's term converge politics,

DOI: 10.4324/9780429264016-3

society, and the city-state. The use of language is integral in building a city, performing theatre, learning and discussing the law in the agora of public matters; that is, to have jurisdiction. Human beings are the only animals who have the ability of *logos* or speech: language is constitutive, inherent and unique to humans.

The state is still the axis of international law and the first entity responsible for human rights protection. This is made clear in the DHRD, and it is not incompatible with the concept or subject of human rights defenders. Fifty years after the adoption of the Universal Declaration of Human Rights, on 9 December 1998, the General Assembly of the United Nations adopted the *Declaration on the Right and Responsibility of Individuals, Groups and Organs of Society to Promote and Protect Universally Recognized Human Rights and Fundamental Freedoms*, set up by Resolution 53/144, 8 March 1999.

According to art. 2 DHRD, human rights defenders must be free to exercise or choose not to exercise their right to promote and protect human rights. This right is in fact a right of action and freedom of thought of individuals, groups, and organs of society; and neither a duty nor a substitute of public action. The responsibility to protect and promote human rights remains with the state, under article 2 DHRD (1998):

> Article 2 1. Each State has a prime responsibility and duty to protect, promote and implement all human rights and fundamental freedoms, inter alia, by adopting such steps as may be necessary to create all conditions necessary in the social, economic, political and other fields, as well as the legal guarantees required to ensure that all persons under its jurisdiction, individually and in association with others, are able to enjoy all those rights and freedoms in practice.
>
> 2. 2. Each State shall adopt such legislative, administrative and other steps as may be necessary to ensure that the rights and freedoms referred to in the present Declaration are effectively guaranteed. (A/RES/53/144, 8 March 1999)

Thus, the main responsibility and duty to protect and promote human rights belongs to states. Today, the individual is no longer a mere object of international law (Peters, 2016). Carrillo Salcedo was one of the first to consider a human being as quasi a subject of international law, when human dignity overcomes sovereignty (1999). Gardbaum goes even further, especially considering that the primary change in this domain identifies individuals as subjects of contemporary international law (in addition to states): "That is, individuals and no longer only states have rights and duties under international law" (Gardbaum, 2009, p. 219). Peters concluded that there is a change in the paradigm of legal personhood due to the individualization of international law in *Beyond Human Rights. The Legal Status of the Individual in International Law (2016)*. Thus, individuals become the new legal subjects (Peters, 2016).

However, this does not mean going beyond human beings or destroying the multilevel legal framework of the state and the cosmopolitan society or university achieved after centuries of social struggles. On the contrary, human rights defenders are part of this synergy under a multilevel system and global international and constitutional trends of individuals and social movements standing for human rights. It is only under the paradigm set by the DHRD (1998) that they become a new active subject of human rights law; out of it, they can never be both subject and object of law. As human rights defenders, this new legal subject and concept is set up to exercise the right to promote and protect human rights. So, it is not based on the entitlement of this right. This new right and subject is a challenge for international and constitutional law. The right to promote and protect human rights does not rely on citizenship and sovereignty; the exercise differs from person to person. After globalization and pandemic declaration, jurisdiction is a concept that, in the twenty-first century, is necessary to build rights. Neither citizenship nor sovereignty, jurisdiction is the ability to set law out of language, which is inherent to human beings. Who has this ability is the crucial question of present times. "Foreigners", "nationals", "others", or "EU citizens" are becoming obsolete terms because states, international organizations, or individuals alone cannot cope with global threats or global changes.

Individuals have become the backbone of the Declaration on human rights defenders. The DHRD gives recognition to individuals, groups, and organs of society, establishing their right to promote and protect human rights. But there is an individual perspective behind giving rights to groups, like NGOs, social movements, and organs of society, or like national human rights institutions and ombudsmen. The right to promote and protect human rights can be exercised "individually and in association with others" (art. 1 DHRD).

The main right, to strive and to promote human rights, is recognized universally in art. 1 of the DHRD. This right is established by instrumental rights recognized throughout the DHRD, like freedom of expression, or the right to communicate with international bodies. But these rights are instrumental to the right contained in art. 1 of the DHRD:

Everyone has the right, individually and in association with others, to promote and to strive for the

> protection and realization of human rights and fundamental freedoms at the national and international levels. (A/RES/53/144, 8 March 1999, art.1)

The right to promote and strive for human rights is recognized at national and international levels.

The synergies between international and constitutional law are increasing in the twenty-first century. So, it is necessary to recognize both national and international levels of convergence. But it is a pity that there is not enough academic doctrine or case law on this right; it is not usually considered outside of academia. However, in Bennet et al. (2015) there is a multilevel system on human rights defenders as developed by the UN. The regional systems of human rights and domestic law (Bennet et al., 2015) must be taken into consideration for the challenges it poses to both international and constitutional law.

The right to promote and protect human rights is anchored by the will of individuals who have the potential to become human rights defenders. To promote and protect human rights is not a legal duty. However, individuals can become human rights defenders by choice, or by a compelling or urgent necessity in instances of human rights violations. Unfortunately, human rights are endangered by the "possession paradox" theorized by Donnelly (2003). The "possession paradox" postulates that human rights become important when they are denied (Donnelly, cit. in Parekh, 2007, p. 126). Further on, human rights defenders suffer threats, killings, and harassment. The case of journalists is paradigmatic. To kill the messenger is a way of hiding violations of human rights from the world (DefendDefenders, 2017).

To be protected, it is necessary to give human rights defenders more than physical protection. The main right of the DHRD is the right to promote and protect human rights. The right to protection is instrumental. Thus, it is necessary to strengthen the guarantees of their rights at the international and national levels, under art.1 of the DHRD. The dialogue and synergy between the two legal corpus, international and constitutional law, are awakening in the twenty-first century. They can be helped by the implementation of international judgements and decisions, hereby legal guarantees for defenders are reinforced.

International and constitutional law are transitioning toward the new rights paradigm. The conventional paradigm of state and sovereignty has been overcome because of globalization. There is a breakdown in the paradigm of human rights as established after the Second World War. However, this does not indicate that the system must be globally erased or substituted, not at all. What the breakdown means is that there are not currently enough mechanisms of protection for human rights at national and international levels, due to the limits of the statist paradigm. In the global world, there is a lack of mechanisms not based in frontiers or sovereignty. This can perpetuate violations of human rights or impunity. However, it is not the task of individuals to be substitutes for state or public action. Nobody must cope with this duty. To promote and to protect human rights is a right that each individual exercises according to their will.

The DHRD recognizes in the "Preamble" the "valuable work of individuals, groups and associations in contributing to the effective elimination of all violations of human rights and fundamental freedoms of peoples and individuals" (A/RES/53/144, 8 March 1999). Bobbio points out that human rights are historical, and constantly in evolution. They are the result of "struggles in favor of the defense for new rights against old powers" (Bobbio, 1991). For instance, this could be the case with new rights against climate and environmental threats. They come mainly from the historical lack of effective measures, and from states as well as businesses and companies. These new rights are dealt with at an international level, sometimes under the umbrella of the right to life, as in the case law of the ECtHR. At a constitutional level, the responsibility for climate change can be dealt with under the umbrella of the right to life too. It is then interesting to follow the 2016 important case of *Juliana v. the United States* (2020). In 2015, 21 children sued the court, alleging the Fifth Amendment in a case against the federal government questioning the responsibility of the US administration on climate change, "asking the court to order the government to act on climate change, asserting harm from carbon emissions" (Reibstein, American Bar Association, Jan. 16, 2018).

But, despite these rising trends on individualization (Peters, 2016), the system of fundamental rights and human rights still remains anchored in a broken state-based legal framework. This statist framework was created after the Second World War and it will soon be obsolete if it is not updated. The emergence of human rights defenders is both evidence and warning about the weakening state paradigm, or the "failed state" (Owen, 2001, p.3). At the dawn of the twenty-first century, Owen (2001) warned about the consequences of weakened or failed states for human rights:

> many of the modern problems of human rights arise not where the state is too strong, but where weak and internally divided states cease to be able to guarantee social order. In the most extreme form, the so called "failed state", "soft interventions" are ineffective. Failed states simply lack the capacity to protect human rights. (Owen, 2001, p.3)

In the context of a "failed state", the action of human rights defenders become compellingly necessary, and often more dangerous. However, it does not mean that we need to trust only in individuals. On the contrary, it is necessary for the constitutional function of states and international organizations to be strong and fair enough to comply with their commitments to human rights. Nowadays, there is an evolution toward global constitutionalism (Suami et al., 2018). In this, the most relevant idea is not having a written global constitution, but a global constitutional function that could be executed or set by international organizations and bodies (Global Constitutionalism—Human Rights, Democracy and the Rule of Law (GlobCon), 2022). Thus, legitimacy comes from the constitutional function still instituted by states, but also by international bodies and organizations, with recurring transfers, synergies, and dialogue between constitutional and international law. Hence, a definition of these constitutionalization trends could be:

> The debate on constitutionalisation suffers from the great variety of meanings assigned to the key terms. I will here use constitutionalisation as the label for the evolution from an international order based on some organizing principles such as state sovereignty, territorial integrity, and consensualism to an international legal order which acknowledges and has creatively appropriated and – importantly – modified principles, institutions, and procedures of constitutionalism. (Peters, 2019b, p. 141)

Under these processes of constitutionalization there are two main relevant trends to be pointed out:

a   The constitutional function usually set in the state evolves beyond borders into international processes (Peters et al., 2009).
b   International sovereignty is overcome by human beings as a changing paradigm (Peters, 2016, 2019a).

Consequently, global constitutionalism could be defined as the following:

> Global constitutionalism is an intellectual movement which both identifies some features and functions of international law (in the interplay with domestic law) as 'constitutional' and even 'constitutionalist' (positive analysis), and also seeks to provide arguments for their further development in a specific direction (normative analysis). The function of constitutional law normally is to establish, organize, integrate and to stabilize a political community, to contain political power, to provide normative guidance, and to regulate the governance activities of law-making, law-application, and law-enforcement. The desired constitutionalist elements are notably the rule of law, containment of political and possibly economic power through checks and balances, fundamental rights protection, accountability, democracy (or proxies such as participation, inclusion, deliberation, and transparency), and solidarity. (Peters, 2019a, p. 141)

The goal of this book is to analyze the right to promote and protect human rights under the trends and synergies between international and constitutional law. These are the main challenges issuing from human rights defenders regarding the changing paradigm toward an active subject of law.

Human rights defenders: individuals and the right to promote and protect human rights

The adoption of the DHRD in 1998 was a legal response to a new reality in international relations: individuals, non-governmental organizations, groups, and even independent national human rights institutions contributed and played an important role in the protection and promotion of human rights. This "humanization" of international law is therefore the result of the paradigm shift in international law (Peters, 2016) brought about by the expansion of human rights law and globalization. The expansive effects of the UDHR led to the development of a system of binding human rights provisions at the international level, which, even today, has continued to evolve, giving rise to increasing synergies between international and constitutional law.

The DHRD is not a legally binding instrument, but still it is an agreement between states and adopted by consensus, which is the result of thirteen years of debates and drafting in the UN Working Group. Even though as a declaration it does not have the binding character of a treaty, it still has international legal value since it represents a commitment of each state to the international community, which is separate from its internal effectiveness (Gómez Sánchez, 2006, pp. 284–285). Similarly, following a 1962 request from the Commission on Human Rights, the UN Legal Adviser provides the following interpretation on the relevance of the "declaration" for the UN (UNESCO, 2020). Note the use of the terms "declaration" and "recommendation" in the Memorandum by the Office of Legal Affairs:

In United Nations practice, a "declaration" is a formal and solemn instrument, suitable for rare occasions when principles of great and lasting importance are being enunciated, such as the Declaration of Human Rights. (Commission on Human Rights, E/CN.4/t.6l0, 1962)

The 1998 DHRD gives the first rule for human rights defenders, set without any specific definition of them (SR on human rights defenders, UN OHCHR, 2022). The UN Declaration on human rights defenders (1998) has strict criteria to fulfil in order to be legally considered a human rights defender. Hence, the legal subject is defined by the exercise of the right by a previous entitlement. This trend presents a changing paradigm of the law. Unlike citizens' rights, which require that subjects meet certain conditions to hold rights based on sovereignty, the right to promote and to protect human rights is *per se* universal, like the academia and university origins. Umberto Eco (2004) distinguishes between the town and the gown, being university independent of power by the reluctant action of students, lecturers and researchers to be controlled by the town in the oldest universities of Oxford, Bologna, Heidelberg or Paris. This is his perspective on the differences between EU and the United States on academic freedom among the campus and the old universities in the middle of a city (2004).

Then, the right to promote and protect human rights depends on each individual's will. But this is not enough, there are some criteria that must be respected in order to be considered human rights defenders.

According to the DHRD and the practice of the Special Procedure of the United Nations on the situation of human rights defenders, the main criteria to be fulfilled to be a human rights defender is as follows:

- An activity for the protection and promotion of rights (not only professional, neither political nor merely social, but having a will, an ethical and an aesthetical commitment and especial effort to promote and protect human rights);
- by peaceful means;
- accepting the universality and interdependence of human rights.

In 2008, the EU Guidelines on human rights defenders were adopted, thus defining human rights defenders (Bennet et al., 2016). This definition is correlative of the UN practice. But in the case of the European Union, it was necessary to set up a specific definition due to the operational nature of the EU Guidelines (Bennet et al., 2016). They are particularly used by the European External Action Service (EEEAS) when EU delegations need criteria to recognize human rights defenders, to enter into dialogue with activists, and to assist them.

The Escazú Agreement, adopted on 4 March 2018, (ECLAC) is the first rule that recognizes human rights defenders in a binding article of an international treaty particularly set for human rights defenders in environmental matters (UN Environment Program 2018, Tripathi). The official name is the Regional Agreement on Access to Information, Public Participation and Justice in Environmental Matters in Latin America and the Caribbean. This agreement runs parallel to the previous Convention on access to information, public participation in decision-making, and access to justice in environmental matters, adopted in Aarhus, Denmark, on 25 June 1998 (UNECE). Parra Cortés (2021) considers the adoption of this agreement a pivotal step toward the enforcement of the UN Environment Rule of Law and the protection of environmental human rights defenders. However, violations of environmental rights and human rights defenders continue to be relevant (Parra Cortés, 2021).

The right to promote and protect human rights includes a negative and a positive dimension. The negative dimension of this right is when the state must abstain from undue interference when citizens exercise the right to promote and protect human rights. The positive dimension occurs when the state is obliged to adopt measures to guarantee the exercise of the right to promote and to protect human rights. Hence, domestic law is the first legal framework for exercising the right to promote and protect human and instrumental rights (art. 2 DHRD). But domestic law must be consistent with the UN Charter and the state's human rights obligations under art. 3 DHRD. Thus, art. 3 is innovative, opening the constitutional function of the UN Charter and the Human Rights Treaties adopted by each state. This will later be analyzed in further depth. Other new relevant rights set under the umbrella of the right to promote and to protect human rights are, for instance: the right to participate in government and public matters, to submit criticism and proposals to public bodies, and the crucial right to HRDs protection:

> The State shall take all necessary measures to ensure the protection by the competent authorities of everyone, individually and in association with others, against any violence, threats, retaliation, de facto or de jure adverse discrimination, pressure or any other arbitrary action as a consequence of his or her legitimate exercise of the rights referred to in the present Declaration. (A/RES/53/144, 8 March 1999, art.12.2)

From my perspective, it is absolutely necessary to point out all the threats that suffer human rights defenders and to provide protection, at international and national levels. Hence, a multilevel system of protection is required (Bennet et al., 2016). But this should not stop us from understanding that the attacks to human rights defenders by non-state actors are related to the dismantlement and weakness of legal guarantees at international, constitutional, and regional levels. The paradox of human rights after the Second World War is that the state that must protect human rights can become the main actor responsible for the violations of human rights, whether it is done by state actors or even by non-state actors. When a human rights defender is silent, a violation of human rights is allowed. This is evidence of the weakness of the broken sovereignty paradigm. What is necessary is to protect their rights and their physical integrity. In a global world, individual action becomes paradoxically both necessary and risky, but only if we are aware of the origin of the human rights defenders' risks and threats these risks could diminish. The loss of control in states opens gaps for an increase in violations of human rights. This reality is unavoidable, but the answer is not in executive measures. Human rights defenders should not risk their lives to protect human rights. It is then necessary to reinforce the connection between constitutional and international law, with respect to individual rights. Then, the necessary legal guarantees for human rights defenders can be respected.

Using a constitutional perspective on fundamental rights, Gavara de Cara reminds us that individuals do not have positive obligations. Even if there can be a horizontal effect on fundamental rights, the opposite would be contrary to the rule of law (Gavara de Cara, 2007, pp. 277–278). This is also the position of the ECtHR, with a short definition on positive obligations:

> Positive obligations place a duty on State authorities to take active steps in order to safeguard Convention rights. In most cases these are not stated explicitly in the text but have been implied into it by the Court. (COE, 2019)

This positive dimension has a twofold perspective in the Declaration on human rights defenders: the state maintains the main responsibility of guaranteeing human rights. According to this responsibility, the state must adopt not only judicial measures, but also educational, legislative, administrative, or other appropriate measures to ensure that the rights laid down in the declaration are effectively guaranteed.

Individuals are bearers of the right to promote and protect human rights. To promote and to protect human rights is not a duty of individuals. This right was set up as a right of action for individuals with a reciprocal duty of respect for states, anchored both in constitutional and international law. This is the legal framework of human rights defenders set by the DHRD. However, the DHRD does not give any specific definition of human rights defenders. This lack of definition can be considered necessary for not narrowing the right to promote and protect human rights but can lead to confusion when identifying human rights defenders, due to this lack of definition. Thus, it is necessary to understand and give an interpretation of the criteria set being respectful of the concept of HRD.

During the Cold War, and throughout the process of discussion in the UN Working Group to draft the DHRD, Eastern states wanted to establish the primacy of the state over the individual (McChesney and Rodley, 1992). This was a trend present in debates between McChesney and Rodley (1992), who were members of the group and consider that:

> Since the inauguration of the Working Group, there has been a constant tension between those who want the proposed instrument to reinforce existing human rights as they apply to "human rights defenders" and those who seek to restrict non-governmental freedom of action through provisions that place duties and limitations on individuals and groups. (Mc Chesney and Rodley, 1992, p. 3)

Analysis of the reports of the debates in the UN Working Group discussion (1985–1998) lead to the same conclusion. Since the Cold War, the primacy of states or communities over individuals is only defended by some states. After the adoption of the Declaration on human rights defenders, in 2001, some states complained about the lack of recognition of peoples or states, and not individuals, defending human rights. This was the case with Cuba, among others. They wrote a verbal note to Hina Jilani, Special Representative of the Secretary General on the situation of human rights defenders (E/CN.4/2001/94). However, to focus the Declaration on human rights defenders, after years of discussion, it was necessary to reach a consensual position on the individual duties set forth in article 18 DHRD:

1   Everyone has duties towards and within the community, in which alone the free and full development of his or her personality is possible.
2   Individuals, groups, institutions and non-governmental organizations have an important role to play and a responsibility in safeguarding democracy, promoting human rights and fundamental freedoms and contributing to the promotion and advancement of democratic societies, institutions and processes.
3   Individuals, groups, institutions and non-governmental organizations also have an important role and a responsibility in contributing, as appropriate, to the promotion of the right of everyone to a social and international order in which the rights and freedoms set forth in the Universal Declaration of Human Rights and other human rights instruments can be fully realized. (A/RES/53/144, 8 March 1999)

These duties, however, are not legal, institutional, or political duties: they are ethical duties. The official name of the declaration (1998) is the Declaration on the Right and Responsibility of Individuals, Groups and Organs of Society to Promote and Protect Universally Recognized Human Rights and Fundamental Freedoms. Thus, responsibility is based on a multilevel framework, but not the right, being the right based in jurisdiction and not in sovereignty. On the one hand, there is the legal responsibility to respect the framework of the DHRD, the UN Charter, and the Human Rights Treaties, as well as the consistency of domestic law. On the other hand, the ethical duties set in art. 18 DHRD dictate that their role and the responsibility is to safeguard democracy and human rights. The UN's official title in Spanish of the Declaration on human rights defenders contains an inappropriate translation of the original English version; it changes the DHRD's framework because "responsibility" is wrongly translated as "deber", meaning it duty, which has a slightly different meaning.

In the contemporary world, we are used to listen individuals claiming to be human rights defenders. But this is not enough. To become human rights defenders, it is necessary to fulfil the three main criteria and to comply with the legal framework of the DHRD. Under art. 3 DHRD, the legal framework for human rights defenders is, firstly, their domestic law being consistent with the Charter of the United Nations and the human rights obligations of the state. This is the constitutional function of the UN Charter set by art. 3 of the DHRD:

Domestic law consistent with the Charter of the United Nations and other international obligations of the State in the field of human rights and fundamental freedoms is the juridical framework within which human rights and fundamental freedoms should be implemented and enjoyed and within which all activities referred to in the present Declaration for the promotion, protection and effective realization of those rights and freedoms should be conducted. (A/RES/53/144, 8 March 1999, art.3)

Human rights are not absolute rights. The right to promote and protect human rights has limits; it does not depend on the ideological discourse promoted by individuals. As for the Special Rapporteur on the situation of human rights defenders—reminds us, the most important thing on HRDs is not "who is right or wrong" (SR on human rights defenders, 2022).

What is most relevant is which is the real action done by human rights defenders to protect or to promote human rights, and their adherence to the DHRD criteria. Within the DHRD there are several instrumental rights, for instance, the right to freedom of expression, or to communicate with international bodies. These can have limitations according to treaties, international law, and constitutional law, because they are not absolute. There are some well-known exceptions such as the interdiction of torture or slavery, and the right to a fair trial set in article 6 ECtHR, that is also present in article 9 DHRD.

If these legal limitations are disproportionate or contrary to human rights, it is another question to be decided according to the case law, human rights, international law, or constitutional law.

Human rights defenders and individual responsibility: criteria and limits on hate speech, international humanitarian law, and abuse of rights

Hannah Arendt wrote about individual responsibility and the danger emerging from individual action. Canneti warned, in 1960, about the dissolution of individuals in the mass, in his book *Masse und Macht*. The annihilation of individuality was conceived in totalitarianism (Arendt, 1951). But reciprocally, we still do not find an absolute answer as to why the dissolution of individual responsibility succeeded and people accepted it.

The main requisite for being considered a human rights defender is to be peaceful, what is, being non-violent. It is a compulsory criterion being a strong ethical commitment to use peaceful means to promote and to protect human rights and refrain from violence. Their historical background and function are closer to dissenters than to guerrillas.

The second criterion is to accept the interdependence of rights and to respect the rights of others without discrimination. Finally, according to art. 3 of the DHRD, it is necessary to exercise the right to promote and protect human rights according to domestic law.

If the law is consistent with the state's human rights obligations and the Charter of the United Nations and human rights treaties, it can be hard to control, being it a diffuse constitutional power. The innovative constitutional function carried out by the UN Charter and human rights treaties is based on the constitutional functions of the instruments of international law, but I regret their asymmetry. From my perspective, there can be states with more human rights obligations than others due to their lack of acceptance of human rights treaties.

The criterion about peaceful means is sometimes challenged by appealing to the right to resistance. But it is something slightly different: being peaceful must be understood not only under constitutional law, but also within the limits of international law. It is particularly controversial if international humanitarian law can or cannot be applying. If someone has the right (or not) to resist against the state depends on the loss of constitutional function that legitimates the contemporary state: mainly the protection of fundamental rights, democracy, and the rule of law, but it is not an individual, group or institutional right. Resistance is a constitutional function allowed or not, but not always an individual will. These constitutional functions are, as for Peters' theory on global constitutionalism, also present in international law (Peters, 2019a).

The foundation of contemporary constitutions is not based in nation-identity or *demos*, being it mostly the obsolete paradigm from the US and French Revolutions (Arendt, 2006). The function of protecting the core values of fundamental rights, rule of law, and democracy is what legitimates the contemporary state. So, it does not only depend on compliance with international law. The right to resist is still recognized by some constitutions, like the Greek or the Portuguese, which maintain this final clause to resist and fight against the dangers of dictatorship. In the case of the Constitution of Greece (2008), there is a right to resist against whoever might try with violence to overthrow the constitution in the final constitutional clause: "Observance of the constitution is entrusted to the patriotism of the Greeks who shall have the right and the duty to resist by all possible means against anyone who attempts the violent abolition of the Constitution".

Thus, the use of violence is beyond the scope of rights to promote and protect human rights. The status of human rights defenders is built under the right to defend human rights, exercised by the limited instrumental rights set up by the DHRD. The DHRD never gives legitimacy to violent action for defending human rights. Even in the case of contradiction with domestic law in the UN Charter, the question of whether violence can be used in a legitimate manner is out of the scope of the DHRD and the concept of human rights defenders. There are indicators to determine if there is a democracy or a dictatorship. Maybe then, the individual's right to resistance cannot be considered under the status of human rights defenders, but as the legitimate opposition to a dictatorial regime, or a usurpation of constitutional power, to be decided according to the characteristics of each individual conflict. However, extending the concept of human rights defenders to other categories or groups is quite dangerous, even for guaranteeing their protection and the protection of their legitimate rights.

Behind the legal subject of human rights defenders there is a strong historical and ethical commitment toward the use of peaceful means. This is more related to dissent rather than to revolt or as a violent answer to the state. What is violence, and what is not, then becomes a prominent question that I will explore further later on in this chapter. Violence, in criminal law, is the use of physical coaction or aggression, but it is also the threat of using violence, coaction, or being complicit, and thus, participating in it.

Human rights can be defended by actions with a material and intellectual dimension, to paraphrase Austin (1955): "Words can do things". Language is performative because discourse can have effects that transform reality (Austin, 1975). Depending on the will of the speaker and their effect on the audience, words can be used for criminal intentions, or to spread hate. This is precisely why freedom of expression has limits in the continental system. In the US, even if freedom of speech is protected by the First Amendment (US Constitution, amend. I), there are some judiciary criteria used to decide on "content neutral" or "hostile audience" and to determine when there are "fighting words". Violence can be enacted physically or by intellectual means, like hate speech, propaganda, incitement, or collaboration to crimes. In these cases, it would be out of the scope of the rights to promote and protect human rights. Intent is necessary for criminal law. As for, genocidal intent does not require to exhaust physically an ethnical group, but the intent of it. The plan or intent is what is relevant for the main crimes against humankind. There are some recent cases that can illustrate this point.

The case of "Hate Media" (*Médias de la Haine*) in Rwanda originates with three journalists who were the creators of the newspaper *Kangura* and the *Radio-Télévision Libre des Mille Collines*, also named RTLM. They were responsible for inciting genocide and spreading hate speech with genocidal intent. Their radio station was popular in Rwanda; it was also known as *Radio Machete*. One of the perpetrators, Nahimana, was a professor of history and dean of the Faculty of Letters at the National University of Rwanda. He was the founder of RTLM and responsible for running the Rwandan Office of Information from 1990 to 1992. The other perpetrator, Barayagwiza, was trained as lawyer, and helped to found the RTLM and the CDR. He was a member of the Radio Steering committee too. The last perpetrator, Ngeze, worked as a journalist and founded the newspaper *Kangura*, holding the post of Editor-in-Chief (Summary Judgement from the Media Trial, 2003). They organized propaganda, and incited publicly and directly to the genocide of the Tutsi community by using their media outlets (*Nahimana, Barayagwiza and Ngeze*, ICTR-99-52, 28 November 2007).

The French journalist Edgar Roskis (1994) wrote an article about the role of foreign media during the genocide in Rwanda using the term "a Genocide without images" (*A Génocide sans images: Blancs filment Noirs*), being published in *Le Monde Diplomatique* newspaper, November 1994 (*Le Monde Diplomatique*, November 1994, No. 32). This article gives a sharp idea of the contemporary trends in photojournalism: the shock and the humanitarian melodrama (Roskis, 2007). There were almost no international media covering the real images of the genocide and not a lot of information was available in the country (Thompson, 2007, p. 4). This article poses strong questions about the ethical and aesthetical role and responsibility of media covering conflicts.

Another relevant case law to consider with regard to violence by non-direct physical means is related to Oskar Gröning, known as "the accountant of Auschwitz". Criminal responsibility was extended to his collaboration in the genocide, though he committed his crimes when he was 21 years old. The appeal was rejected by the Karlsruhe Constitutional Court, which determined that he held criminal responsibility based on the evidence of collaboration by knowledge of murder and participation in it (Peace Palace Library, 2020), (Regional Court of Lüneburg, 15 July 2015), (DW, 29 December 2017). The concept behind this case law is that contributors were necessary to commit genocide.

In the domain of human rights, there is another case to reference from the 2010 case law of the European Court of Human Rights. The case of *Kononov v. Latvia* concerns the command responsibility and violation of the principles of international humanitarian law by a former commandant in the Red Army of the Soviet Union during an operation conducted in 1944 (*Kononov v. Latvia*, 17 May 2010). In this case law, due to the gravity of the charges, which involved setting fire to the property of the civil population as reprisal, resulting in the death of three women (one who was pregnant), who were burned alive, the controversial question was about the retroactivity of criminal law for crimes of war. The applicant complains under art. 7 ECtHR for a retroactive application of criminal law. He considered that, at the time of these facts, they were actually not an offense. The Chamber determined that even if art. 7.2 ECtHR was applicable, the operation of 27 May 1944 did not respect the general principles of law recognized by civilized nations. The ECtHR Grand Chamber concluded that this conviction was not in violation of art. 7 ECHR, and dismissed his complaint

Finally, it is worthwhile to mention the prohibition of the abuse of rights as a final clause for the human rights framework under the ECtHR framework set by art. 17 ECtHR. The abuse of rights would here be developed in connection with dissent.

The will of individuals is necessary to build the status of human rights defenders. But intent is also present in the worst crimes of humankind. Through her work, Arendt inquiries about the reasons for the dispossession of an individual's will under totalitarianism (Arendt, 1951). The concept of individual and individuality in Arendt is relevant to understand the evolution from the human dignity paradigm to the human condition in contemporary law. Thinking about human rights after the Second World War involves thinking about disappointed expectations. The second half of the twentieth century and the entirety of the twenty-first century accounted for other genocides, mass killings, and the deprivation of rights and freedoms coming from states due to the rising responsibility of non-state actors. This perspective brings to mind the future warned by Jaspers in *The Future of Mankind* (1961). Jaspers was a former professor at the University of Heidelberg in the 1930s. He was dismissed for his opposition to Nazism. George Orwell's (1949) *Nineteen Eighty-Four* warns of a dystopian, totalitarian world, that more and more seems to be closer to reality. Jaspers did not believe in the zero hour of

1945, or the *tabula rasa* for the human being (Clark, 2002, p. 201). He was aware that after the Second World War: "We shall not speak jubilantly of the awakening, shall not fall again into the false belief that all will now be good and noble, and that we will become outstanding people in splendid circumstances" (Jaspers, 1946, p. 74, cit. in Clark, 2006).

The UN Charter and the human rights treaties in domestic law: constitutional function under the Declaration on human rights defenders

The Charter of the United Nations and other human rights obligations of any state perform a constitutional function, under art. 3 DHRH, for human rights defenders:

> Domestic law consistent with the Charter of the United Nations and other international obligations of the State in the field of human rights and fundamental freedoms is the juridical framework within which human rights and fundamental freedoms should be implemented and enjoyed and within which all activities referred to in the present Declaration for the promotion, protection and effective realization of those rights and freedoms should be conducted. (A/RES/53/144, 8 March 1999, art. 3)

Human rights treaties and the UN Charter have become limits for state powers that must exercise self-restraint in order not to contradict their international obligations. The constitutional nature of the UN Charter was put on the table by Fassbender (Fassbender, 2009, p. 143). From a functional point of view, the UN Charter constitutional nature was accompanied by international laws such as the two UN 1966 Covenants, the International Convention on the Elimination of All Forms of Racial Discrimination (1965), the Convention on the Prevention and Punishment of the Crime of Genocide (1951), and the Rome Statute of the International Criminal Court (1998).

However, who decides on the limits or violations of the UN Charter and the human rights framework? When domestic law can be considered consistent with them? This function of constitutional control is controversial if it is left sheerly to individuals. It is dangerous to leave it to the state: which can be both responsible for rights and violations of human rights. This paradox leads to the contemporary need to constitutionalize some international synergies and to reinforce these trends with more jurisdiction and guarantees, being both international and constitutional.

More and more, clashes exist among different legal levels. In the European Union, the CJEU considered prioritizing the application of the core values of EU law being in controversy at the *Kadi* case of the CJEU (*Yassin Abdullah Kadi and Al Barakaat International Foundation v. Council of the European Union and Commission of the European Communities*, 3 September 2008). But, as for Fassbender (2009, p. 143), "States have constantly and consistently affirmed the unique place of the Charter in the present structure of international law—accepting, in fact the existence of an 'international legal order *under the United Nations*'". It is worthwhile to note the expression used in the *Kadi* Judgement by the Court of First Instance, 21 September 2005.

The lack of legitimacy remains a shadow on the system of the UN bodies. Charter bodies and unipersonal posts can be undermined by criticism due to the rationale behind the appointments (Bonet Pérez, 2009, pp. 152–159). Another critical issue is the participation of states in the UN human rights bodies that might have committed violations of human rights. Recently, this was the case with the participation of Venezuela in the Council of Human Rights. This trend was particularly criticized in the former Commission of Human Rights, which no longer exists. I agree with the criticism. However, it must be said that, sometimes, obliging a regime to participate in processes on human rights can ultimately have positive long-term effects toward them making a bigger commitment about openness and transparency regarding human rights in their country.

To determine the legal framework of action for human rights defenders, the double constitutional check of art. 3 DHRD is applied, first, by domestic law then, second, by the UN Charter and the human rights treaties, under their constitutional function set by the Declaration on human rights defenders.

Consequently, the domestic legal framework must be consistent with the UN Charter and the other state obligations on human rights and fundamental freedoms. But human rights defenders are neither judges nor a constitutional court. The determination of the consistency of domestic laws, according to the UN Charter and human rights treaties is, of course, a question that can be discussed.

Article 3 of the DHRD defines a clear objective framework that is mainly based on domestic law, because it is presumed to be consistent with human rights. When domestic law is not consistent with the UN Charter and human rights obligations, then the conclusion must be drawn that it is not the appropriate framework to apply, being then applied the UN Charter and other international obligations of the state in the field of human rights. This is a radical change with strong constitutional consequences that must be considered.

The rights of the others being it political, civil, economic, and social rights cannot be however restricted or derogated by the exercise of the right to promote and to protect human rights, and they are instrumental rights:

> Nothing in the present Declaration shall be construed as impairing or contradicting the purposes and principles of the Charter of the United Nations or as restricting or derogating from the provisions of the Universal Declaration of Human Rights, the International Covenants on Human Rights and other international instruments and commitments applicable in this field. (A/RES/ 53/144, 8 March 1999)

If we remember the requisites for being a human rights defender, these criteria come both from the Vienna Declaration (1993): interdependence and interrelation of rights, both criteria are for individuals and duties for the international community and states. In federal or quasi-federal states, decentralized power is not exempt from this binding rule. Thus, human rights treaties must apply as usual: without discrimination; even if some individuals believe or do not believe in a particular ideology, or if they are right or wrong. The limit depends on the commission of illegal actions. Consequently, this is a strong democratic conception on pluralism. The contrary would be to justify discrimination. Hence, what is necessary is to analyze the actions of human rights defenders, not their thoughts.

If rights were determined only by the will of the majority, there would exist a biased conception of democracy and the rule of law. Canetti (1960) warned about this after the experiences of literal interpretation in majoritarian democracy, considering the legitimacy of the state only in terms of numbers of individuals supporting it. Majorities cannot determine the scope of the right to promote and to protect human rights. These are political, ethical, and even aesthetical limits to mass.

Then, it is worthwhile to remember that behind the constitutional functions created by state power, legitimacy comes not only from majoritarian principles. The majoritarian principle is valid for electing representatives, but is not the criterion used for passing laws that must respect discussion, pluralism, fundamental and human rights. So, the constitutionality of a law does not depend only on the will of individuals or political parties. If it did, such circumstances could lead to historical tragedies, as has already happened in recent history.

In cases of adopting decisions with constitutional transcendence for the rights of other individuals, it is worthwhile to remember that: "Democracy, development and respect for human rights and fundamental freedoms are interdependent and mutually reinforcing", as set before by the VIII Principle of the Vienna Conference (1993) as precedent.

While thinking of the constitutional function of the UN Charter and human rights treaties for each state, we can reason that constitutional control comes from UN bodies or states and individuals. From my perspective, the Declaration of human rights defenders opened, in 1998, the door to the future; it is not an attribution to individuals of the function of constitutional control.

For some authors, it is important then to avoid the privatization of constitutional functions, both at international and constitutional levels, because individualism and privatization are not exactly the same (van den Meerssche, 2016). It is necessary to avoid privatization since it can have a non-desirable effect. As Martin-Ortega (2008) states, it is necessary to have more public control of private non-state actors, such as transnational business companies, but this is something quite different.

References

Agamben, G. (2003). *Homo Sacer: el poder soberano y la nuda vida*. Valencia: Pre-Textos.
Arendt, H. (1951). *The Origins of Totalitarianism*. New York: Brace, Harcourt.
Arendt, H. (2006). *On Revolution*. London: Penguin Classics.

Aristotle (1944). *Aristotle in 23 Volumes*, Vol. 21, translated by H. Rackham. London: Heinemann & Cambridge, MA: Harvard University Press. Retrieved 26 May, 2022, from: www.perseus.tufts.edu/hopper/text?doc=Perseus:abo:tlg,0086,035:1:1253a

Austin, J. L. (1975). *How to Do Things With Words: The William James Lectures delivered at Harvard University in 1955.* Harvard: Harvard University Press.

Bennet, K., Ingleton, D., Nah, M. A., and Savage, J. (2016). *Critical Perspectives on the Security and Protection of Human Rights Defenders.* Oxon & New York: Routledge.

Bennett, K., Ingleton, D., Nah, A. M., and Savage, J. (2015). "Critical perspectives on the security and protection of human rights defenders". *International Journal of Human Rights*, 19(7), 883–895. Retrieved 26 May, 2022, from: https://doi.org/10.1080/13642987.2015.1075301.

Bobbio, N. (1991). *El tiempo de los derechos.* Madrid: Sistema.

Bonet Pérez, J. (2009). *De la Comisión de Derechos Humanos al Consejo de Derechos Humanos: Entre la continuidad y el cambio*, B. Altemir & R. Cortado (Eds). Madrid: Tecnos.

Canetti, E. (1960). *Masse und Macht.* Hamburg: Claassen.

Carrillo Salcedo, J. A. (1999). *Dignidad frente a barbarie. La Declaración Universal de Derechos Humanos cincuenta años después.* Madrid: Trotta.

Clark, M. W. (2002). "A prophet without honour: Karl Jaspers in Germany 1945–1948". *Journal of Contemporary History*, 37(2), 197–222.

Clark, M. W. (2006). *Beyond Catastrophe. German Intellectuals and Cultural Renewal After World War II: 1945–1955.* Lanham: Lexington Books.

DefendDefenders (2017). "Don't shoot the messenger! Journalists as human rights defenders in the East and Horn of Africa". Retrieved 4 June, 2022, from: www.defenddefenders.org/wp-content/uploads/2017/11/DontShootTheMessenger.pdf.

Donnelly, J. (1989). *Human Rights in Theory and Practice.* Ithaca & London: Cornell University Press.

Eco, U. (2004). "La Universidad y los mass media". *CIC (Cuadernos de Información y Comunicación)*, 9, 149–159.

Fassbender, B. (2009). "Rediscovering a forgotten constitution". In J. L. Dunoff & J. P. Trachtman (Eds), *Ruling the World: Constitutionalism, International Law and Global Governance.* Cambridge: Cambridge University Press.

Gavara de Cara, J. C. (2007). "La vinculación positiva de los poderes públicos a los derechos fundamentales". *Teoría y Realidad Constitucional*, 20, 277–320.

Gavara de Cara, J. C. (2011). *La proyección interna de la dimensión objetiva de los derechos fundamentales: el art.10.1 CE.* Barcelona: J.M. Bosch Editor.

Gardbaum, S. (2009). "Human rights and international constitutionalism". In J. L. Dunoff & J. P. Trachtman (Eds), *Ruling the World: Constitutionalism, International Law and Global Governance.* Cambridge: Cambridge University Press.

Gómez Sánchez, Y. (2020). *Constitucionalismo multinivel. Derechos Fundamentales.* Madrid: Sanz y Torres.

Jaspers, K. (1961). *The Future of Mankind.* Chicago: Chicago University Press.

Martin-Ortega, O. (2008). *Empresas multinacionales y derechos humanos en derecho internacional.* Barcelona: J.M. Bosch Editor.

McChesney, A. and Rodley, N. (1992). "Human rights defenders. Drafting a declaration". *International Commission of Jurists Review*, 48.

Orwell, G. (1949). *Nineteen Eighty-Four.* London: Secker & Warburg.

Owen, N. (2001). *Human Rights, Human Wrongs. The Oxford Amnesty Lectures 2001.* Oxford: Oxford University Press.

Parekh, S. (2007). "Resisting dull and torpid assent: Returning to the debate over the foundations of human rights". *Human Rights Quarterly*, 29(3), 754–778.

Parra Cortés, R. (2021). "Protección de defensores ambientales en el Acuerdo de Escazú: sinergias entre Derechos Humanos y Medio Ambiente". In N. Saura-Freixes (Ed.), *Derechos Humanos, Derecho Constitucional y Derecho Internacional: Sinergias Contemporáneas. Human Rights, Constitutional Law and International Law: Contemporary Synergies* (pp. 511–531). Madrid: Centro de Estudios Políticos y Constitucionales.

Peters, A. (2016). *Beyond Human Rights: The Legal Status of the Individual in International Law*. Cambridge: Cambridge University Press.

Peters, A. (2017). "Constitutionalisation". *MPIL Research Paper Series*, 8.

Peters, A. (2019a). *Humanisme, constitutionalisme, universalisme. Etude de droit international et comparé*. Paris: Editions Pedone.

Peters, A. (2019b). "Constitutionalisation". In J. Aspremont and S. Singh, *Concepts for International Law. Contributions to Disciplinary Thought*. Cheltenham & Northampton: Edward Elgar.

Peters, A., Klabbers, J., and Ulfstein, G. (2009). *The Constitutionalization of International Law*. Oxford: Oxford University Press.

Reibstein, R. (2018). "Can our children trust us with their future?". *American Bar Association*.

Roskis, E. (2007). "A genocide without images: White film noirs". In A. Thompson, *The Media and the Rwanda Genocide*. London: Pluto Press.

Roskis, E. (1994). "Un genocide sans images: Blanc filment Noirs". *Le Monde Diplomatique*, 32.

Saura-Freixes, N. (2016). *Human rights defenders: el derecho a promover y proteger los derechos humanos*. Madrid: UNED.

Suami, T., Peters, A., Kumm, M., and Vanoverbeke, D. (2018). *Global Constitutionalism from European and East Asian Perspectives*. Cambridge: Cambridge University Press.

Thompson, A. (2007). *The Media and the Rwanda Genocide*. London, Kampala & Ottawa: Pluto Press, IDRC, Fountain Publishers.

van den Meersche, D. (2016). "Exploring constitutional pluralism(s): An ontological roadmap". Retrieved 4 June, 2022, from: https://ssrn.com/abstract=2880469LAW2016/21 https://ssrn.com/abstract=2880469.

van Trigt, E. (2018). "Former Nazi officer's plea for mercy rejected". *Blog Peace Palace Law Library*. Retrieved 4 June, 2022, from: https://peacepalacelibrary.nl/blog/2018/former-nazi-officers-plea-mercy-rejected.

WZB Berlin Social Science Center (2022). "Global constitutionalism". *Global Constitutionalism. Human Rights, Democracy, Rule of Law*. Retrieved 4 June, 2022, from: www.wzb.eu/en/research/completed-research-programs/center-for-global-constitutionalism/global-constitutionalism-journal.

Documents

Treaties

African Charter on Human and Peoples' Rights (adopted 27 June 1981, *entered into force 21 October 1986) CAB/LEG/67/3 rev.* 5, 21 I.L.M. 58 (1982) (African Charter)

American Convention on Human Rights (adopted 22 November, 1969, entered into force 18 July 1978) 1144 UNTS 123; OASTS. No. 36 ("Pact of San Jose, Costa Rica", ACHR)

Charter of the United Nations, (adopted 24 October 1945) 1 UNTS XVI

Consolidated Version of the Treaty on European Union [2012] OJ C 326/13

Convention for the Protection of Human Rights and Fundamental Freedoms, as amended, (adopted 4 November 1950, *entered into force 3 September 1953*) ETS No. 005 (ECHR)

Convention on access to information, public participation in decision-making and access to justice in environmental matters (adopted 25 June 1998, entered into force 30 October 2001) 2161 UNTS 447 (Aarhus Convention)

International Covenant on Civil and Political Rights (adopted 16 December 1966, entered into force 23 March 1976) 999 UNTS 171 (ICCPR)

International Covenant on Economic, Social and Cultural Rights (adopted16 December 1966, entered into force 3 January 1976) 993 UNTS 3 (ICESCR)

International Convention on the Elimination of All Forms of Racial Discrimination (adopted 21 December 1965, entered into force 4 January 1969) 660 UNTS 195

Convention on the Prevention and Punishment of the Crime of Genocide (adopted 9 December 1948, entered into force 12 January 1951) 78 UNTS 277

Optional Protocol to the International Covenant on Civil and Political Rights (adopted 16 December 1966, *entered into force 23 March 1976)*. 999 UNTS 171

Regional Agreement on Access to Information, Public Participation and Justice in Environmental Matters in Latin America and the Caribbean (adopted 4 March 2018, entered into force 22 April 2021) C.N.195.2018 (The Escazu Agreement)

United Nations

Universal Declaration of Human Rights UNGA Res. 217A (III) (10 December 1948)

Declaration on the Right and Responsibility of Individuals, Groups and Organs of Society to Promote and Protect UniversallyRecognized HumanRights and Fundamental Freedoms UNGA A/RES/53/144 (8 March 1999)

UNCHR *"Report submitted by Ms. Hina Jilani, Special Representative of the Secretary-General on human rights defenders in accordance with Commission resolution 2000/61"* (2001) UN Doc E/CN.4/2001/94. Retrieved 3 June, 2022, from: https://digitallibrary.un.org/record/450010?ln=es

UNCHR "Report submitted by Ms. Hina Jilani, Special Representative of the Secretary-General on human rights defenders in accordance with Commission resolution *2000/61. Annexes: 1. Note verbale dated 17 Nov. 2000 from the Permanent Mission of Cuba to the United Nations Office at Geneva addressed to the Special Representative of the Secretary-General; 2. Letter dated 5 Jan. 2001 from the Special Representative of the Secretary-General to the Permanent Representative of Cuba to the United Nations Office at Geneva* (2001)

UN Doc E/CN.4/2001/94. Retrieved 3 June, 2022, from: https://digitallibrary.un.org/record/434315?ln=es

UNCHR *"Use of the terms "Declaration"* and "Recommendation". Memorandum by the Office of Legal Affairs". (1962) *UN Doc E/CN.4/t.610.* Retrieved 4 June, 2022, from: https://digitallibrary.un.org/record/757136

OHCHR (2022). "*Special Rapporteur on the situation of human rights defenders*". Retrieved May 28, 2022, from: www.ohchr.org/en/special-procedures/sr-human-rights-defenders#:~:text=Ms.,of%20Business%20and%20Human%20Rights

OHCHR (2022). "About human rights defenders" *Special Rapporteur on human rights defenders*. Retrieved 4 June, 2022, from: www.ohchr.org/en/special-procedures/sr-human-rights-defenders/about-human-rights-defenders

ONU programme pour l'environnement. (27 September 2018). *"Statement on early ratification of the Escazú Agreement By Satya Tripathi, Assistant Secretary-General of the United Nations and Head of the New York Office at UN Environment"*. Retrieved 4 June, 2022, from: www.unep.org/fr/node/23805 (accessed 28 May 2022)

World Conference on Human Rights in Vienna. Vienna Declaration and Programme of Action (25 June 1993). *Retrieved 3 June, 2022* from: www.ohchr.org/sites/default/files/vienna.pdf

EU

Council of the EU (Foreign Affairs). Ensuring protection. European Union Guidelines on human rights defenders [2008]. Retrieved 4 June, 2022, from: www.eeas.europa.eu/sites/default/files/eu_guidelines_hrd_en.pdf

CJEU

Joined Cases C-402/05 and C-415/05 *Yassin Abdullah Kadi and Al Barakaat International Foundation v Council of the European Union and Commission of the European Communities* [2008] EU:C:2008:461

Case T-315/01 *Judgment of the Court of First Instance (Second Chamber, extended composition) of Yassin Abdullah Kadi v Council of the European Union and Commission of the European Communities* [2005] EU:T:2005:332.

COE

COE (2022) *"Some definitions"*. Retrieved 28 May, 2022, from: www.coe.int/en/web/echr-toolkit/definitions

ECtHR

Kononovv.Latvia, [GC] App. no. 36376/04, (EctHR 17 May 2010)

ICTR

TheProsecutorv.Ferdinand Nahimana, Jean-Bosco Barayagwiza, HassanNgeze (Appeal Judgment), ICTR-99–52-A (28 November 2007). *Retrieved 4 June*, 2022, from: www.refworld.org/cases,ICTR,48b5271d2.html

Greece

Constitution of Greece, as revised by resolution dated May 27th, 2008*by the H' revisionary Parliament session*. Retrieved 4 June, 2022, from: www.hellenicparliament.gr/UserFiles/f3c70a23-7696-49db-9148-f24dcc6a27c8/001-156%20aggliko.pdf

Germany

Regional Court of Lüneburg, Judgment, 27 Ks 1191 Js 98402113 (9/14) "Oskar Gröning" case

US

US Constitution, amend. I, December 15, 1791

Kelsey Cascadia Rose Juliana, et al. v.United States of America, 947 F.3d 1159 (9th Cir. 2020)

4 Human rights defenders
Concept, subject, limits, and challenges

Human rights defenders became legal subjects in 1998 due to the DHRD, but the idea was not invented then. The former Special Rapporteur on the situation of human rights defenders, Michel Forst, reminded us that the Declaration on human rights defenders did not originate with them, in fact, it was vice versa (2018). The DHRD contains the necessary legal recognition of the contribution of individuals and groups as crucial stakeholders and actors in the human rights system. But what was most relevant for the Special Rapporteur was the changing paradigm arising from this new active subject, which is coincident with my thesis (Saura Freixes, 2016):

> To be clear, human rights defenders were not born of the Declaration, rather the Declaration was born of the recognition of human rights defenders. The Declaration recognized a new approach to human rights as its founding principle: the centrality of individuals and groups within society to the realization of the human rights project. As such, it represents a paradigm shift away from a top-down, State-centric approach to the realization of human rights. (SR on human rights defenders, A/73/215, 2018, para. 10)

Theoretically, the recognition of this new subject in law could be closer to Bobbio or even Marx, not in terms of setting a right to revolution, but due to the recognition of individuals and groups as a driving force for the law. According to Bobbio, rights historically emerged due to the action of humans in social struggles for new freedoms against old powers (Bobbio, 1991).

In this sense, the DHRD recognizes "the right, individually and in association with others, to develop and discuss new human rights ideas and principles and to advocate their acceptance" (A/RES/53/144, 8 March 1999, art.7). But, even from a historical perspective, the main change brought about by the DHRD is the recognition of their action of protecting and promoting human rights as a right, instead of merely as a status of protection. This action is the axiological basis of this new legal subject: human rights defenders. Human rights defenders cannot then be defined *per se*, in order to exercise the right, so, the right is universal. But I suggest that they can be identified as having the status of human rights defenders and their guaranteed rights. It would then be necessary to follow a legal perspective based on the criteria outlined in the Declaration on human rights defenders.

DOI: 10.4324/9780429264016-4

Hence, we must remember that public officers have some differences or limitations toward becoming human rights defenders. Public institutions can be considered human rights defenders, as in the case of real independent national human rights institutions, complying with the Principles relating to the Status of National Institutions—the "Paris Principles" (SR on human rights defenders, A/HRC/22/47, 2013). In the case of public bodies, they cannot be considered fully human rights defenders due to their public nature and legitimacy. Finally, public officers cannot be considered only or fully human rights defenders, because to qualify them they have a twofold regime, subject to limitations different from those of individuals or even groups. Public officers working in public bodies are the holders of public powers. They do not work only in defence of human rights, but also for public interest. Paradoxically, they can then be considered human rights defenders when acting for human rights under the qualification criteria of interpretation based in their "special effort" to defend human rights, as for their work is "mixed increasingly" (SR on human rights defenders, 2022):

> Those who contribute to assuring justice—judges, the police, lawyers and other key actors—often have a particular role to play and may come under considerable pressure to make decisions that are favourable to the State or other powerful interests, such as the leaders of organized crime. Where these actors in the judicial process make a special effort to ensure access to fair and impartial justice, and thereby to guarantee the related human rights of victims, they can be said to be acting as human rights defenders. (SR on human rights defenders, 2022)

Representatives or officials can defend human rights, but they are bound by their mandate as an elected politician or official appointed to undertake a public function. So, they can direct their actions under the axiological basis of promoting or protecting human rights. Mainly, they must respect human rights. They also have a public legal framework—constitutional or international—that can condition their defence of human rights. Thus, they have a different legal framework *ad origine*. They can be considered human rights defenders when they are defending human rights under an individual framework. Some examples of this include politicians advocating for human rights in electoral campaign, or public officers in court who have a status different than individuals acting as human rights defenders. Once elected, the legal status of representatives differs according to the requisites and limits of constitutional, parliamentary, and administrative law. They are executing a public function of representation, as representatives, and not merely holders of an individual right. However, there are certain cases under the qualification of "special effort" in which politicians can be considered human rights defenders. For instance: "A politician who takes a stand against endemic corruption within a Government is a human rights defender for his or her action to promote and protect good governance and certain rights that are threatened by such corruption" (SR on human rights defenders, 2022). However, it is important to remind the individual criteria and legal framework, under the doctrine of interpretation based in the "special effort" qualification to consider them as human rights defenders.

In the case of public officers, usually, the rule is the same. Once in the post, the public office must comply with the principles of administrative law, like institutional neutrality. This can be considered unpopular, but it is important to avoid the arbitrariness of emerging populisms and maintain democratic guarantees, not only for people enforcing these positions, but for people living in a democracy.

Whistleblowers have a particular status that is coincident with human rights defenders. The main criterion is an action to defend human rights, not a previous entitlement to do it. The new directive (EU) 2019/1937 of the European Parliament, and of the Council of 23 October 2019, refers to the protection of persons who report breaches of union law. Whistleblowers are persons who report breaches of EU law in some specific areas. However, there is a sizable gap in the EU's internal legal framework without any reference to human rights defenders per se. The EU framework for EU Member States is mostly focused on whistleblowers, who have a different nature due to their twofold status related to: "Reporting persons working in the private or public sector who acquired information on breaches in a work-related context" (Directive (EU) 2019/1937, art.4). This is slightly different from human rights defenders, but they can be considered both human rights defenders and whistleblowers. The personal scope of the directive on the protection of persons who report breaches of the EU law can be found under article 4:

1 This Directive shall apply to reporting persons working in the private or public sector who acquired information on breaches in a work-related context including, at least, the following:
2 persons having the status of worker, within the meaning of Article 45(1) TFEU, including civil servants;
3 persons having self-employed status, within the meaning of Article 49 TFEU;
4 shareholders and persons belonging to the administrative, management or supervisory body of an undertaking, including non-executive members, as well as volunteers and paid or unpaid trainees;
5 any persons working under the supervision and direction of contractors, subcontractors and suppliers.
6 This Directive shall also apply to reporting persons where they report or publicly disclose information on breaches acquired in a work-based relationship which has since ended. (Directive (EU) 2019/1937 of the European Parliament and of the Council of 23 October 2019 on the protection of persons who report breaches of Union law). (Directive (EU) 2019/1937, art. 4)

This regulation accepts a wider range of persons as whistleblowers. From my perspective, giving so broad a definition opens the door to controversial situations and difficulties for implementation. But, despite the inner paradox of their apparent double public and individual condition, whistleblowers serve a public function and they comply with their duty to enforce the law and protect human rights. This is slightly different from the promotion of human rights, but related to human rights defenders. However, human rights defenders do not enforce law, they hold a right. Thus they can have a duplication of framework applying in the EU area.

There is not a closed binding definition of human rights defenders in the UN and the other regional systems:

> In accordance with this broad categorization. Human rights defenders can be any person or group of persons working to promote human rights, ranging from intergovernmental organizations based in the world's largest cities to individuals working within their local communities. Defenders can be of any gender, of varying ages, from any part of the world and from all sorts of professional or other backgrounds. In particular, it is important to note that human rights defenders are not only found within NGOs and intergovernmental organizations but might also, in some instances, be government officials, civil servants or members of the private sector. (SR on the situation of human rights defenders, 2022)

There is an exception in the EU guidelines on human rights defenders with a definition, set first in 2004, and revised in 2008. Bennet reminds us that "support to HRDs is identified as a major priority of European Union (EU) external policy in the field of human rights" (Bennet et al., 2016, p. 27). The goal of the EU guidelines is to set both "policy objectives and practical initiatives to be implemented by the EU and its Member States in support of HRDs in third country missions worldwide" (Bennet et al., 2016, p. 27). Under this perspective, from an operational point of view it makes sense to use this definition for human rights defenders. This can help to identify who in the field is a human rights defender. Furthermore, this definition in the EU guidelines is consistent with those delineated by the UN Special Representative of Human Rights Defenders, created in 2000:

> Human rights defenders are those individuals, groups and organs of society that promote and protect universally recognized human rights and fundamental freedoms. Human rights defenders seek the promotion and protection of civil and political rights as well as the promotion, protection and realization of economic, social and cultural rights. Human rights defenders also promote and protect the rights of members of groups such as indigenous communities. The definition does not include those individuals or groups who commit or propagate violence. (EU Guidelines on human rights defenders 2004, revised 2008)

This definition provides a strong synthesis of the criteria required to be considered a human rights defender. This is not something easy or banal; these criteria are the result of a long debate of more than ten years in the UN Working Group to draft a Declaration on human rights defenders.

Human rights defenders in environmental matters: the Escazú Agreement and the United Nations environment programme

Only recently, 20 years after the Declaration on human rights defenders, is there a new binding rule on human rights defenders in environmental matters (or environmental human rights defenders), as set by the "Escazú Agreement" in 2018 (ECLAC). This new regional treaty applies to the Latin America and the Caribbean ECLAC area. The official name of the treaty is: the Regional Agreement on Access to Information, Public Participation and Justice in Environmental matters. In the European region, there is the Aarhus Convention on access to information, Public Participation in Decision-Making and Access to Justice in Environmental Matters, as previously explained, adopted on 25 June 1998, by the member states of the Economic Commission for Europe UNECE, as well as states having consultative status with the Economic Commission for Europe. At the beginning only five states ratified the "Escazú Agreement", despite possessing twenty-two signatories (UN CEPAL 2019), but "after meeting the conditions set out under article 22, the Agreement entered into force on 22 April 2021" ("Observatory on Principle 10 in Latin America and the Caribbean"). The Escazú Agreement is the first legal treaty in the world that includes a binding reference to human rights defenders. The UN Secretary General, Antonio Guterres, considers it the "region's first treaty on environmental matters and the world's first to include provisions on human rights defenders in environmental matters" (Guterres, 2018).

Using the term "human rights defenders in environmental matters" is adequate and interchangeable with "environmental human rights defenders". There is an unnecessary controversy between human rights defenders and environmental defenders. In 2016, the UN Special Rapporteur on the situation of human rights defenders launched a report on environmental human rights defenders, using these terms (A/71/281, 3 August 2016). He was particularly concerned by the rise of violence against them, as exemplified by the case of Berta Cáceres, who was shot on 2 March 2016. She was an environmental human rights defender who protested against a project threatening indigenous communities and land resources (A/71/281, 3 August 2016). Berta Cáceres "opposed hydroelectric dams in the sacred Gualcarque river basin" (A/71/281, 3 August 2016, para.1). This is why in 2016 the UN Special Rapporteur on the situation of human rights defenders focused on environmental defenders:

> The present report is dedicated to the heroic activists who have braved the dangers facing them and defended the rights of their communities to a safe and healthy environment, to a future with dignity and respect, and to their traditional land and livelihood. They spoke truth to power, and were murdered in cold blood. (A/71/281, 3 August 2016, para.1)

Michael Forst, the Special Rapporteur on human rights defenders has used both the terms "environmental human rights defenders" and "human rights defenders in environmental matters", as in the Escazú Agreement. He considers this agreement a new step necessary for the protection and safeguarding of human rights defenders in environmental matters:

> This agreement is a major leap forward in the protection and safeguarding of human rights defenders in environmental matters. By establishing specific binding provisions, Latin American and Caribbean States are not only recognizing the acute and alarming situation faced by environmental defenders in countries of the region, but are also taking concrete steps to reaffirm their role and respect, protect and fulfil all their rights. (OHCHR, Special Procedures, 13 September 2018)

In 2019, the Human Rights Council adopted the landmark resolution "Recognizing the contribution of environmental human rights defenders to the enjoyment of human rights, environmental protection and sustainable development" (A/HRC/40/L.22/Rev.1). Furthermore, it is important to remember that environmental matters are also human rights concerns. The Escazú Agreement brought this to the forefront as a part of the environmental rule of law. The concept of the environmental rule of law was used for the first time in 2013 by the UN Environment Programme's Governing Body, adopting Decision 27/9, on Advancing Justice, Governance and Law for Environmental Sustainability (UNEP/GC.27/17, 2013). The rising concern about environmental defenders is related to human rights. There are some important causes: "At least 40% of internal conflicts over the last 60 years have a link to natural resources" (UNEP, 6 November 2015). But environmental protection can't be out of the principles of the rule of law. This is why the UN Environment Programme (UNEP) is working to reinforce the environmental rule of law, which can be defined as:

> Environmental rule of law is central to sustainable development. It integrates environmental needs with the essential elements of the rule of law, and provides the basis for improving environmental governance. It highlights environmental sustainability by connecting it with fundamental rights and obligations. It reflects universal moral values and ethical norms of behavior, and it provides a foundation for environmental rights and obligations. Without environmental rule of law and the enforcement of legal rights and obligations, environmental governance may be arbitrary, that is, discretionary, subjective, and unpredictable. (UNEP, 2022)

Individuals have responsibility for safeguarding the core concepts and principles of constitutionalism—such as the rule of law—democracy, promotion of human rights, and contribution to the "advancement of democratic societies" (art. 18.2 DHRD). Thus, environmental defenders can be considered human rights defenders in environmental matters too, which is highlighted by this definition from the UNEP:

> UN Environment considers an environmental defender to be anyone who is defending environmental rights, including constitutional rights to a clean and healthy environment, when the exercise of those rights is being threatened. (UNEP, 8 February 2018)

They have a responsibility to the planet and the protection of environmental rights. Thus, the protection of environmental rights and defenders falls into the scope of the Declaration on human rights defenders. There are two recent milestones worthwhile to mention in this field. Firstly, the historical Resolution A 76/300 passed by the UN Assembly on 28 July 2022 recognizing *"the human right to a clean, healthy and sustainable environment"* opens new legal perspectives in this domain. Secondly, the UNECE adopted, during its seventh session held in Geneva 18–20 October 2021, the Decision VII/9 on a rapid response mechanism to deal with cases related to article 3 (8) of the Convention on Access to Information. It will be necessary to consider the challenges and trends emerging from these two landmark decisions.

Human rights defenders: a new legal subject? Limits and challenges on governance, democracy, constitutional, and international law

Individuals, in addition to states, have become subjects of rights and obligations under international law (Gardbaum, 2009), (Peters, 2016). Non-state actors, such as NGOs, play a crucial role in the defence of human rights defenders (Decaux and Bernard, 2011). The individualization of international law adheres to similar synergies as international and constitutional law, as indicated by Peters (2016). The constitutionalization of international law (De Wet, 2012) is increasingly important to the evolution of international human rights law. This individualization has led to a paradigm shift in international law to pave the way for the humanization of international law (Peters, 2019).

Some of these synergies and trends come from the incorporation of human rights treaties into domestic law. For instance, some constitutions, like the Spanish Constitution in 1978, have a clause of referral to human rights treaties as a criterion for the interpretation of fundamental rights, under art. 10.2:

> The principles relating to the fundamental rights and liberties recognised by the Constitution shall be interpreted in conformity with the Universal Declaration of Human Rights and the international treaties and agreements thereon ratified by Spain. (Spanish Constitution, 1978)

In the case of the UK, there is the Human Rights Act (1998), and in France there is an integration of the Charter for the Environment in the French Fifth Republic Constitution of 2005 (Marrani, 2014). In the Spanish constitutional system, there is a constitutional review leading to Constitutional reform in case of contradiction between the Constitution and the treaties to be accepted (art. 95 Spanish Constitution). This is particularly relevant for the cession of competences to international organizations, such as the International Criminal Court, with the transference in criminal law of one of the main state powers, such as the *ius puniendi* or *ius iudicandi*.

However, there are still obstacles to end with impunity around the world: first, the lack of political will interfere with some individual cases that remain uninvestigated. In this sense, the ECtHR considers the absence of a necessary investigation a violation of the right to life:

> For example, in the context of the conflict in Chechnya, the Court has concluded that when a person is detained by unidentified servicemen without any subsequent acknowledgement detention, this can be regarded as life-threatening. (ECtHR *Baysayeva v. Russia*, 2007, para. 119; ECtHR *Beksultanova v. Russia*, 2011, para. 83)

Second, there are also states that remain openly reluctant to accepting international treaties to enforce responsibility, such as the US. To defend this position, they could argue that their system is strong enough to cope with any illegal action, even if it is committed outside their borders. This approach makes it particularly complicated in some cases, since it is difficult to enforce human rights treaties or international humanitarian law. However, there are global challenges that do not depend on the unilateral enforcement of treaties or laws, such as the climate change. In *The Washington Post*, on 13 August 2019, an article states that an increase in 2 Celsius degrees was most striking in US states like Alaska, New Jersey, and Rhode Island, but also overcome New York and Los Angeles: "These winters do not exist anymore" (Mufson et al., *Washington Post*, 13 August 2019).

After the Second World War it was necessary to accept that what happens in one country is not only the business of that country. Violations of human rights concern humankind. That is why there are rules of *Jus Cogens*, which go even further than sovereignty or agreement by states. A decisive criterion can be examined according to the Vienna Convention on the Law of Treaties (1969) and the ICJ's landmark opinion *Nicaragua v. United States: Military and Paramilitary Activities in and Against Nicaragua* (ICJ, 26 November 1984). According to Bassiouni, there are international crimes forbidden by *Jus Cogens* that constitute an obligation, *erga omnes*, in times of peace and in times of war (Bassiouni, 1997). If a genocide, illegal international use of force, or torture is committed, it concerns the whole of humankind. In terms of human rights, there is still strong dependence on the acceptance of treaties, despite the existence of other mechanisms like special procedures, where legitimacy comes from the Charter of the United Nations. Climate change represents a clear example of the need for legal commitments beyond state borders. If the lakes in New Jersey no longer ice over in winter, it is a global concern. If habitats disappear in Africa, it is also a relevant global concern. But the Presidential should not be the only relevant consideration. For example, in May 2019, the US House of Representatives passed a bill to keep the US in the Paris Agreement. However, it was the former President Trump who decided to leave the Paris Agreement, even against the House of Representatives will. But fortunately, on the 20 January 2021, President Biden signed the instrument to bring the United States back into the Paris Agreement (Blinken, 2021).

Some constitutional synergies are endangered at international if they are only considered in procedural, not functional terms; for instance, dilemmas on direct democracy. I consider that decisions of special constitutional relevance require the consideration of a further check on the executive power, with some limits on presidential power. The decision cannot be passed by referendum because it can harm minorities, human rights, pluralism, and fundamental rights. Constitutional control should be decided before the referendum instead of after. For instance, thus, it would create a strong problem to explain to the population that their supposed will is unconstitutional, even though it is.

In Spain, the constitutional doctrine changed in precisely this manner with the L.O. 12/2015, 22 September 2015. In Spanish Constitution there is a federal system almost *de facto* that was set in 1978, after the civil struggle against the Franco dictatorship. Inspired by the Basic Law for the Federal Republic of Germany, the Spanish constitutional framework recognizes legislative and executive powers to autonomous regions, similar to *Länder* or federate states.

After the 1978 Constitution, the historical autonomous regions of Catalonia, Euskadi, and Galizia had, at the beginning, a higher threshold of competences than other autonomous regions. This different condition comes from their previous recognition and vote within the framework of II Republic Constitution (1931), prior to the Spanish Civil War (1936). The main rule of each autonomous region is generally called the Estatuto de Autonomía (Statute of Autonomy). Until recently, three statutes were set and voted in by referendum in Catalonia: the first was *Estatut de Núria*, voted in 1931, set in 1932, during II Republic before Spanish Civil War, and later abolished by Franco's dictatorship between 1939 and 1977; the second was *Estatut de Sau* in 1979; and the last controversial statute was set in Miravet in 2006. After years of dictatorship and struggle, the Constitution in 1978 was a turning point for democratic transition to a democratic social state under the rule of law in Spain. Individuals could not even be a part of legal political parties until 1977. The last statute in 2006 had some controversial limits due to further Constitutional Court revisions. The 1978 Constitution states, as a legal framework, that a referendum is required after parliamentary discussion and approval of the main rules for autonomous regions via statutes. But this is compulsory only for the historical autonomous regions with the highest threshold of competences, or those set in the statute. In 2006, the latest standing constitutional revision of the Statute of Catalonia was quite disappointing for some sectors of the society. To avoid social rejection this constitutional provision had a new interpretation by legislative amendment: constitutional revision is allowed before the referendum, but not after. First, it must be verified what in the new rule is constitutional. The regional rule must be voted in a referendum in the region (not in all the state). This prior constitutional review is a new measure to avoid the disappointment of the population, if later on the Constitutional Court rules against it. The Spanish Constitutional Court framework follows the continental model of concentrated constitutional control, much like the Karlsruhe Court in Germany. It is not a judiciary system of constitutional control like the Common Law or the US Supreme Court.

Human rights defenders: memory and resistance at the breakdown of the human rights' paradigm from the Second World War

In case of doubt regarding the need for respect toward minorities, it is just necessary to have a look into history and memory. Maybe then it is important to examine the *Angelus Novus* (1920) painted by Klee. Walter Benjamin (1940) wrote about the painting in *On the concept of history*. His *Theses on the Philosophy of History*, that reads as follows:

> There is a picture by Klee called Angelus Novus. It shows an angel who seems about to move away from something he stares at. His eyes are wide, his mouth is open, his wings are spread. This is how the angel of history must look. His face is turned toward the past. Where a chain of events appears before up, he sees one single catastrophe. (Benjamin, 2003, p. 392)

This *Angelus Novus* (Klee, 1920) is the angel of history, but for Benjamin it is impossible to look at the future as representative of progress, because it comes from barbarism:

> Where a chain of events appears before us, he sees one single catastrophe which keeps piling wreckage and hurls it in front of his feet. The angel would like to stay, awaken the dead, and make whole what has been smashed. But a storm is blowing in from Paradise; it has got caught in his wings with such a violence that the angel can no longer close them. The storm irresistibly propels him into the future to which his back is turned, while the pile of debris before him grows skyward. This storm is what we call progress. (Benjamin, 2003, p. 392)

It is important to remember that the Second World War is behind the foundation of human rights. The paradigm of human rights was made while looking at the future. The main principle of the Nuremberg Trials is universal individual criminal responsibility, despite orders or official charges. The setting of this principle is a guarantee for the neutrality of criminal law and for a fair trial.

But the Trials of Nuremberg were, for some, a *tabula rasa*. However, not for all authors. Jaspers was a professor at the University of Heidelberg. He considered that pretending there was a new utopian era of rights seemed fallacious (Clark, 2002), as further historical events have confirmed. When Hannah Arendt later wrote about Eichmann (Arendt, 1963) and the "banality of evil", she was criticized for her approach. In the twenty-first century, the idea of necessary collaboration arrived in German criminal law as it applied to those who collaborated in the concentration camps.

Once the Second World War finished, Jaspers was conscious of the risks of a *tabula rasa*.

At this time, it was hard for the Soviet Union to accept the abuses committed by their troops and the authoritarianism of Stalin. See, for instance, the further judgement of *Kononov v. Lettonie*, ECtHR (2010), or the Massacre of Katyn case-law in *Janowiec and Others v. Russia* (2013). It was necessary at that time to build a discourse on the aftermath, not to watch behind, under the treat to fall, like the angels of Wenders film (1987), *Der Himmel über Berlin* (Wings of Desire). It was only filmed, however, 30 years later, and two years before the fall of the Berlin Wall in 1989.

If I can dare to say it, there is a certain confusion about individual legal guilt and political collective responsibility and patterns. This is not a relief; on the opposite, what makes it all more worrying and disturbing is the banality of evil present in Eichmann (Arendt, 1963).

Not all human beings are Eichmann. During my research, I was interested in researching individual cases of resistance to Nazism in Germany. Even during this most extreme example of totalitarianism, some human beings said no. This is necessary to understand the origins of human rights and the limits of individual actions of resistance against oppression—looking at individual resistance under totalitarianism is one way of thinking about history without coming to an easy answer based on good and evil. This is not as terrifying as thinking about the banality of evil developed by Arendt (1963).

Obeying orders is forbidden even in the army when the order is manifestly illegal. Command responsibility after the Second World War is based on the command-and-control principle of responsibility. Troops are obliged to comply with IHL. Those obeying are obliged only by legal orders in IHL. Wondering if there was or was not a possibility for individual choice in the 1930s and the Second World War is a dangerous path to tread almost a hundred years later, always leading to an uncomfortable question to answer. Still, it is not acceptable to later condemn the vulnerable. Pérez-Reverte (2001) reminds about it, in his picture of a French woman with a baby from a German soldier made by Robert Capa in Chartres, July 1944. In this sense, Pérez-Reverte reminds us how many of those women laughing would not have done the same before because of fear, hunger, and privileges (or even rage). Later, it is always easy to condemn for those who before didn't want, dare or could resist to totalitarianism.

Canetti (1960) wrote that individuals lose freedom of choice and become part of the collective mass; this is a way to live without guilt or responsibility (Fromm, 1942).

The problem of responsibility is also related to the conditions of the will. To explain everything sheerly in terms of the collective is a way to find an answer for power, but not for individual freedom or lack of freedom.

However, there are many cases of strong individual resistance to Nazism, and I will describe several examples below:

The philosopher and professor, Dr. Karl Jaspers, continued to live in Heidelberg an inner exile during the Second World War after being dismissed from Heidelberg University (Clark, 2002). He continued to live in a house close to the city centre, in Plöck 66, Heidelberg. Jaspers refused to divorce his wife of Jewish origin, Gertrud Mayer.

Willy Brandt, who took his famous pseudonym from a Norwegian comrade, was a correspondent during the Spanish Civil War, and later became the leader of the

SPD, and German chancellor from 1969 to 1974. Brandt was awarded with the Nobel Prize in 1971 (Britannica, 2021).

The lawyer Josef Haubrich "continued collecting forbidden modern and vanguardist art despite Nazis forbidding private individuals to do so" (Ludwig Museum Kohlm, The Haubrich collection 2019).

Gerda Taro, a young woman born in Stuttgart, in the 1930s fled to combat fascism during the Spanish Civil War with her camera, changing the history of photojournalism and sharing a pseudonym with her lover, Robert Capa. She died in battle in 1937.

Walter Reuter, an international correspondent in the Spanish Civil War, fled from Germany, going into exile in Mexico later.

The philosopher Hannah Arendt worked from exile in the US.

In academia, there was the opposition of the scientist Einstein.

Bertolt Brecht, the playwright and poet, suffered following the persecution of the Hollywood Ten in the US because of the witch hunt. The resistance students in Munich—*The White Rose*—and the *Swingjugend* opposed the Nazi regime by dancing to forbidden, "degenerate" music. And finally, the members of the School of Frankfurt, "who moved to Columbia University after the Nazis come to power" (Scheuerman, 2013). The group includes Theodor Adorno, Herbert Marcuse, the legal scholar, Otto Kirchheimer, and Erich Fromm. All these individuals said no.

In Europe, we can find the painting of the *Angelus Novus* (1920) looking back through history. This is particularly flagrant in the case of the Soviet Union and the crimes of Stalinism. The tragedy of Katyn in Poland resulted in a massive execution of thousands of officers in 1940 while the country was under Soviet control. Polish officers were killed and buried in mass graves in the Katyn forest. Since the graves were discovered in 1942–1943, the official version of the Soviet Union insists that German Nazis were responsible for the killings (Britannica, 2022). In 1990, President Mikhail Gorbachev recognized the Katyn executions (ECtHR *Janowiec and others v. Russia*, 21 November 2013) during a visit to Poland. In 2013, the European Court of Human Rights ruled in the judgment, *Janowiec and others v. Russia*. The application to the court was submitted by relatives of the officers who were killed in the Katyn tragedy. The final ruling concluded that there was no violation of art. 3 ECtHR, and no violation of art. 2 ECtHR for the lack of investigation, but that Russia failed to comply with their obligations under article 38 ECHR. The court considered that it had *no competence temporis*, using what Kaminski describes as the "Convention values" test and the "genuine connection" criterion (Kaminski, 2013). However, from my perspective, I do not understand how it was then possible to rule in the case *Kononov against Latvia* (2010) for a war crime committed by the Red Army in 1944. The ECtHR remarks that the violation of art. 38 is for the lack of cooperation of the Government of Russia and declassification of papers.

In the United States, in 1947, just one year before the DHRD was formed, the Hollywood Ten refused to answer before the House Un-American Activities Committee. As a result, these producers, directors, and playwriters were blacklisted—among them, the writer Bertolt Brecht, who then flew to the controversial German

Democratic Republic (Britannica, 2020). During the 1950s, Senator McCarthy undertook a witch hunt against supposed communists that included intellectuals, writers, artists, Hollywood screenwriters: "The accused had two options. They could refuse to testify and risk losing their jobs and friends. Or they could cooperate and accuse friends and colleagues of being Communists" (American Museum Natural History, 2002–2003). However, Eleanor Roosevelt, who was heading the commission, charged with drafting the 1948 Declaration of Human Rights, wrote about McCarthyism and the next president of the US, John Fitzgerald Kennedy:

> I think McCarthyism is a question on which public officials must stand up and be counted", I added. "I still have not heard Senator Kennedy express his convictions. And I can't be sure of the political future of anyone who does not willingly state where he stands on that issue. (Roosevelt, 1958)

All the complexity of history can be found in human rights, especially if we consider the Universal Declaration of Human Rights adopted in 1948 as the point of departure. However, the main danger to human rights in the aftermath of the Second World War stems from the possibility of a state becoming totalitarian. This is true because the state held the greatest power in the paradigm of the Second World War. But after 1948, states continued being both guarantors and violators of human rights. This is perhaps the main paradox of the system of human rights after the Second World War, in international and constitutional law. Today, while reinforcing structures for human rights in states, we have the danger of the abuse of rights coming from individuals in power—like authoritarian presidents, or political parties—as well as the proliferation of non-state actors who can be even more powerful than states. In the twenty-first century, the answer to the abuse of rights from state or non-state actors comes too often from individuals acting as human rights defenders and civil society, particularly in the case of failed states, and despite the existence of international organizations. This is another paradox.

Since the creation of the United Nations and the adoption of the Universal Declaration of Human Rights, there has been an increasing participation of the individual as a key actor in international society. A cornerstone on this system is the notion of participation. Even while the DHRD recognizes groups as human rights defenders, collective action comes from the individual will to exercise rights collectively. In this sense, the ECtHR in case law often recognizes that the right to association of art. 11 ECtHR can be considered a collective exercise of freedom of expression, art. 10 ECtHR. Both rights are instrumental in the main right to promote and protect human rights.

The idea of participation could be the key to overcome the dichotomy between subject and object in international law. In this sense, Higgins, former president of the ICJ, referred to the notion of *participant* in the process of decision making as a criterion to be considered in international legal subjects (Higgins, cited in McCorquodale 2014, p. 287).

In the *Reparation for Injuries Suffered in the Service of the United Nations,* the CIJ established the principles of international legal personhood for non-state

84 *Concept, subject, limits, and challenges*

actors. The first idea is that it recognizes an evolving notion of the subject in international law:

> It recognizes that, while the State is the primary subject of the international legal system, the subjects of that system can change and expand depending on the 'needs of the [international] community' and 'the requirements of international life'. (McCorquodale, 2014, p. 287)

Breitenmoser identified three phases of increasing participation for individuals in the international system (Breitenmoser, 2008). First, after 1945, the adoption of treaties recognizes the individual as a bearer of rights at the international level. Second, there is a rising recognition of the individual's right to complain at international institutions and courts, and to even being held responsible at the international criminal level in the ICC. Third, there has been increase in the development of case law and decisions from courts and committees, with a consolidation of the universality of human rights, horizontal effect, and positive obligations, even recognizing some human rights as *jus cogens* (Breitenmoser, 2008, pp. 245–246).

Hence, the ICJ in the *Reparation for Injuries Suffered in the Service of the United Nations* recognizes a subject different from the state, "capable of possessing international rights and duties, and that it has capacity to maintain its rights by bringing international claims" (ICJ *Reparation of injuries suffered in the service of the United Nations*, Opinion, 11 April 1949).

In this manner, Clapham (2006) reminds us that disparity of rights and obligations among subjects of international law would not be problematic to recognize. He advocates for a more practical approach rather than a theoretical one based "on the mysteries of subjectivity". Clapham makes an interesting point on the content, nature of obligations and rights, among international subjects:

> A state could not claim to have been subjected to torture under the law of human rights; a state could not claim that she had been denied the right to marry. We need to admit that international rights and duties depend on the capacity of the entity to enjoy those rights and bear those obligations; such rights and obligations do not depend on the mysteries of subjectivity. (Clapham, 2006, p. 68)

He makes reference to the ICJ case *Lagrand* from 27 June 2001, *Germany v. United States*. This case law considers the thesis of the pre-eminence of state against individuals right in consular protection not enough consistent. The ICJ decision rules on a violation of the article 36.2 of the 1963 Vienna Convention on Consular Relations.

The approach used in the *Reparation for Injuries* decision is helpful for outlining criteria to identify a subject of international law, albeit it lets still unresolved if individuals would become an international recognized legal subject or an eternal candidate to it. McCorquodale considers the broad principles set forth in the

Reparation for Injuries opinion principles "that could be applied to any non-State actor on the International plane" (McCorquodale, 2014, p. 287).

Human rights defenders are legal subjects created by the exercise of a right, and not *vice versa*—a legal subject possessing a right to due to an entitlement-based approach.

Consequently, the key point is that there is a new legal subject with implications at constitutional and international levels that does not depend on citizenship or sovereignty. What does the recognition of individuals as bearers of this right mean? Most relevant is the new paradigm of personhood on human rights defenders: "As such, it represents a paradigm shift away from a top-down, State-centric approach to the realization of human rights" (A/73/215, 23 July 2018, para. 10).

Kumm asserts that there must be a Copernican turn on constitutionalism to move from a state-based paradigm toward a cosmopolitan paradigm of constitutionalism (Kumm, 2013). Human rights defenders come to this conclusion too. However, as stated by Arendt, any kind of "global government" is not the sole solution to the problem of human rights. Brunnée and Toope consider the realistic approach that states are "still-dominant actors" (Brunnée and Toope, 2018). This is true. The answer is to think about how "transposing the concept of rule of law to the international level is not only possible but necessary" (Waldron, 2006 cited in: Brunnée and Toope, 2018). In this theoretical turn individuals must play an important role. For these authors, states cannot be conceived worldwide without thinking about individuals:

> Although it is argued that we cannot compare states to individuals, this argument tends to reify states and to disconnect them from their social reality. States are, in their ambitions and actions, controlled by people. People, be they state leaders or international lawyers, experience interactions in international society that can induce social learning, reinforcing commitments to legality, just as they can in the domestic sphere. That is why individual autonomy and equality before the law in domestic law have equivalents in state sovereignty and sovereign equality at international level.
> (Brunnée and Toope, 2018, p. 178)

Internationalization of fundamental rights guarantees is opening constitutions to international law and *vice versa*. The recognition of human rights defenders in international law cannot become a trigger for undermining the rule of law. Kumm points out a necessary distinction between the rule of law and the rule of persons (Kumm, 2017, p. 122):

> The idea of one person or a group of persons ruling over another implies that the will of one or one group can bind the rest. Insisting on the rule of law rather than the rule of persons means rejecting a conception of law that ties the law to the will of an individual or a group of rulers. This idea implies a rejection of 'any purely voluntarist account of law'. (Kumm, 2017, p. 199)

This is why it is important to think of human rights defenders from a constitutional point of view, that is, in synergy with international law. This does not mean ignoring their valorous contribution to human rights or democracy. Human rights defenders are not contrasted against the rule of law, they are a part of it.

There are recent experiences of populism, extreme nationalism, and rising authoritarianism in the twenty-first century. Individuals are no longer a mere receptacle of international and constitutional rights; they are becoming more powerful due to social and constitutional changes. They possess fundamental and human rights, and a legitimate right to promote and protect human rights, but there is a responsibility in exercising this right.

Human rights are not absolute rights. In the case law of the European Court of Human Rights there is an insistence on the social dimension of individuals rights, such as freedom of expression. There are limitative clauses of the rights set in the second paragraph of art. 8, 9, 10, 11 ECtHR. All these rights are instrumental to the right to promote and protect human rights, but they are not absolute.

When exercising instrumental rights established by the Declaration on human rights defenders, defenders are bound by domestic law, the UN Charter, and the treaty obligations of each state with respect to human rights. This is not only a legal commitment, but an ethical one. The right to promote and protect human rights is legitimate under the rule of law, not only because of the "rule of persons" (Kumm, 2017, pp. 199–200), the opposite would mean to legitimize the will of imposition. The rule of law is against the arbitrary exercise of power. Hence, it cannot be acceptable to leave the door open to arbitrariness.

However, this connection with the rule of law has two sides. Recognition of the primary rights established in the Declaration on human rights defenders cannot be eroded without, at the same time, eroding the rule of law. For Kumm, these rights are an inherent and necessary part of the rule of law (Kumm, 2017, p. 200), and his use of the term "rights enabling individuals" is interesting. The term highlights the performative nature of law and rights, and their power to enable individuals, not only as a normative dimension of the "rule by law" (Kumm, 2017).

Individuals have a responsibility to safeguard the core concepts and principles of constitutionalism, such as the rule of law, democracy, the promotion of human rights, and the contribution to the "advancement of democratic societies" (art. 18.2 DHRD), but also, they have a responsibility to the planet and the protection of environmental rights—these are also recognized as human rights.

Some principles in the Declaration of human rights defenders are present in global constitutionalism and lead to a correlative responsibility for any individual to contribute to the "right of an international order" where human rights "can be fully realized" (art. 18.3 DHRD). But this individual responsibility is ethical; it is not a legal duty to undertake positive obligations and public action that appertains to states or international organizations. The legal duty and the prime responsibility (art. 1 DHRD) to protect human rights remains with states (art. 18.1 DHRD). If states and international organizations would comply with their duties, the actions of human rights defenders would be less risky. Their rights could be real, not forced duties for individuals that assume responsibility that appertains to the public and statist domain.

The duties of the state and the responsibility of the individuals do not erode the international organizations' duty to protect and promote human rights. Rovira Viñas (2013) states that democracy claims the instauration of the global system of protection and responsibility toward human rights to combat the impunity created under the principle of non-intervention, a conception that is still anchored in the borders of states. According to the author, this is only possible because of the globalization of guarantees and rights (Rovira Viñas, 2013, p. 21). The emergence of international guarantees, for Rovira Viñas, is also parallel to the crisis of traditional guarantees in fundamental rights under a state framework. It grows weaker following globalization (Rovira Viñas, 2013, p. 20).

Consequently, we can point out three main aspects important to the creation of this multilevel system of human rights defenders that are necessary given considerations to constitutional and international law:

a   Internationalization occurs because international control organs have emerged to act whenever states fail to fulfil their human rights obligations
b   Individualization goes hand in hand with social action. In this case, individuals and groups act when states fail to fulfil their obligations, or in order to force them to comply with their role as the prime guarantor of rights. This action, however, is axiologically individual—the collective exercise of these individual rights leads to collective action—. These collectives, as such, do not hold all human rights. From an axiological perspective, in the twenty-first century these rights derive from the human condition, thus excluding abstract entities such as peoples, identity, or nations, after globalization
c   Multilevel constitutionalism is the result of reciprocal synergy with individualization and internationalization. Constitutional systems include referrals to international organs and rules, thus fundamental rights become part of a multilevel protection system. Human rights, in spite of their international or supranational origin, become part of the constitutional corpus, either by the incorporation of international law into domestic law, by interpretation, or by recognition of the different levels of guarantees. Although the degree of multilevel constitutional development does vary from state to state, particularly in the case of human rights defenders

Hence, human rights defenders are a key example to be considered when theorizing on the constitutionalizing of international law (Peters, Kumm) or the internationalization of constitutional Law (Chang and Yeh, 2012). They are a particular subject that creates tension and challenges the balance between the individual state, international organizations, and globalization. Consequently, the concept of the sovereign state should evolve toward the concept of the responsible state (art. 1 DHRD). A responsible state is capable of protecting and promoting human rights both at the domestic level and the international level. When the promotion and protection of human rights at the domestic or international level falls short, human rights defenders become relevant. Parallel to the displacement of the state as a centre of power and the emergence of new international actors, increasingly individuals, groups, and independent institutions are relied on to promote and protect human rights:

- When treaty-based and state mechanisms for the protection and guaranteeing of human rights fail
- When treaty-based and state mechanisms for the protection and guaranteeing of human rights need to be strengthened
- When treaty-based and state mechanisms for the protection and guaranteeing of human rights need to be complemented
- When treaty-based and state mechanisms for the protection and guaranteeing of human rights do not exist.

In the case of human rights defenders, it is therefore important to not only have in mind the rights of human rights defenders but also their responsibilities, from legal and ethical perspectives, in international and constitutional law. The universal right to promote and protect human rights cannot be used as an umbrella for the abuse of power and rights. Because it is not an absolute right, it must be exercised according to the DHRD and their multilevel system of law. The abuse of rights is forbidden by the main human rights instruments (art. 17 ECtHR, art. 54 ECFR), but it is often ignored. Democracy and individuals are interconnected axiologically and this must be present. There are dangers coming from the assimilation of political majority or masses as the only democratic force, the individual must be respected as subject. Crowds and individuals are in tension in our contemporary world with dangers emerging from the destruction of the constitutional framework and their substitution by populist majoritarian decisions. That can be interesting from electoral perspective and good for the power, but with disastrous consequences for individuals.

Canetti's book *Masse un Macht* (*Crowds and Power*, 1960) studies the dynamics of crowds and how they are related to the dissolution of individuality. The individual's dissolution to masses is reciprocal to individual non-responsibility (Canetti, 1960). Crowds do not necessarily make the best decisions in democracy. But democracy is something political, and there is a wide range of political decisions, all of them acceptable, from a democratic perspective on pluralism that can't be destroyed. What is most relevant to the law is that majorities cannot destroy human and fundamental rights. Keeping in mind recent historical, political, and controversial decisions and events, the abuse of rights emerges when, in the name of "rights" or even a supposed majoritarian legitimacy, the other's rights can be diminished. This goes against the core concept of human rights defenders. This is why constitutional law also developed the rule of law: to counterbalance a massive democracy based only on majoritarian decisions made by a sole leader. The disasters that occurred under totalitarian and fascist regimes provide ample evidence of this. However, despite trends in global constitutionalism, the lack of sufficient constitutional enforcement at the international level, as well as the lack of jurisdictions and guarantees or the weakness of the constitutional-framework after globalization, are factors that explain also the rising importance of human rights defenders.

The case law doctrine of the European Court of Human Rights asserts that there can be "no democracy without pluralism" (*Refah Partisi v. Turkey*, 2003, para. 44). "Democratic necessity" is a necessary criterion to be fulfilled in the application of the limitative clauses on ECtHR rights set by art. 10.2; limits on freedom of expression; art. 11.2 on limits on the rights to freedom of assembly and association; art. 8.2 setting the right to respect for private and family; and art. 9.2, limits on freedom of thought, conscience and religion. All of them are instrumental rights explaining the increasing importance of the right to promote and protect human rights. This is why, in the ECtHR, the core of democracy can be found in the debate and proposal of political programmes, limited by not going against democracy itself: "It is of the essence of democracy to allow diverse political programs to be proposed and debated, even those that call into question the way a state is currently organized, provided that they do not harm democracy itself" (COE, 2018). The advocacy for political change is possible via a political party, but also for human rights defenders. However, there are two conditions to be fulfilled:

> A political party may promote a change in the law or the legal and constitutional structures of the State on two conditions: firstly, the means used to that end must be legal and democratic; secondly, the change proposed must itself be compatible with fundamental democratic principles. It necessarily follows that a political party whose leaders incite to violence or put forward a policy which fails to respect democracy or which is aimed at the destruction of democracy and the flouting of the rights and freedoms recognized in a democracy cannot lay claim to the Convention's protection against penalties imposed on those grounds. (*Yazar, Karataş, Aksoy and the People's Labour Party (HEP) v. Turkey*, 9 April 2002, para. 49)

Even if we use the ECtHR as an example, each state will have a different multilevel system of human rights. After the 1998 DHRD, in 2000 the UN created a Special Representative of the Secretary General on human rights defenders. This had an irradiation effect (Bennet et al., 2016) on the other systems of human rights. So, to know if a legal system applies to a human rights defender, it would be necessary to know domestic law, the UN Charter, obligations under international human rights treaties, and hence, the regional system of human rights, and the UN DHRD framework.

Throughout this book, the multilevel framework of human rights defenders will be analyzed, but to understand the requisites for human rights defenders becoming a subject of law, it is necessary to attend to their origins and precedents.

References

Arendt, H. (1963). *Eichmann in Jerusalem. A Report on the Banality of Evil*. New York: Viking Press.

Bassiouni, C. (1997). "International crimes: *Jus Cogens* and *Obligatio Erga Omnes*". *Law and Contemporary Problems*, 59(4), 63–74.

Benjamin, W. (2003). "On the concept of history". In H. Eiland and M. Jennings (Eds), *Walter Benjamin Selected Writings. 1938–1940* (Vol. 4). Cambridge: Harvard University Press.

Bennet, K., Ingleton, D., Nah, M. A., and Savage, J. (2016). *Critical Perspectives on the Security and Protection of Human Rights Defenders.* Oxon & New York: Routledge.

Blinken, A. J. (2021). "The United States officially rejoins the Paris Agreement". Press statement. *US Department of State.* Available at: www.state.gov/the-united-states-officially-rejoins-the-paris-agreement/ (accessed 17 May 2022).

Bobbio, N. (1991). *El tiempo de los derechos.* Madrid: Sistema.

Breitenmoser, S. (2008). "The protection of groups and groups rights in Europe". In K. de Feyter and J. Pavlakos (Eds), *The Tension Between Group Rights and Human Rights. A Multidisciplinary Approach.* Oxford: Hart Publishing.

Encyclopedia Britannica (2020). "Hollywood Ten". Retrieved 30 October 2022 from www.britannica.com/topic/Hollywood-Ten

Encyclopedia Britannica (2021). "Willy Brandt". Retrieved 30 October 2022 from www.britannica.com/biography/Willy-Brandt

Encyclopedia Britannica (2022). "Katyn Massacre". Retrieved 30 October 2022 from www.britannica.com/event/Katyn-Massacre

Brunnée, J. and Toope, S. (2018). "Interactional legal theory, the international rule of law and global constitutionalism". In A. F. Lang and A. Wiener (Eds), *Handbook on Global Constitutionalism* (pp. 170–182). Cheltenham: Edward Elgar.

Calderón-Valencia, F. and Escobar-Sierra, M. (2020). "Defensores ambientales en Colombia y razonamiento abductivo en el acceso a la justicia". *Veredas Do Direito, Belo Horizonte,* 17(38), 69–112.

Canetti, E. (1960). *Masse und Macht.* Hamburg: Claassen.

Chang, W. H. and Yeh, R. R. (2012). "Internationalization of constitutional law". In M. Rosenfeld and A. Sajó (Eds), *The Oxford Handbook of Comparative Constitutional Law.* Oxford: Oxford University Press.

Clapham, A. (2006). *Human Rights Obligations on Non State Actors.* Oxford: Oxford University Press.

Clark, M. W. (2002). "A prophet without honour: Karl Jaspers in Germany 1945–1948". *Journal of Contemporary History,* 37(2), 197–222.

Clark, M. W. (2006). *Beyond Catastrophe. German Intellectuals and Cultural Renewal After World War II: 1945–1955.* Lanham: Lexington Books.

De Wet, E. (2012). "The Constitutionalization of Public International Law". In M. Rosenfeld and A. Sajó (Eds), *The Oxford Handbook of Comparative Public Law.* Oxford: Oxford University Press.

Decaux, E. and Bernard, A. (2011). "Les défenseurs des droits de l'homme". In *Droit, liberté, paix, developement. Mélanges en honneur de Mahjid Benchick* (pp. 23–33). Paris: Pedone.

Fromm, E. (1942). *Fear of Freedom.* London: Routledge & Kegan Paul.

Gardbaum, S. (2009). "Human Rights and International Constitutionalism". In J. L. Dunoff and J. Trachtman (Eds), *Ruling the World? Constitutionalism, International Law and Global Governance.* Cambridge: Cambridge University Press.

Kaminski, I. (2013). "The Katyn Massacre before the European Court of Human Rights: A personal account". *Polish Yearbook of International Law,* 33, 205–226.

Kumm, M. (2013). "The cosmopolitan turn in constitutionalism: An integrated conception of public law". *Indiana Journal of Global Legal Studies,* 20(4).

Kumm, M. (2017). "Global constitutionalism and the rule of law". In *Handbook on Global Constitutionalism.* Cheltenham: Edward Elgar.

Marrani, D. (2014). "The intersection between constitution, human rights and the environment: The French charter for the environment and the new ex post constitutional control in France". *Environmental Law Review*, 16(2), 107–121.

McCorquodale, R. (2014). "The individual and the international legal system". In M. D. Evans (Ed.), *International Law*. Oxford: Oxford University Press.

Mufson, S., Mooney, C., Eilperin, J., Muyskens, J., and Salwans, G. (2019, August 13). "2° C beyond the limit. Extreme climate change has arrived in America". *The Washington Post*. Available at: www.washingtonpost.com/graphics/2019/national/climate-environment/climate-change-america/ (accessed 17 May 2022).

Pérez-Reverte, A. (2020, May 26). "La risa de las ratas". *El Bar de Zenda*. Available at: www.zendalibros.com/perez-reverte-la-risa-de-las-ratas/ (accessed 16 May 2022).

Peters, A. (2016). *Beyond Human Rights: The Legal Status of the Individual in International Law*. Cambridge: Cambridge University Press.

Peters, A. (2017). "Constitutionalisation". *MPIL Research Paper Series No. 2017–08*.

Peters, A. (2017). "Proportionality as a global constitutional principle". In F. A. Lang and A. Wiener (Eds), *Handbook on Global Constitutionalism*. Cheltenham: Edward Elgar.

Peters, A. (2019). *Humanisme, constitutionalisme, universalisme. Etude de droit international et comparé*. Paris: Editions Pedone.

Roosevelt, E. (1958, March 8) "On my own". *Saturday Evening Post*. Retrieved 1 November 2022 from: www2.gwu.edu/~erpapers/mep/displaydoc.cfm?docid=jfk15

Rovira Viñas, A. (2013). "Gobernanza y Derechos Humanos". In A. Rovira Viñas (Ed.), *Gobernanza Democrática*. Madrid: Marcial Pons.

Saura-Freixes, N. (2016). *Human rights defenders. El derecho a promover y proteger los derechos humanos*. Madrid: UNED.

Scheuerman, W. E. (2013). "Review: The Frankfurt School at war: The Marxists who explained the Nazis to Washington". *Foreign Affairs*, 92(4), 171–176.

Wenders, W. (1987). *Der Himmel über Berlin*.

Documents

Treaties

Charter of the United Nations, (adopted 24 October 1945) 1 UNTS XVI

Consolidated Version of the Treaty on European Union [2012] OJ C 326/13

Convention for the Protection of Human Rights and Fundamental Freedoms, as amended, (adopted 4 November 1950, *entered into force 3 September 1953) ETS No. 005 (ECHR)

Convention on access to information, public participation in decision-making and access to justice in environmental matters (adopted 25 June 1998, entered into force 30 October 2001) 2161 UNTS 447

International Covenant on Civil and Political Rights (adopted 16 December 1966, entered into force 23 March 1976) 999 UNTS 171 (ICCPR)

International Covenant on Economic, Social and Cultural Rights (adopted 16 December 1966, entered into force 3 January 1976) 993 UNTS 3 (ICESCR)

The Paris Agreement (adopted 12 December 2015, entered into force 4 November 2016) 3156 UNTS

Regional Agreement on Access to Information, Public Participation and Justice in Environmental Matters in Latin America and the Caribbean (adopted 4 March 2018, entered into force 22 April 2021) C.N.195.2018 (The Escazú Agreement)

Rome Statute of the International Criminal Court (adopted 17 July 1998, entered into force 1 July 2002) 2187 UNTS 3

Vienna Convention on the Law of Treaties (adopted 23 May 1969, entered into force 27 January 1980) 1155 UNTS 331

Vienna Convention on Consular Relations (adopted 24 April 1963, entered into force 19 March 1967) 596 UNTS 261

UN

Universal Declaration of Human Rights UNGA Res. 217A (III) (10 December 1948)

Declaration on the Right and Responsibility of Individuals, Groups and Organs of Society to Promote and Protect UniversallyRecognized HumanRights and Fundamental Freedoms UNGA A/RES/53/144 (8 March 1999)

UNGA "*Situation of human rights defenders. Note by the Secretary General. Report of the Special Rapporteur on the situation of human rights defenders*" (23 July 2018) UN Doc A/73/215. Retrieved May 28, 2022, from: https://documents-dds-ny.un.org/doc/UNDOC/GEN/N18/234/82/PDF/N1823482.pdf?OpenElement

UNGA "*National institutions for the promotion and protection of human rights, Annex. Principles relating to the status of national institutions*" (20 December 1993) UN Doc A/RES/48/134. Retrieved 4 June, 2022, from: www.legal-tools.org/doc/b38121/pdf/.

UNGA "*Situation of human rights defenders, Note by the Secretary-General. Report of the Special Rapporteur on human rights defenders*" (3 August 2016) UN Doc A/71/281. Retrieved May 29, 2022 from:https://documents-dds-ny.un.org/doc/UNDOC/GEN/N16/247/09/PDF/N1624709.pdf?OpenElement

UNGA Resolution The human right to a clean, healthy and sustainable environment (28 July 2022) UN Doc A/RES/76/300

UNECE. Decision VII/9 on a rapid response mechanism to deal with cases related to article 3 (8) of the Convention on Access to Information (18–20 October 2021), ECE/MP.PP/2021/2/Add.1, 2.

HRC "*Report of the Special Rapporteur on the situation of human rights defenders, Margaret Sekaggya*", (16 January 2013) UN Doc A/HRC/22/47. Retrieved 4 June, 2022, from: https://documents-dds-ny.un.org/doc/UNDOC/GEN/G13/101/79/PDF/G1310179.pdf?OpenElement

HRC "*Recognizing the contribution of environmental human rights defenders to the enjoyment of human rights, environmental protection and sustainable development*" (20 March 2019), UN Doc A/HRC/40/L.22/Rev.1. Retrieved June 1, 2022, from: https://documents-dds-ny.un.org/doc/UNDOC/LTD/G19/071/97/PDF/G1907197.pdf?OpenElement

Guterres, A. (2018). "Foreword", *Regional Agreement on Access to Information, Public Participation and Justice in Environmental Matters in Latin America and the Caribbean*, Santiago: United Nations

OHCHR (13 September 2018). "*UN experts urge prompt ratification of landmark Latin America and Caribbean environment treaty*". [Press Releases- Special Procedures]. Retrieved May 29, 2022, from: www.ohchr.org/en/press-releases/2018/09/un-experts-urge-prompt-ratification-landmark-latin-america-and-caribbean?LangID=E&NewsID=23557

OHCHR (20 November 1993). "*Principles relating to the Status of National Institutions (The Paris Principles)*" Retrieved May 30, 2022, from: www.ohchr.org/en/instruments-mechanisms/instruments/principles-relating-status-national-institutions-paris

Governing Council of the United Nations Environment Programme "*Decision 27/9: Advancing justice, governance and law for environmental sustainability*" (12 March 2013) UN Doc UNEP/GC.27/17. Retrieved 4 June, 2022, from: https://documents-dds-ny.un.org/doc/UNDOC/GEN/K13/509/45/PDF/K1350945.pdf?OpenElement

UNEP (6 November 2015). "*UNEP marks International Day for Preventing the Exploitation of the Environment in War and Armed Conflict*", [Press-Release-Disasters and conflicts]. Retrieved 4 June, 2022, from: www.unep.org/news-and-stories/press-release/unep-marks-international-day-preventing-exploitation-environment-war

UNEP (6 March 2018). "*Promoting Greater Protection for Environmental Defenders. Policy*". Retrieved 4 June, 2022, from: https://wedocs.unep.org/bitstream/handle/20.500.11822/22769/UN%20Environment%20Policy%20on%20Environmental%20Defenders_08.02.18Clean.pdf?sequence=1&isAllowed=y

UNEP (2022). "*Promoting Environmental Rule of Law*". Retrieved 29 May, 2022, from: www.unep.org/explore-topics/environmental-rights-and-governance/what-we-do/promoting-environmental-rule-law

ICJ

Case concerning military and paramilitary activities in and against Nicaragua (*Nicaragua v. United states of America*) (Jurisdiction and Admissibility, Judgment), [1984] ICJ Rep 1984, p. 392

LaGrand (*Germany v. United States of America*) (Merits) [2001] ICJ Rep 2001, p. 466

Reparation for Injuries Suffered in the Service of the United Nations. (Advisory Opinion) [1949]. I.C.J Rep 1949, p. 174

International Law Commission

ILC "*Principles of International Law Recognized in the Charter of the Nürnberg Tribunal and in the Judgment of the Tribunal 1950*", (1950) Yearbook of the International Law Commission, 1950, vol. II. UN Doc A/CN.4/L.2. Retrieved 4 June, 2022, from: https://legal.un.org/ilc/documentation/english/a_cn4_l2.pdf

EU

Charter of Fundamental Rights of the European Union [2012] OJ C 326

Directive (EU) 2019/1937 of the European Parliament and of the Council of 23 October 2019 on the protection of persons who report breaches of Union law [2019] OJ L 305

Council of the EU (Foreign Affairs). Ensuring protection. European Union Guidelines on human rights defenders [2008]. Retrieved 4 June, 2022, from: www.eeas.europa.eu/sites/default/files/eu_guidelines_hrd_en.pdf

ECLAC

ECLAC (2022). "*Text of the Regional Agreement*". Retrieved May 29, 2022, from: www.cepal.org/en/subsidiary-bodies/regional-agreement-access-information-public-participation-and-justice/text-regional-agreement

COE (June 2018). *"Freedom of expression and the broadcast media. Thematic Factsheet"*. Retrieved May 29, 2022, from: https://rm.coe.int/factsheet-on-broadcasting-june2018-docx/16808b3dd6

ECtHR

Baysayeva v. Russia App no 74237/01 (ECtHR 5 April 2007)
Beksultanova v. Russia App no 31564/07 (ECtHR 27 September 2011)
Janowiec and others v. Russia [GC] App nos 55508/07 and 29520/09 (ECtHR 21 October 2013)
Kononov v. Latvia [GC] App no 36376/04, [GC] (ECtHR 17 May 2010)
Refah Partisi (The welfare party) and others v. Turkey [GC] App nos 41340/98, 41342/98, 41343/98 and 41344/98 (ECtHR 13 February 2003)
Yazar, Karataş, Aksoyand thePeople'sLabour Party (HEP) v.Turkey App nos 22723/93, 22724/93 and 22725/93 (ECtHR 9 April 2002)

France

France. Constitution of October 4, 1958. *Retrieved 4 June,* 2022, from: www.conseil-constitutionnel.fr/sites/default/files/as/root/bank_mm/anglais/constiution_anglais_oct2009.pdf
LOI constitutionnelle n° 2005–205 du 1er mars 2005 relative à la Charte de l'environnement, JORF n° 0051 March 2005

Spain

The Spanish Constitution. BOE 29 December 1978, *no* 311, p. 29313–29424 www.boe.es/legislacion/documentos/ConstitucionINGLES.pdf
Ley Orgánica 12/2015, de 22 de septiembre, de modificación de la Ley Orgánica 2/1979, de 3 de octubre, del Tribunal Constitucional, para el establecimiento del recurso previo de inconstitucionalidad para los Proyectos de Ley Orgánica de Estatuto de Autonomía o de su modificación. BOE 23 September 2015, *no* 228, pp. 84470–84472. Retrieved May, 29, 2022, from: www.boe.es/diario_boe/txt.php?id=BOE-A-2015-10196
Ley Orgánica 6/2006, de 19 de julio, de reforma del Estatuto de Autonomía de Cataluña. BOE 20 July 2006, *no* 172, pp. 84470–84472 (Estatut de Miravet) Retrieved 4 June, 2022, from: www.boe.es/buscar/act.php?id=BOE-A-2006-13087
Ley Orgánica 4/1979, de 18 de diciembre, de Estatuto de Autonomía de Cataluña. BOE 22 December 1979, *no* 306, pp. 29363–29370. (Estatut de Sau). Retrieved May 29, 2022, from: www.boe.es/buscar/doc.php?id=BOE-A-1979-30178 (accessed 29 May 2022)
Estatut de Catalunya de 1932, (Estatut de Núria, 1931). Gaceta de Madrid 21 September 1932, no 265, BOGC 15 October 1932, no 19. Retrieved May 29, 2022, from: www.gencat.cat/eapc/revistes/RCDP/Documents_interes/RCDP_41/9_Estatut_1932.pdf

Germany

Basic Law for the Federal Republic of Germany, 23 May 1949. Last amended on 29 September 2020. Retrieved May 29, 2022, from: www.btg-bestellservice.de/pdf/80201000.pdf

UK

Good Business Implementing the UN Guiding Principles on Business and Human Rights, Cm 8695. (September 2013) Retrieved 26 May, 2022, from: https://assets.publishing.service.gov.uk/government/uploads/system/uploads/attachment_data/file/236901/BHR_Action_Plan_-_final_online_version_1_.pdf

Human Rights Act 1998

5 Human rights defenders
The intellectual dimension of individuals and collectives

To truly understand the concept of human rights defenders it is necessary to be reminded their origins. Soviet dissent establishes an important precedent in the relationship between the state and the individual. The story of Soviet dissent influenced the creation of the Declaration on human rights defenders, and the discussion that took place inside the UN Working Group charged with the drafting of the declaration (McChesney and Rodley, 1992). Debates inside the UN Working Group stretch from 1985 until the final adoption in 1998. These debates were done under the pressure of the world division in two opposite blocs (McChesney and Rodley, 1992). Bennett (2016) reminds us that this "long genesis" was a product of a "slow and drawn-out drafting process" that was marked by "tension, disagreement, and compromise" (Bennet, et al., 2016, p. 1).

The Soviet dissenters were different from other movements of their time. Other social movements used violence, like the guerrilla warfare, or openly advocated for the use of violence against the state, for the consecution of their controversial "fair" objectives. But at the core of human rights defenders is the unavoidable criterion that they act peacefully. However, this criterion goes further than mere non-violence, or the abstention of the use of violent methods. This requisite appears in the DHRD, particularly in these articles:

- Article 5, the right to meet or assemble peacefully.
- Article 12.1, the right to protest: "Everyone has the right, individually and in association with others, to participate in peaceful activities against violations of human rights and fundamental freedoms".
- Article 12.3, the right to be protected:

    In this connection, everyone is entitled, individually and in association with others, to be protected effectively under national law in reacting against or opposing, through peaceful means, activities and acts, including those by omission, attributable to States that result in violations of human rights and fundamental freedoms, as well as acts of violence perpetrated by groups or individuals that affect the enjoyment of human rights and fundamental freedoms. (A/RES/53/144, 8 March 1999)

This criterion is sometimes contested when placed in contexts of oppression. But as previously noted, the right to legitimate defence, or the right of resistance, are legitimate and different from the right to promote and protect human rights. For instance, the international law of human rights and international humanitarian law are not the same, being IHL the *lex specialis* in times of war (ICJ *Nuclear Weapons advisory opinion*, 8 July 1996, para. 25). Consider that, according to the DHRD structure, protecting and promoting human rights by peaceful means is not only a legal requisite, but a moral commitment that gives legitimacy to the concept of human rights defenders and their protected status under international and constitutional law; other considerations fall outside the purview of this book because they are not within the scope of the right to promote and protect human rights.

Enrique Eguren Fernández and Champa Patel consider human rights defenders from a contextual perspective (Eguren Fernández and Patel, 2015, p. 7), but it is important for the exegesis of the concept to have an interpretation that is not only contextual or political—so that it can lead to different applications of the same right—both historically and theoretically. Otherwise, maybe different political considerations can be applied to the narrow legal status of human right defenders, and there can be discrimination in the criteria used in exercising the rights that constitute this universal subject.

A precedent for human rights defenders: individuals, the Helsinki Final Act, and Soviet dissent

The relationship of human rights defenders to the precedent of Soviet dissent emerges in the Final Helsinki Act. On 1 August 1975 ended in Helsinki the Conference on Security and Co-operation in Europe, with attendance from the West and the East bloc states (McChesney and Rodley, 1992, p. 49). The adoption of the Helsinki Final Act influenced the development of dissent and human rights in the Eastern countries, particularly in the Soviet Union.

The heading of VII Chapter of the Helsinki Final Act is: "Respect for human rights and fundamental freedoms, including the freedom of thought, conscience, religion or belief". In Chapter VII, there is a sentence that is crucial to the future of human rights and dissent in the East: "They confirm the right of the individual to know and act upon his rights and duties in this field". McChesney and Rodley consider this clause to be of great significance for the eastern states; it anchors dissenters and serves as a tool for reproving the (former) eastern countries:

> During the Cold War representatives of Western Governments relied upon this tenet to chide members of the Eastern bloc for hampering the activities and lives of political dissidents. Some of these activists had organized specifically to promote the human rights principles proclaimed in the Helsinki Act. The oppression that such individuals experienced was a regular topic at the Conference on the Security and Cooperation in Europe, which meets periodically to build upon and to monitor the implementation of the Helsinki Accord and subsequent accord. (McChesney and Rodley, 1992, p. 49)

The Helsinki Act was an agreement, not a conventional treaty. But according to Brett, it was considered binding for the participant countries and later under customary nature (Brett, 1996).

Nevertheless, when the Helsinki Act was adopted, the drafters could not predict the wider impact it would have on human rights. As a result of its adoption, a social movement for dissent in the eastern countries gained a particular legal umbrella under the "right to know and act" with regard to human rights (McChesney and Rodley, 1992). However, when it was implemented, as Ku reminds us (2012), even the dissenters were not at first conscious of its wide impact, and were sceptical of the real probability of the collapse of the Soviet Union, and the possibilities under the Helsinki Act (Ku, 2012, p. 19).

The adoption of the Final Helsinki Act was a catalyst for dissent against the regime, and it arose from an open claim for human rights against the totalitarian system. But at the time, the opposition against the Soviet Union was mainly based on individual dissent against the state, more than massive opposition. It is difficult to ask for massive resistance when totalitarianism or a dictatorship is in power. Throughout history, resistance by oppressed states depended on the action of individuals or small groups of resistance. Only in the last steps of a state breakdown, society and population react usually when they are not afraid or they have nothing more to lose.

In the case of eastern dissent, human rights activists arose and created a transnational net of dissent organized by pro-human rights groups:

> These movements were made up of the human rights activists who dared to press for the right to travel and other individual liberties after the conclusion of the 1975 Helsinki Final Act of the Conference on Security and Cooperation in Europe (the CSCE Helsinki Final Act). In a series of follow-up conferences that grew out of the Helsinki Final Act, these individuals formed into coherent transnational social movements and became an effective international political force through networking and capacity-building. (Ku, 2012, p. 19)

This movement of dissent emerged from civil society to find a point of reference in the Helsinki Final Act "right to know and act" for human rights, a binding element for the dissent written in Chapter VII of the Act. This civil movement had different manifestations, stemming from different ways to oppose a regime. Hence, the opposition began by individuals dissenting with forbidden readings in public squares, private pro-human rights groups, the *Samizdat* system of carbon copy, and the moral commitment of scientists and intellectuals, such as Andréi Sakharov. This scientist gave name to the European Parliament Prize for Freedom of Thought: "The prize is named after the Soviet scientist, dissident and Nobel Peace Prize laureate Andrei Sakharov (1921–1989). The European Parliament awards the prize to those who, like Sakharov, dedicate their lives to the peaceful struggle for human rights" (European Parliament Sakharov Prize, 2022). The European Parliament celebrated the 30th anniversary of the Prize in 2019.

I consider particularly relevant to remark the intellectual dimensions of dissent and dissidents, this being a way of protecting and promoting human rights, not just through political parties. A prominent moral commitment existed in individuals to fight against the totalitarian state and its methods. This side of the argument has often been ignored or lost to oblivion, but dissent mainly relates to freedom of thought. Dissent can find different forms for expression according to time and context, but at its core is freedom of thought—according to individual convictions and choices. Hence, the methods and forms of dissent are not just formal questions, but inherent ones. This precedent is at the very core of human rights defenders. Let us summarize and explore the more relevant methods used by dissenters.

In the former Soviet Union, the freedom to read, write, and publish openly did not exist. There were even threats to life, or punishment, despite the fact that freedom of expression was recognized by the Soviet Constitution. Access to publication had to be authorized by the Soviet state and follow the official guidelines. However, *Samizdat* was a key element and channel for dissent. *Samizdat* published censored works. When typesetting a banned book with carbon paper, the copy was then passed on to another member of the *Samizdat* circle, who then repeated the same process successively, therefore perpetuating access to forbidden readings, as explained by Joo (Joo, 2004, p. 572). In 1968, Horvath recalled that the anonymous publishers of *Samizdat* also created and published *The Chronicle of Current Events* (Horvath, 2014, p. 153). Alexeyeva situates the origin of the human rights movement to the first demonstration in Moscow's Pushkin Square in 1965. The slogan, "Respect the Soviet Constitution", paradoxically guaranteed the restricted freedom of expression in the constitutional text (Alexeyeva, 1985). Article 19 of the Universal Declaration of Human Rights was advertised on the cover of *The Chronicle of Currents Events*. This continual reference to claims to human rights is a rising characteristic of Soviet dissent. It later became a precedent for human rights defenders, and for the drafters of the Declaration on human rights defenders.

What seems more relevant to these dissidents is the challenge by the individual against the state. This movement came from individuals firstly using tools such as censored books, *Samizdat*, poetry or a legal basis for complaints, even claiming freedom of expression, that paradoxically was codified in the Soviet Constitution (Horvath, 2014, p. 153). Later, the adoption of the Helsinki Final Act lead to the creation of the Helsinki Watch Group in Moscow, and the Polish Worker's Defence Committee in Poland (Brier, 2013, pp. 104–127).

In the United Nations, some western states—with Canada and Norway as the main proponents—and NGOs working in human rights—such as Amnesty International and the International Commission of Jurists—recognized the usefulness of the "right to know and act". After the Final Helsinki Act, they decided to create a declaration of this right, which later became the Declaration on human rights defenders, based entirely on the right to promote and to protect human rights:

> Having seen the usefulness of Principle VII in the support of political dissidents in Central and eastern Europe, some Western nations and non-governmental

organizations (NGOs) worked in the 1980's to create a Declaration on the "Right to Know and Act" within the United Nations system. Canada and Norway were the main governmental proponents of such a Declaration. (McChesney and Rodley, 1992, p. 49)

The UN Working Group that drafted the Declaration on human rights defenders discussed and debated if the activity on human rights was the most relevant aspect for the paradigm of human rights defenders. But the too often neglected freedom of thought and their intellectual dimension were inherent to the defence of human rights. Human rights defenders have included, since their drafting origins in the UN Working Group, different kinds of defenders, including of course, writers, journalists, doctors, or teachers:

Along with many lawyers, paralegals, and judges, there are numerous kinds of human rights defenders:

> [The] community of human rights defenders includes journalists and other writers who report objectively about human rights violations which… governments would rather keep in the shadows. They are doctors who refuse to assist in torture, teachers who tell others about their rights, and people who assist organizations of women, indigenous and minority groups, peasants, workers or refugees. (McChesney, 1995, p. 55)

To summarize, the core concept for human rights defenders remains the individual dissident acting for human rights, either individually or within a collective. According to McChesney, representative of the International Commission of Jurists in the UN Working Group to draft the Declaration on human rights defenders:

> The UN initiative to develop a declaration on the rights of human rights defenders was partly inspired by the experience of the Conference on Security and Cooperation in Europe Security and Cooperation in Europe (CSCE) during the Cold War. Principle VII of the CSCE's Helsinki Final Act (1975), containing a "right of the individual to know and act upon" human rights, was one rallying point in discussions of the rights of political dissidents and human rights activists in the Second World. (McChesney, 1995, p. 43)

However, the Declaration on human rights defenders has not had this only influence. The requirement of respecting the interdependence and universality of human rights emerged from the Vienna World Conference on Human Rights, held on the 14–25 June 1993, in Vienna, Austria. Under the Vienna Declaration of 1993, "All human rights are universal, indivisible and interdependent and interrelated", (para. 5); thus, establishing the principle of interdependence and universality in human rights. This principle applies to human rights defenders too. They can choose, according to their will, which rights they decide to defend. But in 1996, the protection of defenders about economic, social, and cultural rights was a point of contention within the debates of the UN Working Group to draft the Declaration on human rights defenders (McChesney, 1995, p. 39). It was thus impossible to achieve the necessary consensus on the issue to draft an article in the sessions of the UN Working Group (McChesney, 1995, p. 39).

McChesney, as a representative of the International Commission of Jurists in the UN Working Group to Draft the Declaration on human rights defenders in 1995 stated that: "If all of the enumerated rights are universal and interdependent, no state pressure should be exerted to force human rights defenders to adopt particular rights or categories of rights as their focus" (McChesney, 1995, p. 42). Hence, it is the defender's will and choice about which rights they decide to defend: "It would be illogical for defenders of human rights and fundamental freedoms to be unable freely to select their own priorities from among the catalogue of universal rights" (McChesney, 1995, p. 42). This choice is not an obligation to defend all human rights at the same time. It respects all individuals' rights as universal and interdependent.

The notion of dissent is thus at the core of the concept of human rights defenders as a legal subject since the beginning of the debate in the UN Working Group, but a human rights defenders do not only defend civil and political rights.

This is why they considered it better not to narrow human rights defenders with a definition. But it does not mean that anyone claiming to be a human rights defender must be considered one under the status of human rights defender. This is a critical approach, and maybe controversial. I present it in this book because strong commitments on the human rights' action are at the core of the human rights defenders' status.

Intellectual human rights defenders, conscientious objectors, artists, academics, and asylum: pluralism and freedom of thought

The right to promote and to protect human rights does not only cover the external action of promoting or protecting human rights. The intellectual dimension of human rights defenders is also a part of this right. The official terms used in art. 1 of the DHRD are "to promote and to strive" for human rights, "individually and in association with others".

However, even if the right to promote and protect human rights have instrumental rights, not all of them are comprehensively covered by the declaration. Sometimes, intellectual human rights defenders promote and protect human rights via their teaching, essays, thoughts, words, or art, and find it difficult for them to be recognized as human rights defenders (Quinn and Levine, 2014).

For Quinn and Levine, the inclusion of academic freedom along with other rights, such as freedom of expression, remains problematic since they are not exactly the same (Quinn and Levine, 2014). I would like to add that the right to artistic freedom creates a similar problem.

Quinn and Levine distinguish between two categories of academics that can be considered human rights defenders. The first group is academics working at universities. Due to their study or intellectual work and research on human rights, they can be considered human rights defenders:

Many of these academics, researchers and lecturers would recognize themselves as human rights defenders because their academic research, publishing and/or teaching is consciously paired with rights-promoting education and advocacy activities. (Quinn and Levine, 2014, p. 210)

The second group, however, includes academics who are targeted because of the impact their work has on human rights, even when they are not focusing specifically on human rights academic research (Quinn and Levine, 2014). Within this second group, Quinn and Levine make a distinction between those who "may be targeted because of the specific content of their scholarly research, publishing or teaching", and others "who may be targeted not because of the content of their work, but due to their prominent standing in the intellectual community, especially if they are members of a religious, ethnic or geographic sub-community" (Quinn and Levine 2014, pp. 210–211).

The Declaration on human rights defenders contains several articles that cover human rights promotion and protection based on intellectual action of human rights; thus articles 6, 7 and 11 are particularly relevant in the DHRD. Article 6 outlines rules for instrumental rights related to freedom of expression and information:

Everyone has the right, individually and in association with others:

a) To know, seek, obtain, receive and hold information about all human rights and fundamental freedoms, including having access to information as to how those rights and freedoms are given effect in domestic legislative, judicial or administrative systems;
b) As provided for in human rights and other applicable international instruments, freely to publish, impart or disseminate to other views, information and knowledge on all human rights and fundamental freedoms;
c) To study, discuss, form and hold opinions on the observance, both in law and in practice, of all human rights and fundamental freedoms and, through these and other appropriate means, to draw public attention to those matters. (A/RES/53/144, 8 March 1999, art. 6)

Under article 6 DHRD, there are specific groups of intellectual human rights defenders concerned, such as journalists, writers, academics, or students. Journalists, students, and environmental defenders are some of the most targeted groups of human rights defenders, according to the Special Rapporteur on human rights defenders (A/HRC/19/55, 21 December 2011). The risks and threats would be even greater if the rights in article 6 were exercised by women, because these are rights of interaction in the public domain. Traditionally, women only exist in the private sphere. Thus, exercising the article 6 rights is not only dangerous for defenders, it is even more dangerous for women challenging the traditional role dictated by their gender. Depending on geography, there could be an increased risk of violence, for instance, in Latin American countries. However, threats of gender violence are also prevalent in Europe, where gender-discrimination still persists. Despite rules on equality and non-discrimination, women in the public sphere face challenges due to conditions and expectations around motherhood, as well as traditional gender roles.

In the 2019 annual report by the Special Rapporteur on human rights defenders, he posits that HRDs are particularly exposed to risks because they are "defenders of land, the environment, peace, access to justice, sexual diversity, freedom of expression and gender equality" (A/74/159, 2019, para. 17). Human rights defenders all use the internet as a tool, but the internet is not a neutral mean for communicating. The ECtHR case law (particularly in *Editorial Board of Pravoye Delo and Shtekel v. Ukraine*, 5 May 2011) establishes that states have positive obligations "to create an appropriate regulatory framework to ensure effective protection of journalists' freedom of expression on the Internet" (Research Division ECtHR, 2015, p. 18). Hence, the internet is considered under the scope of the European Convention of Human Rights, in particular, the application of article 8 on the right to respect for private and family life, and article 10 of freedom of expression.

But the internet is also a dangerous tool that is being used against human rights defenders. They are exposed to digital attacks such as the blocking of sites, hacking, or the denial of services online (A/74/159, 15 July 2019, para. 20, 21). The problem of fake news is particularly dangerous for HRD because they can be a tool for critiquing the voices of defenders and silencing them through digital media:

In the case of human rights defenders, it is common for digital media to be used to violate their rights to privacy, honour or personal integrity, for example, through threats of sexual violence, comments on their sexuality, publication of private information about an individual on the Internet by a third party ("doxing") and publication of fake or manipulated videos. In his report on the situation of women human rights defenders, the Special Rapporteur examined the risks related to gender and the specific violations faced, including sexual violence (A/74/159, 15 July 2019, para. 20).

Even in the description of the vulnerabilities faced by defenders, it is important to recall that the rights spelled out in the Declaration on human rights defenders are not exclusive to any group; they are the rights of all individuals: "The rights outlined in the Declaration belong to all human beings, they are the rights of all of us, not the entitlements of a privileged elite or professional class" (A/73/215, 23 July 2018, para. 14). This is why human rights defenders and the right to promote and to protect human rights are universal if they comply with the requisite of peaceful means: "Everyone is a human rights defender when they take up the human rights project through peaceful means" (A/73/215, 23 July 2018, para. 14).

If we analyze the different instrumental rights that come into play, such as freedom of thought, freedom of expression, freedom of information, freedom of education, artistic freedom, or academic freedom, each of them has their own particular scope and limits.

In the CJEU case of *Andre Lawrence Shepherd v Bundesrepublik Deutschland* (2015) there is an interesting approach taken in the opinion of the Advocate General Sharpston in this case about conscientious objectors. The origins of the *Andre Lawrence Sheperd* case can be found in a refusal of asylum for a mechanic deserting their service from the US armed forces. After being transferred to Germany in 2004, the mechanic deserted in 2007 because he disagreed on the Iraq War. He came to the conclusion that the war was contrary to international law and he refused to obey considering it was an illegal order. Under danger of prosecution in the US for desertion, in 2008 he applied for asylum in Germany. His petition was refused in 2011. For the Advocate General, the scope of "conscientious objection" is larger than simply objecting to the military:

However, the term "conscientious objection" has more than one meaning. It is understood to cover pacifists (such as Quakers) where the objection to military action is absolute. It may also refer to persons who object to a particular conflict on legal, moral or political grounds or who object to the means and methods used to prosecute that conflict. (*Opinion of Advocate General Sharpston delivered on 11 November 2014. Andre Lawrence Shepherd v Bundesrepublik Deutschland,* C-472/13, para. 53)

The right to conscientious objection is allowed by article 10. 2 of the Charter of Fundamental Rights to national laws: "The right to conscientious objection is recognized, in accordance with the national laws governing the exercise of this right". However, with regard to the Advocate General, even if the right to conscientious objection is not recognized by the art.10.1 of the Charter of Fundamental Rights, the ECtHR recognized it, and it must be interpreted equally under the umbrella of the right to freedom of thought, conscience, and religion.

Even if the term "conscientious objector" does not appear in the Article 10 (1) of the Charter on Fundamental Rights or in the Article 9(1) of the ECtHR, the ECtHR recognized it in the case of an opposition to military service "where it is motivated by a serious and insurmountable conflict between the obligation to serve in an army and a person's conscience—constitutes a conviction of sufficient cogency, seriousness, cohesion and importance to be protected by Article 9(1) of the ECtHR". Article 10 (1) of the Charter should therefore be interpreted in a similar manner. (*Opinion of Advocate General Sharpston delivered on 11 November 2014. Andre Lawrence Shepherd v Bundesrepublik Deutschland,* C-472/13, para. 52)

However, I disagree with the final ECJ judgment in this preliminary ruling in this case considering the imposition of a prison sentence or discharge is not so disproportionate or discriminatory as to be considered persecution. This is under article 9(2)(b) and (c) of Directive 2004/83 on the minimum standards for the qualification for refugee status.

There are cases where the status and protection of human rights defenders and refugees could overlap. However, as Jones reminds us, little attention is given to this overlap, and the regime of asylum and refugees' protection could be misused:

> The response of the international community and civil society to human rights defenders at risk has thus far failed to openly acknowledge an important remedy for human rights violations that pre-exists the contemporary human

rights movement: the international commitment to offer asylum to refugees from persecution. The two solitudes of human rights defenders at risk and refugee protection have not always been so unconnected. (Jones, 2015, p. 936)

Article 7 of the Declaration on human rights defenders is related to freedom of thought as well: "Everyone has the right, individually and in association with others, to develop and discuss new human rights ideas and principles and to advocate their acceptance". This freedom of discussion and development of human rights is also a turning point in the Declaration on human rights defenders. Even the ECtHR needs to develop "an evolutive approach" in the case-law interpretation in the light of "present-day conditions" (ECtHR *Goodwin v. United Kingdom*, 11 July 2002, para. 74).

Jones reminds us that temporary international relocation initiatives relocate at risk human rights outside of their state. This is a recent concept, but "the organized provision of international protection by civil society has a long history" (Jones, 2015, p. 945). This author reminds how the NGO, CARA, Council for At-Risk Academics, comes from the academic council system that was created in 1933 to help academics and scholars fleeing the persecution of Nazism (Jones, 2015, p. 945). The NGO CARA works across the borders of these two systems: the asylum and human rights defenders' protection regime (Jones, 2015, p. 945). CARA not only helps those who meet refugee status, "Cara helps many who are at great risk but do not see themselves as 'refugees', and instead still hope to return to their home countries when conditions allow" (CARA, 2022).

Many German academics were threatened and expelled from universities by Nazis on racial and political grounds. The former director of the London School of Economics, William Beveridge, conscious of the danger, decided to create an organization for assisting with the urgent rescue of scholars fleeing Nazi persecution. Thus, the Academic Assistance Council (AAC) was founded. Later it evolved towards a permanent organization, the Society for the Protection of Science and Learning as precedent for CARA, changing the name to the Council for Assisting Refugee Academics (CARA) in 1999. During their history, this organization also helped the academics flee persecution because of Stalinism, as well as apartheid, and dictatorships in Latin America (CARA, 2022).

In this sense, it is also necessary to be reminded of the actions of Varian Fry and the Emergency Rescue Committee, who helped 2000 intellectuals and artists, such as Marc Chagall, André Breton, and Marcel Duchamp leave Europe and escape Nazi persecution (United States Holocaust Memorial Museum, 2022).

Before leaving Europe in 1933, Albert Einstein made a speech standing up for intellectual freedom; it is a worthwhile reminder that:

> If we want to resist the powers which threaten to suppress intellectual and individual freedom we must keep clearly before us what is at stake, and what we owe to that freedom which our ancestors have won for us after hard struggles. Without such freedom, there would have been no Shakespeare, no

Goethe, no Newton, no Faraday, no Pasteur and no Lister. Most people would lead a dull life of slavery. It is only men who are free who create the inventions and intellectual works which to us moderns make life worthwhile.
(Einstein, 1933)

Intellectual freedom is the core concept of human rights defenders, because freedom of thought is a necessary condition for being a human being. However, too often academics and intellectual human rights defenders are forgotten due to the intellectual nature of their work.

National human rights institutions and human rights defenders

National institutions on human rights (NHRI) are public bodies created by constitutional or legal mandates (sometimes even presidential decrees). They are also considered under the framework of human rights defenders, but they must fulfil specific criteria. In 2013, Margaret Sekaggya, the Special Rapporteur on the situation of human rights defenders, dedicated the Annual Report to the Human Rights Council to NHRIs: "The main focus of the report is the role of national human rights institutions in the promotion and protection of human rights, highlighting the fact that they can be considered as human rights defenders" (A/HRC/22/47, 2013). Ombudsman, commissions on human rights, institutes for human rights (FRA 2010), or similar bodies can be considered NHRIs acting as human rights defenders if their goal is to promote and protect human rights (FRA 2010), if they comply with the Principles relating to the Status of National Institutions—The Paris Principles— and the framework of the Declaration on human rights defenders.

The goal of NHRIs is to promote and protect human rights (OHCHR, 2010, p. 13). With their action, they can have a strong influence on public policies relating to human rights different however to the action of NGOs: "The differences between NGOs and NHRIs are perhaps most pronounced with regard to the investigation of complaints. National Human Rights Institutions are neutral fact finders, not advocates for one side or another" (Office of the United Nations High Commissioner for Human Rights, United Nations, 2010, p. 13).

The United Nations' Paris Principles were adopted in 1993 by the General Assembly. Under the Paris Principles, the Global Alliance for National Human Rights Institutions (GANHRI) serves as the International Association of National Human Rights Institutions (NHRIs) and is comprised of members from all parts of the globe. The Sub-Committee on Accreditation legitimizes NHRIs (OHCH, GANHRI, 2022), and NHRIs must comply with some specific criteria defined by the Paris Principles. They must:

Protect human rights, including by receiving, investigating and resolving complaints, mediating conflicts and monitoring activities; and
Promote human rights, through education, outreach, the media, publications, training and capacity building, as well as advising and assisting the Government.
(OHCHR, GANHRI, 2022)

In summation, the Paris Principles can be synthesized by the six criteria required to be considered NHRIs:

- Mandate and competence: a broad mandate, based on universal human rights norms and standards;
- Autonomy from Government;
- Independence guaranteed by statute or Constitution;
- Pluralism;
- Adequate resources; and
- Adequate powers of investigation. (OHCHR, GANHRI, 2022)

They can be considered human rights defenders when their members and staff comply with the Paris Principles. It is interesting that the legal text, by law or constitutional provision, must define its composition and their sphere of competence. Hence, the NHRI's composition is particularly relevant. To comply with the guarantees of independence and pluralism, it "shall be established in accordance with a procedure which affords all necessary guarantees to ensure the pluralist representation of the social forces (of civilian society)" (UN Paris Principles, 1993) with representatives from:

a Non-governmental organizations responsible for human rights and efforts to combat racial discrimination; trade unions, concerned social and professional organizations, for example, associations of lawyers, doctors, journalists and eminent scientists.
b Trends in philosophical or religious thought.
c Universities and qualified experts.
d Parliament.
e Government departments (if they are included, their representatives should participate in the deliberations in an advisory capacity only). (UN Paris Principles, 1993)

The members and the staff of NHRIs must cope with significant personal and public challenges to human rights. They are for a long time subject to attacks and threats, as well as intimidation, harassment, arrest, and detention in connection with their human rights activities (A/HRC/13/22, 2009, para.3). It is relevant that the legal text, by law or constitutional provision, must define its composition and sphere of competence.

NHRIs are often labelled with different names. Their legal framework in the EU area is related to article 47 in the European Charter on Fundamental Rights (FRA, 2010). There are multiple synergies among NHRIs, constitutional law, and international law. Murray and Steinerte remind us of the importance of National Preventive Mechanisms (NPM's) under the Optional Protocol to the Convention against Torture and other Cruel, Inhuman or Degrading Treatment or Punishment (Murray et al., 2009). Each state must develop NPM's and there is an international subcommittee on the Prevention of Torture and other Cruel,

Inhuman or Degrading Treatment or Punishment ("SPT"). This system is different from the traditional UN treaty mechanisms. NPM's can usually be ombudsmen or national human rights commissions (Murray and Steinerte, 2009): "It would be wrong to conclude that an ombudsperson is better suited to be an NPM than a HRC (or vice versa) *per se*; it depends on the specific context" (Murray and Steinerte, 2009). This is yet another synergy between international and constitutional law in this twofold system.

The EU "Equality Directives" also require that each state implement an equality body:

> In addition to their obligations under Directives 2000/43/EC, 2004/113/EC, 2006/54/EC and 2010/41/EU as regards designating bodies for the promotion of equal treatment (hereinafter 'equality bodies'), all Member States should consider designating an equality body to cover the discrimination on the grounds of religion or belief, disability, age or sexual orientation within the scope of application of Directive 2000/78/EC. (Commission Recommendation on standards for equality bodies, 22 June 2018).

Hence, the composition and independence of these "Equality bodies" are correlatives. The Member States must focus in particular "on the procedures for appointing and dismissing staff, including persons holding leadership positions" (Commission Recommendation on standards for equality bodies, 22 June 2018).

In the Human Rights Council, national human rights institutions with "A" status accreditation can participate directly after their country and be accredited as observers (UN Human Rights Council, 2022). NHRIs with an "A" status accreditation, the GANHRI, and regional coordinating bodies can all undertake these functions:

- make an oral statement under all substantive agenda items of the Human Rights Council;
- participate through video messages in the HRC plenary debates, including during the adoption of the outcome of the UPR of the country by the Council, the interactive dialogue following the presentation of a country mission report by a special procedures mandate holder and panels or annual discussions;
- submit documents, which will be issued with UN document symbol;
- take separate seating in all sessions. (UN Human Rights Council, 2022)

However, some authors like Decaux remind us that NHRIs possess a hybrid nature as public bodies and human rights defenders. But they cannot replace the NGOs that are working in the field (Decaux and Bernard, 2011). I consider in this sense that the valuable work done by most NHRIs cannot be considered a substitute of civil society. NGOs, social movements, civic associations and individuals as human rights defenders are important stakeholders of the system of human rights. They are the groups that can be considered human rights defenders too, from the perspective of individuals in association with others to defend human rights.

Groups and human rights defenders: collective rights, trade unions, and NGOs

The Preamble in the Declaration on human rights defenders mentions the contributions of individuals and groups toward the elimination of human rights violations. This is consistent with the structure of the right to promote and protect human rights set in art. 1 of the DHRD. Article 1 establishes an individual and collective exercise of this right: "Everyone has the right, individually and in association with others, to promote and to strive for the protection and realization of human rights and fundamental freedoms at the national and international levels" (A/RES/53/144, 8 March 1999).

This collective dimension of the right to promote and protect human rights was controversial during discussions in the UN Working Group that drafted the Declaration on human rights defenders. However, there are many reasons to recognize the right of groups (not nations or states) composed of individuals acting in a collective way for human rights defence.

It is necessary to recognize the essential roles and actions for human rights executed by NGOs and INGOs, as well as civic associations, and social movements on an irregular or unregistered basis. Many environmental social movements have mobilized against projects that harm human rights, and students have acted without appertaining to an established movement or NGO. For instance, indigenous peoples also have some particularities as a group that merit consideration.

Behind all these groups, however, it is important to remember that there is an individual perspective. Under art. 1 of the DHRD, the aforementioned groups are considered human rights defenders, and they are individuals exercising their right to promote and protect human rights in association with others. Hence, the DHRD's legal framework applies to them, but complexities emerge from the groups' collective characters.

The legal recognition of human rights defenders in the declaration implies the recognition of a legal basis geared toward individuals, and not toward states or abstract entities such as peoples, nations, or communities. Abstract entities, such as people or nations, do not have a human condition for rights, as they are political concepts more than subjects of rights. Only individuals can possess the conditions of humanity. Other rights, of a different nature, do not derive from human dignity, but from other sources. Even while at the constitutional level fundamental rights have been attributed to legal persons, there are still certain rights, which by their nature, cannot be held by legal persons. The DHRD directly attributes the right to promote and protect human rights to groups as well as NGOs because they collectively exercise individual rights that derive from the paradigm of human condition.

The concept of "human rights defender" causes the debate to shift from the legal subject of rights to the application of these rights. The codification, attribution, and content of rights constitutes a legal paradigm of constitutional and international analysis. However, the right to promote and protect human rights undermines the constitutional and international paradigm when the DHRD construes the legal subject based on the exercise of fundamental rights, and not *vice versa*. As a result of this process, we can observe an erosion of the constitutional paradigm by the contemporary reality, in which constitutional functions are no longer necessarily and intrinsically associated with the state. Beginning with the process of the individualization of international law, and prompted by human rights, a change of paradigm in constitutional law leads to the development of a paradigm that can no longer be identified exclusively with the binomial state or nation, but where the dichotomy between the state and the individual is increasingly relevant. In this way, the individual is no longer a mere beneficiary of rights or a victim of human rights violations, but is able to act as a human rights defender, becoming a legal actor. The ultimate goal of the declaration is to recognize that power defined as the capacity to create, protect, and promote legal rules, according to Torres del Moral (Torres del Moral, 2015). This idea is not rooted in peoples, states, or nations, but in individuals. The ultimate basis for this legal power is found in the human condition.

This recognition of the right to promote and to strive for the protection of human rights individually or in association with others, constitutes a harsh historical reality. During the course of history, men and women have struggled for the codification, guarantees, protection, and promotion of their rights. Because of this, law as manifestation of power is not just a state matter. It is neither simply part of the internal affairs of a state, nor merely constituted on the basis of the aspirations of abstract collective entities such as peoples or nations. It is built using the synergy that exists in codification, therefore guaranteeing that individuals may exercise their rights as individuals. Consequently, individual action, individually or collectively exercised, is a factor for change in the legal sphere. The International Criminal Court, for instance, might not have existed if it had not been for all the NGOs that promoted its creation, neither would the United States have succeeded in ending racial segregation if it had not been for the Civil Rights Movement. Many European constitutions are the result of a fight against dictatorship and were adopted due to the efforts of individuals who, anonymously and peacefully, fought individually or in social movements for the protection and promotion of rights, demanding their codification as fundamental rights to act as limits, and as the *raison d'être* of state power. It is necessary to recognize the effort of those individuals, who, for instance, fought individually or in social movements during the Spanish transition to a constitutional system, such as the 1978 Spanish Constitution, inspired by the German Basic Law, that guarantees their fundamental rights. In this case, trade unions had an important role, as in the case of the *Atocha Lawyers*. On 24 January 1977, four labour lawyers and a trade union co-worker were killed by the shooting of far-right fascist gunmen in their office located in Madrid at 55 Atocha Street, and other four lawyers were wounded there. They belonged the trade union *Comisiones Obreras*, and were also close to the then clandestine Communist Party in Spain. This was a turning point in the Spanish Transition to democracy. Since the 1960s, there was a rising opposition to Franco's dictatorship in the streets, universities, and social movements. The day before, a student was also shot in a demonstration. The spirit and goal of all these protests were to achieve democracy after decades of dictatorship. However, they chose peaceful protest. The iconic painting of Juan Genovés, *El abrazo* (1920), (The Hug), shows this spirit of consensus in the Spanish revolts, leading to the end of dictatorship and the transition to democracy. The 24 January was chosen *in memoriam*, as the International Day of the Endangered Lawyer: "as a day to call for the attention of lawyers all over the world who are being harassed, silenced, pressured, threatened, persecuted, tortured" (Day of the endangered lawyer, 2022).

The right to promote and protect human rights has both an individual and a collective dimension. This right may be exercised collectively: associations and groups also have the right to promote and protect human rights. The declaration recognizes that human rights defenders may exercise the rights that are instrumental to their activities, such as the right of assembly, the right of association, the freedom of expression and opinion, as well as the right to protest. The recognition of the rights of groups does not preclude the recognition of the rights of associations. This also includes the rights of unregistered organizations, which may be exercised both through private gatherings as well as in public. The requirements to be met by human rights defenders also correspond to the nature of the right exercised. The universality and interdependence of rights, and the use of non-violent action through peaceful means constitute the foundations and limits of the right to promote and protect human rights, even for social movements, groups or organizations. Thus, violent action and the related modes of coaction or collaboration from a passive or active manner are not covered by the right to promote and protect human rights. This establishes a clear limit to the activities aimed at the promotion and protection of human rights. Therefore, the violent exercise of this right is excluded, as the promotion and protection of human rights must be peaceful. If we look at historical precedents of human rights defenders, we see that they defended dissident positions and questioned power peacefully, making them no less coherent or effective. One must not forget that this is a right each individual decides to exercise freely; no one may be obliged to bear a situation of peaceful resistance against authority or power abuse.

The human rights framework is necessary in an active, civil society. Critical media, organizations reporting human rights violations, groups promoting new rights in response to new social needs, dissidents that resist and organize themselves against the abuse of power, women who are active both in the public and the private sphere, NGOs that collaborate with national and international mechanisms for the protection of rights, individuals who raise their voices against laws that are contrary to human rights: all of these are necessary actors for the protection and promotion of human rights in a globalized world. At the legal level, this reality must be recognized, both internationally and constitutionally. Without the participation of individuals and civil society, the mechanisms for the protection of human rights cannot be used effectively. Individuals, groups and NGOs are therefore an essential part of the system for the protection of human rights. A multilevel legal system must be established that recognizes not only the need for the physical protection of the declaration's subject (the human rights defenders), but also the need to guarantee the right to promote and protect human rights, as well as the rights which are instrumental to its exercise. This means that synergies must be established between international and constitutional law, as well as guarantees of these rights. These are not only operative when they have already been violated, but also before and during the exercise of these rights, by means of legislative guarantees that may be translated into administrative, social, political, and educational measures.

Gómez Sánchez reminds us that they are collective rights or individual rights, depending on their subject (Gómez Sánchez, 2018). There are even individual rights that can be exercised in a collective manner. The Interamerican Court of Human Rights recognized the common property of land in the instance of indigenous people after the prominent case of *Awas-Tigny v. Nicaragua* (Ferrero Hernández, 2016, pp. 66–67). In the European Court of Human Rights, there is consistent case law that considers the right of assembly, demonstration, and in certain cases, association, (Art.1.1 ECtHR) as a collective exercise of the right of freedom of expression (art. 10 ECtHR). It is important to remember that in the ECtHR paradigm, both rights (right of freedom of expression and right of freedom of association), are not absolute rights with a specific limitative clause in their second paragraph, setting the criteria to be fulfilled if there is a limitation, that is: legal provision, necessity in a democratic society, and legitimate goals (with slight differences among these rights).

In the case of the indigenous peoples, the communal law is built to be a collective right. (Ferrero Hernández, 2016, pp. 66–67). The Interamerican Court considers it a law appertaining to the whole community, even if the beneficiaries are each one of the individuals in the community (Ferrero Hernández, 2016, p. 71). Another relevant aspect here is the need of consultation of the indigenous coming from the practice of the UN Rapporteurship on the rights of indigenous peoples, the ILO's Convention 169, and the UN Declaration on the Rights of Indigenous Peoples (Ferrero Hernández, 2016, pp. 86–88). All this is particularly relevant, because, as González Domínguez reminds us, human rights defenders defend indigenous people, land or environment. Human rights defenders on indigenous issues, land and environmental human rights defenders are among the most vulnerable groups of defenders (González Domínguez, 2016, p. 112). In 2016, the 40% of the HRDs killed were appertaining to these vulnerable groups.

Groups and the right to freedom of assembly

The DHRD recognizes the right to the freedom of assembly (art. 5.a and art. 12 DHRD). The right to the freedom of assembly is absolutely necessary to promote and protect human rights. Without the right to freedom of assembly it is not possible to carry out actions to defend human rights. Hence, this right allows for the collective exercise of the right to promote, to protect, and to strive for human rights and the articulation in the public and private spheres of individual and social claims for human rights (Saura-Freixes, 2015, p. 95). It is a twofold right within the framework of the Declaration on human rights defenders: "In articles 5 and 12 the Declaration on Human Rights Defenders recognizes the right to freedom of assembly and the legitimacy of participation in peaceful activities to protest against violations of human rights" (A/66/203, 2011, para. 21).

To be entitled to this right it is necessary to fulfil two criteria: peaceful activity and the universality of human rights. In the DHRD framework several activities of protest, including challenging actions against power, are possible: "from meetings inside private residences to conferences in public places, demonstrations, vigils, marches, picket lines and other kinds of assemblies" (A/66/203, 2011, para. 23). However, assemblies must be non-violent. This does not mean a lesser degree of protest, it just means that violence is not a legitimate method to promote and protect human rights. Gillion considers the efficacy of protest according to its impact, being considered a continuum of information on an issue, as for instance, minority claims on government (Gillion, 2013, p. 10). Thus, massive demonstrations may be more effective if they are peaceful rather than violent. Freedom of assembly is inherent to "social movements", who may also be subject to the right to promote and protect human rights, according to the Declaration on human rights defenders. Tilly and Wood characterize social movements, from 1750 to the present, according to three aspects:

1   A sustained, organized public effort making collective claims on target authorities (let us call it a campaign)
2   Employment of combinations form among the following forms of political action: creation of special-purpose associations and coalitions, public meetings, solemn processions, vigils, rallies, demonstrations, petition drives, statements to and in public media, and pamphleteering (call the variable ensemble of performances the social movement repertoire); and
3   Participants' concerted public representatives of WUNC: worthiness, unity, numbers, and commitment on the part of themselves and/or their constituencies (call them WUNC displays). (Tilly and Wood, 2016)

Freedom of assembly and social movements go together. Consequently, restrictions on the freedom of assembly must be balanced and limited by international standards. Nevertheless, by limiting the freedom of assembly, the right to promote and protect human rights may also be restricted. Limitation clauses are present in different human rights systems. In the United Nations system, article 21 of the International Covenant on Civil and Political Rights is the point of departure for the DHRD framework (A/66/203, 2011, para. 25).

Following ICCPR, three requirements must be fulfilled in order to be a legitimate restriction on the freedom of assembly: first, restrictions must be imposed by law; second, restrictions must be necessary in a democratic society; and finally, restrictions must be justified on legitimate grounds of national security or public safety, public order (*ordre public*), the protection of public health or morals, or the protection of the rights and freedoms of others (A/66/203, 2011, para. 25). Using unjustified restrictions or an excessive use of force is not allowed under the Declaration on human rights defenders or other significant human rights treaties. There must therefore be a reciprocal commitment in national law at the constitutional, legislative, and local levels with respect to this framework.

Groups and the right to freedom of association

The right to the freedom of association is also an indispensable tool for the promotion and protection of human rights. By means of the freedom of association, non-state agents such as NGOs can perform activities for the defence of human rights without unjustified obstacles (Saura-Freixes, 2015, p. 95). But this is a right not only of registered associations and organizations, it also includes groups within the scope of the Declaration on human rights defenders. There are two criteria to be fulfilled to possess this right: the principles of universality of human rights and non-violence (A/66/203, 2011, para. 29). This right is directly linked with participation in the public domain. Over time, human rights claims have been conducted by means of collective action. Moeckli considers "freedom of association is the freedom to pursue collective action" (Moeckli et al., 2014, p. 231). This collective action is carried out by three different types of organizations within the scope of freedom of association: political parties, trade unions, and civil organizations, such as NGOs (Moeckli et al., 2014, p. 231).

The Declaration on human rights defenders focuses especially on civil organizations. According to the framework and draft of the Declaration on human rights defenders, civil organizations can be also human rights defenders. The Special Rapporteur on the situation of human rights defenders thinks that leaders of trade unions or even politicians can be considered human rights defenders, but only if they are undertaking a particular action to protect or promote human rights (SR on the situation of human rights defenders, 2022). However, this action resides under the framework of their public action, and then it is overlapped. In the case of leaders of political parties, they are also restrained by the legal framework of political parties. What would be more controversial is to consider the political party a human rights defender; then, questions with regard to constitutional law emerge too. Remember, however, that under art. 1 of the DHRD, domestic law needs to be applied since it is the first legal framework for HRDs.

Let us consider the hybrid nature that can coexist in social movements. For instance, in 2000 the Sakharov Prize of the European Parliament was awarded to *¡BASTA YA!* The movement *¡BASTA YA!* was "a citizens' initiative against terrorism and political violence in Spain's Basque Country, formed in 1999 by intellectuals, human rights and political activists, trade unionists and other civil-society representatives" (European Parliament, 2016). In this case, the European Parliament recognized a social movement that transcended its country of origin and was relevant to all Europe. This is why the prize was awarded:

> The movement was opposed to all forms of nationalism and also criticised the Basque Country authorities for nationalistic policies and rhetoric. ¡BASTA YA! brought a flood of thousands to the streets of San Sebastián, calling for adequate policies to defeat terrorism and for the respect of the constitution in two large demonstrations in 2000. ¡BASTA YA! was recognized by the European Parliament that same year for its active campaigning for human rights, democracy and tolerance in the Basque Country. The prize was not only a recognition of ¡BASTA YA!'s work, but an acknowledgement that terrorism in

the Basque Country was a European problem, rather than only a Spanish one. (European Parliament, 2016. p. 62)

This new subject recognized human rights for non-state actors, such as individuals acting in groups for human rights. Thus, it becomes absolutely necessary in the international human rights system. Fact-finding depends on NGOs, they usually participate in international standard setting, and international and local advocacy (Ladmann and Abraham, 2004, p. 1). They are entitled to lodge individual complaints, to have a consultative status in the United Nations (Kamminga, 2005, p. 96) where now NGOs can also participate in the Universal Periodic Review. Finally, the Statute of the International Criminal Court (art. 15.2) recognizes that NGOs are an information source for the Prosecutor.

This right has both a negative and a positive dimension to it. On the one hand, one has the right to adhere to an association; but on the other hand, one has the right not to adhere. This is why freedom of association is also linked with ideological freedom, as well as with the freedom of expression.

The right to freedom of assembly and the right to freedom of association are the main collective rights. The other rights, such as the right to protest, the right to communicate with international bodies, the right to be protected or the right to an effective remedy are also held by groups as instrumental rights when they act as human rights defenders.

Groups as human rights defenders are more specifically recognized by the Inter-American Court of Human Rights in connection with the article 16 of the American Convention on Human Rights:

> El artículo 16 de la Convención Americana comprende también el derecho de toda persona a formar y participar libremente en organizaciones, asociaciones o grupos no gubernamentales orientados a la vigilancia, denuncia y promoción de los derechos humanos. Dada la importancia del papel que cumplen los defensores de derechos humanos en las sociedades democráticas, el libre y pleno ejercicio de este derecho impone a los Estados el deber de crear condiciones legales y fácticas en las cuales puedan desarrollar libremente su función. (Case *Kawas Fernandez c. Honduras*, 3 April 2009, para. 146)

From this perspective, Vogelfanger (2015) reminds us that in the first report about the situation of human rights defenders in the Americas, *Informe sobre la Situación de las Defensoras y Defensores de Derechos Humanos en las Américas*, there is an explicit recognition of the collective dimension of the right to promote and to protect human rights, thus establishing a difference between the individual dimension, the collective dimension, and the social dimension of this right. Then, according to the author, the collective dimension of the right can be defined as a defence of human rights in the public interest, where several individuals participate in association, with the right of assembly and certain aspects of freedom of expression (Vogelfanger, 2015, p. 281).

My thesis (2016) is coincident with this author because human rights defenders need protection not because they are a "group in a situation of vulnerability", but because of the individuals' right to promote and protect human rights, individually or in association with others (Vogelfanger, 2015, p. 293).

NGOs are also considered in the communications directed to the Special Rapporteur on the situation of human rights defenders and mentioned in the article 16 of the DHRD. However, Decaux (2005) points out that if there is an international law about states and international organizations, historically, as in the case of NGOs, there is no uniformity, and each international organization sets their own criteria to interact with NGOs (Decaux, 2005). Decaux and Bernard emphasize how states try to control the participation of independent NGOs in international organizations, like the United Nations (Decaux and Bernard, 2011, p. 25). Inside the Working Group, certain states have attempted to impose domestic law submission criteria to the submission to national legislation, control of activities, or even funding (Decaux and Bernard, 2011, p. 25). I agree with these authors when they remind us that the recognition of NHRIs and the Principles of Paris should not result in a diminished role for NGOs and INGOs working in the field (Decaux and Bernard, 2011, p. 26).

If there is no definition for human rights defenders, there is not a specific rule about them collectively (Decaux and Bernard, 2011, p. 25). But there are some exceptions, such as *La Convention européenne sur la reconnaissance de la personnalité juridique des organisations internationales non gouvernementales* (n° 124), 24 April 1986.

Adhering to Bobbio's theory (1991), over the course of history rights have not simply emerged because of decisions made by the ruling powers. Instead, rights have emerged through individual and social struggles, specifically with respect to the areas of life in which the state should refrain from intervening in, or on the contrary, should intervene with, in order to create guarantees and protection. Human rights transcend the statist dimension and generate international obligations to be fulfilled even in the absence of state control organs, yet even so their creation is driven by social needs. Up until the Declaration on human rights defenders, human rights were codified as a result of these social claims. The DHRD, however, for the first time gives legal recognition to the act of promoting the creation of new rights and protection for existing ones. The right to promote and protect human rights is a right of action. It constitutes a legal recognition which is in keeping with the historical character of human rights as the result of the individual and collective struggle against the abuse of power over the course of history. In addition, the declaration also represents an expansion of the personal scope of the application of human rights, as it is not just aimed at states, but at everyone. Other individuals and non-state actors must also respect the rights of the Declaration on human rights defenders, the DHRD legal framework and, in particular, the right to promote and protect human rights.

Human rights defenders: a subject built on the exercise of the right to strive for human rights

Contemporary global society created the necessity for a legal analysis' paradigm based on multilevel citizenships not limited by borders. Constitutionalism needs to understand the processes and synergies between legal orders involved in the protection of fundamental rights and human rights. The increase of referrals between these different legal orders have led to the emergence of synergies between constitutional and international law.

Peters' work on the individualization of international law (2016) changed the legal status of the individual in international law. For Peters, "the dichotomy between States and all other international legal subjects, is no longer fully tenable" (Peters, 2016, p. 44). Individuals emerge as a new actor, even as a subject with personhood, currently: "The individual—not the State—is the 'natural' person under international law" (Peters, 2016, p. 44). Human rights defenders' emergence is evidence of this change toward the paradigm of the subject, and further: human rights defenders are an active new subject in international law, leading to a reciprocal challenge in constitutional law. This is precisely why this new subject begs to be analysed in the academic domain, and also at the international and constitutional level.

In 1948, the Universal Declaration of Human Rights (UDHR) set a paradigm for the protection of human rights based on limiting the power of the state. Within this system of human rights, human beings hold rights that do not derive from state sovereignty, but from the human dignity. Human rights' protection was characterized by two aspects: universality of rights (leading to international control) and the role of the state as the one responsible for compliance to the right. Hence, human dignity and sovereignty were the two main axiological principles in tension under the UDHR. This responsibility could be gradually claimed internationally by individuals (Peters, 2016). But in the initial phase, even the Commission on Human Rights of the United Nations declared itself incompetent to act in cases of human rights violations. This created the necessity to have other international treaty-based guarantees for the protection of human rights that still depended on the agreement of sovereign states. The protection, and/or, violation of rights, were no longer an internal affair of the state.

As a result of globalization, the aspects of universality and state responsibility have both evolved. In contemporary times, whenever we refer to the universality of human rights, we mean a universal legal basis deriving not only from human dignity, from the human condition. Rights are universal, but what differs is the exercising of these rights from one individual to another. Current problems on rights must focus more on the processing of exercising rights, because it is in the exercise where unequal conditions can be found. This must not be only considered as opposed, as it is obvious that rights can be exercised in a different manner among individuals, cultures, and countries. For instance, this is something dealt with the margin of appreciation, as in the case law of the European Court of Human Rights. However, after globalization, there is a strong paradox as to when the state should guarantee rights when it no longer has a monopoly on power. Hence, it is no more tenable that states are the only legal subject, as Peters states:

> For instance, no one would claim that individuals can declare war or acquire territory with international legal effect. But then, for the sake of consistency, the State should also be considered merely a limited legal subject. States do

not—even potentially—possess the totality of all legal positions possible in international law. For instance, they are unable to enjoy human rights. (Peters, 2016, pp. 42–43)

I would like to remark on the importance of this last sentence: "they are unable to enjoy human rights" (Peters 2016, p. 43). It lets us see the path behind the increasing subjectivity of individuals in international, and reciprocally, constitutional law. To arrive at the contemporary concept of human rights, and the evolution of the axiological paradigm from human dignity to the human condition, it is important to understand the system of law after the Second World War.

Following the Second World War paradigm, the obligation of international protection emerges once national protection fails. For example: the international obligation to protect refugees, which some states still refuse to carry out. The first phase in the evolution of human rights (1948–1966) revolves around the idea of codification, but unfortunately, and at present, there are not enough multilevel mechanisms that may be used to claim responsibility from non-complying states if the responsibility is not based on a previous agreement. Currently, the treaty rights will hardly be effective if measures are not adopted under domestic law to guarantee their effectiveness. This includes international decisions, which impact in the constitutional sphere.

At the national level, democracies have included fundamental rights as positive rights in their constitutions, with increasing references to international law. Following the Second World War paradigm, article 1 of the 1949 German Basic Law can be considered a tool to understand the constitutional legitimacy for contemporary states:

1 Human dignity shall be inviolable. To respect and protect it shall be the duty of all state authority.
2 The German people therefore acknowledge inviolable and inalienable human rights as the basis of every community, of peace and of justice in the world.
3 The following basic rights shall bind the legislature, the executive and the judiciary as directly applicable law.

In contemporary democracies, the legitimacy of state power derives from the state's obligation to guarantee the rights of citizens first, evolving to individuals, and whoever is under their jurisdiction, even beyond borders. Hence, the criterion of state jurisdiction seems more adequate than the criterion of state sovereignty to understand the constitutional function of the contemporary states. I consider it more adequate to think about the state's constitutional function, which also has repercussions at the international level.

To avoid abuses of power by the state, the classic paradigm of human rights dictates that the international community should act through their international mechanisms to ensure the compliance of state obligations laid down in treaties. But treaty-mechanisms between parties is still based on vestiges of the sovereignty principle, with refers to constitutional law, and from constitutional law. This system was necessary because it allowed the development of the entire framework for the protection of human rights after the Second World War. However, as a result of globalization, the breakdown of the state-nation is a cause for the breakdown of the human rights treaty-guarantees around the world. Hence, it is important that the twofold guarantees on human rights are currently interdependent. The system of human rights guarantees' is then *per se* asymmetric, so even if the subject of rights is universal, the human rights' exercise seems to be condemned to become unequal and asymmetrical among individuals, for better and worse.

Human rights defenders are a new legal non-state actor in international and constitutional law. But, the main change, in my opinion, is that individuals are considered to be actors, and not mere passive subjects of law with a twofold perspective, at the constitutional and international level, under art. 1 and art. 3 of the DHRD.

Rights—as shown by totalitarian states—should not depend on the sovereignty of the state, and going further, not on respect for human dignity. Respect for the human condition demands the individualization of rights, putting the focus on the exercising of rights, and not only on the personhood of rights. The turning point that arrives under globalization is this change of paradigm.

Following the phase of codification, another phase may be observed during which a legal system is progressively created with different levels of protection, as well as rules on the international and regional level, including a process of European integration leading to the creation of a supranational system for the protection of fundamental rights. Marrani (2012) finds a synergy among globalization and multilevel constitutionalism. However, legal pluralism and multilevel governance are not at the same level of integration:

> The problem of a global space—the European Union (EU) and European integration being one example—is therefore, fundamental to the problem of multilevel governance, of pluralism, and particularly, of legal pluralism; hence, the consideration given here to the point of interconnection. The first observation that can be made is that one individual may come to understand our world in a different way to another individual. To be more specific, one individual may perceive the world as a series of nation-states while others may not. (Marrani, 2012, p. 34)

Marrani (2012) contends that there are several phenomena in this second modernity: dissolution of nations in a cosmopolitan society, fading concepts such as state-nation and sovereignty, emergence of supranational elements at regional level, but also the redefinition of communities and minorities in an era of multilevel governance. This pluralism leads to a legal pluralism where the monopoly of the state to create law is under attack: "These attacks come from official and nonofficial norms, created both within and outside the state" (Marrani, 2012, p. 35).

There is a need to configure rights that do not depend exclusively on a territorial or legal relation with the state. The fundamental "right to have rights" emanates from the human condition and not from status as a citizen. Hence, any human being possesses the "right to have rights" (Arendt, 1951), but each individual would exercise the rights in a different manner.

For this reason, in order to neutralize the political capacity of the state to violate human rights, fundamental rights were introduced into constitutions at the national level, and human rights at the international level. But a contradiction arises between the constitutional and the international spheres when the sovereignty of the state, expressed through the concept of citizenship, prevails over human dignity as the foundation of human rights. Ultimately, as the Spanish Constitutional Court has ruled, there are fundamental rights that emanate from human dignity and therefore pertain to all individuals.

The legal system established in 1998 with the Declaration on human rights defenders presents a new paradigm of personhood based on the exercising of rights, not on personhood or citizenship, but based on the human condition. Any individual can become a human rights defender, or not, depending on their will. This distinction builds the criteria to be fulfilled for being considered a human rights defender. This paradigm is not a substitute for the responsibility of states to comply with human rights. It is a flexible idea to put on the table since individuals are not only abstract entities under law, but realistic entities not dependent on the will of the state, but on their own individual will. This individual will is not absolute; there are some criteria to be fulfilled to gain status. Hence, this is quite Aristotelian, and subsequently Arendtian: human beings need (not only) other human beings, but a legal framework to be individuals. The turning point is that this framework is no longer only based on the state-nation or the human rights treaties-human dignity, but on their human condition. In the ability to hold rights and obligations at the international and constitutional levels, they can be considered a new subject for the law that still requires attention.

References

Alexeyeva, L. (1985). *Soviet Dissent. Contemporary Movements for National, Religious and Human Rights*. Middletown, Connecticut: Wesleyan University Press.
Arendt, H. (1951). *The Origins of Totalitarianism*. New York: Brace, Harcourt.
Bennet, K., Ingleton, D., Nah, M. A., and Savage, J. (2016). *Critical Perspectives on the Security and Protection of Human Rights Defenders*. Oxon & New York: Routledge.
Bobbio, N. (1991). *El tiempo de los derechos*. Madrid: Sistema.
Brett, R. (1996). "Human rights and the OSCE". *Human Rights Quarterly*, 18(3).
Brier, R. (2013). "Broadening the cultural history of the Cold War: The emergence of the Polish Workers' Defense Committee and the rise of human rights". *Journal of Cold War Studies*, 15(4), 104–127.
Decaux, E. and Bernard, A. (2011). "Les défenseurs des droits de l'homme". In *Droit, liberté, paix, developement. Mélanges en honneur de Mahjid Benchick* (pp. 23–33). Paris: Pedone.
Decaux, E. (2005). "La contribution des organisations non gouvernementales à l'élaboration des règles du droit international des droits de l'homme". In D. Cohen-Jonathan & J. F. Flauss (Eds), *Les organisations non gouvernementales et le droit international des droits de l'homme*. Brussels: Bruylant.

Eguren Fernández, L. E. and Patel, C. (2015). "Towards developing a critical and ethical approach for better recognising and protecting human rights defenders". *The International Journal of Human Rights*, 19(7), 896–907.

Einstein (1933). "*Programme*". London: Refugee Assistance Fund.

Ferrero Hernández, R. (2016). "Protección de la propiedad comunal indígena por la Corte Interamericana". *Revista Instituto Interamericano de Derechos Humanos*, 63, 65–104.

FRA (2010). "National Human Rights Institutions in the EU Member States Strengthening the fundamental rights architecture in the EU I". Available at: https://fra.europa.eu/en/publication/2012/national-human-rights-institutions-eu-member-states-strengthening-fundamental (accessed 24 May 2022).

Gillion, D. Q. (2013). *The Political Power of Protest: Minority Activism and Shifts in Public Policy*. Cambridge: Cambridge University Press.

González Domínguez, M. (2016). "El derecho a defender los derechos humanos como un derecho autónomo". *Revista Instituto Interamericano de Derechos Humanos*, 63, 105–146.

Horvath, R. (2014). "Breaking the totalitarian ice: The initiative group for the defense of human rights in the USSR". *Human Rights Quarterly*, 36(2014).

Jones, M. (2015). "Protecting human rights defenders at risk: Asylum and temporary international relocation". *International Journal of Human Rights*, 19(7), 935–960. Retrieved 4 June, 2022, from: https://doi.org/10.1080/13642987.2015.1075304.

Joo, H. (2004). "Voices of Freedom: Samizdat". *Europe-Asia Studies*, 56(4).

Kamminga, T. (2005). "The evolving status of NGOs under international law: A threat to the inter-state system?" In P. Alston (Ed.), *Non-State Actors and Human Rights*. Oxford: Oxford University Press.

Ku, C. (2012). *International Law, International Relations and Global Governance*. London: Routledge.

Ladmann, T. and Abraham, M. (2004). "Evaluation of nine non-governmental human rights organisations". *IOB Working Document*, February 2004.

Marrani, D. (2012). "'Mission impossible': Interconnecting the common law legal culture and civil law legal systems in the European integration". In R. Freixes, J. Remotti, D. Marrani, J. A. Bombin, & L. Vanin-Verna (Eds), *La Gouvernance Multi Level: Penser-l'enchevêtrement* (pp. 33–55). Bruxelles: EME Editions.

McChesney, A. (1995). "Protecting the rights of all human rights defenders". *The Review. International Commission of Jurists*, 55, 39–58.

McChesney, A. (1995). *The Protection of Human Rights Defenders*. International Commission of Jurists.

McChesney, A. and Rodley, N. (1992). "Human rights defenders. Drafting a declaration". *International Commission of Jurists Review*, 48.

Moeckli, D., Shah, S., and Sivakumaran, S. (2014). *International Human Rights Law*. Oxford: Oxford University Press.

Murray, R. and Steinerte, E. (2009). "Same but different? National human rights commissions and ombudsman institutions as national preventive mechanisms under the Optional Protocol to the UN Convention against Torture". *Essex Human Rights Review*, Special Issue, 54–72.

OHCHR (2010). *National Human Rights Institutions. History, Principles, Roles and Responsibilities*. New York & Geneva: United Nations.

Peters, A. (2016). *Beyond Human Rights: The Legal Status of the Individual in International Law*. Cambridge: Cambridge University Press.

Quinn, R. and Levine, J. (2014). "Intellectual-HRDs and claims for academic freedom under human rights law". *The International Journal of Human Rights*, 18(7–8), 898–920.

Saura-Freixes, N. (2015). *Libertad de expresión y derecho a promover y proteger los derechos humanos*. Barcelona: J.M. Bosch Editor.

Saura-Freixes, N. (2016) *Human rights defenders. El derecho a promover y proteger los derechos humanos*. Madrid: UNED.

Tilly, C. and Wood, L. J. (2016). *Social Movements. 1768–2012*. New York: Routledge.

Torres del Moral, A. (2015). *Estado de Derecho y Democracia de Partidos*. Madrid: Universitas.

Vogelfanger, A. D. (2015). "El Status jurídico de defensores y defensoras de derechos humanos". *Revista Instituto Interamericano Derechos Humanos*, 63, 267–294.

Documents

Treaties

American Convention on Human Rights (adopted 22 November, 1969, entered into force 18 July 1978) 1144 UNTS 123; OASTS No. 36 ("Pact of San Jose, Costa Rica", ACHR)

Charter of the United Nations, (adopted 24 October 1945) 1 UNTS XVI

Consolidated Version of the Treaty on European Union [2012] OJ C 326/13

Convention for the Protection of Human Rights and Fundamental Freedoms, as amended, (adopted 4 November 1950, *entered into force 3 September 1953) ETS No.* 005 (ECHR)

Convention européenne sur la reconnaissance de la personnalité juridique des organisations internationales non gouvernementales (24 April 1986), ETS No. 124

International Covenant on Civil and Political Rights (adopted 16 December 1966, entered into force 23 March 1976) 999 UNTS 171 (ICCPR)

International Covenant on Economic, Social and Cultural Rights (adopted 16 December 1966, entered into force 3 January 1976) 993 UNTS 3 (ICESCR)

ILO Indigenous and Tribal Peoples Convention C169 (27 June 1989)

Optional Protocol to the International Covenant on Civil and Political Rights (adopted 16 December 1966, entered into force 23 March 1976) 999 UNTS 171

Optional Protocol to the Convention against Torture and Other Cruel, Inhuman or Degrading Treatment or Punishment, (18 December 2002) 2375 UNTS 237 (OPCAT)

Optional Protocol to the Convention on the Elimination of All Forms of Discrimination against

Women New York, 6 October 1999 (22 December 2000) 2131 UNTS 83

UN

Universal Declaration of Human Rights UNGA Res. 217A (III) (10 December 1948)

Declaration on the Right and Responsibility of Individuals, Groups and Organs of Society to Promote and Protect UniversallyRecognized HumanRights and Fundamental Freedoms UNGA A/RES/53/144 (8 March 1999)

Declaration on the Rights of Indigenous Peoples: resolution/adopted by the General Assembly, UN Doc A/RES/61/295, (2 October 2007)

UNGA "National institutions for the promotion and protection of human rights, Annex. Principles relating to the status of national institutions" (20 December 1993) *UN Doc A/RES/48/134.* Retrieved 30 May 2022, from: www.legal-tools.org/doc/b38121/pdf/

UNGA "*World Conference on Human Rights: resolution/adopted by the General Assembly*" A/RES/48/121, (14 February 1994). *UN Doc A/RES/48/121 Retrieved 29 May*, 2022 https://digitallibrary.un.org/record/180196?ln=es

UNGA "*Situation of human rights defenders. Note by the Secretary-General. Report of the Special Rapporteur on the situation of human rights defenders*" (23 July 2008) UN Doc A/73/215. Retrieved 29 May, 2022, from: https://digitallibrary.un.org/record/1639412?ln=es

UNGA "Human rights defenders. *Note by the Secretary-General.* Report of the Special Rapporteur on the situation of human rights defenders" (28 July 2011) *UN Doc A/66/203*. Retrieved 4 June, 2022, from: https://digitallibrary.un.org/record/709670?ln=es

UNGA "*Situation of human rights defenders. Note by the Secretary-General. Report of the Special Rapporteur on the situation of human rights defenders*" (15 July 2019) UN Doc A/74/159. Retrieved 4 June, 2022, from: https://digitallibrary.un.org/record/3824600?ln=es

HRC "*Report of the Special Rapporteur on the situation of human rights defenders, Margaret Sekaggya*" (30 December 2009) UN Doc A/HRC/13/22. Retrieved 4 June, 2022, from: https://digitallibrary.un.org/record/679324?ln=es

HRC "Report of the Special Rapporteur on the situation of human rights defenders, Margaret Sekkagya (21 December 2011) UN Doc A/HRC/19/55. Retrieved 4 June, 2022, from: https://digitallibrary.un.org/record/719453?ln=es

HRC "*Report of the Special Rapporteur on the situation of human rights defenders, Margaret Sekaggya*" (16 January 2013) UN Doc A/HRC/22/47. Retrieved 4 June, 2022, from: https://digitallibrary.un.org/record/742868?ln=es

HRC (2022). "*NGO and NHRI Information*". Retrieved 30 May 2022, from: www.ohchr.org/en/hr-bodies/hrc/ngo-nhri-info

OHCHR "*Principles relating to the Status of National Institutions (The Paris Principles) (20 November 1993)*" UN Doc A/RES/48/134. Retrieved 30 May 2022, from: www.ohchr.org/en/instruments-mechanisms/instruments/principles-relating-status-national-institutions-paris

OHCHR (2022). "*GANHRI Sub-Committee on Accreditation (SCA)*". Retrieved May 30, 2022, from: www.ohchr.org/en/countries/nhri/ganhri-sub-committee-accreditation-sca

Special Rapporteur on the rights of indigenous peoples. (2022). *Retrieved 4 June*, 2022, from: www.ohchr.org/en/special-procedures/sr-indigenous-peoples#:~:text=about%20this%20mandate.-,Current%20mandate%20holder,role%20on%201%20May%202020

World Conference on Human Rights in Vienna. Vienna Declaration and Programme of Action (25 June 1993). *Retrieved 3 June*, from: www.ohchr.org/sites/default/files/vienna.pdf

ICJ

Legality of the threat or use of nuclear weapons (Advisory opinion) [1996] ICJ Rep 1996, p. 226

ECtHR

ECtHR Research Division. (2005) "*Internet: case-law of the European Court of Human Rights*" Updated: June 2015. Council of Europe. Retrieved 29 May, 2022, from: https://echr.coe.int/Documents/Research_report_internet_ENG.pdf (accessed 29 May 2022)

Editorial Board of Pravoye Delo and Shtekel v. Ukraine App. no. 33014/05 (ECtHR 5 May 2011)

ChristineGoodwinv.TheUnited Kingdom, [GC] App. no. 28957/95 (ECtHR 11 July 2002)

EU

Sakharov Prize European Parliament (2022) "FAQs". Retrieved 29 May, 2022, from: www.europarl.europa.eu/sakharovprize/en/the-prize/faqs (accessed 29 May 2022)

Charter of Fundamental Rights of the European Union [2012] OJ C 326

Directive (EU) 2019/1937 of the European Parliament and of the Council of 23 October 2019 on the protection of persons who report breaches of Union law [2019] OJ L 305

Council of the EU (Foreign Affairs). Ensuring protection. European Union Guidelines on human rights defenders [2008]. Retrieved 4 June, 2022, from: www.eeas.europa.eu/sites/default/files/eu_guidelines_hrd_en.pdf

Council Directive 2000/78/EC of 27 November 2000 establishing a general framework for equal treatment in employment and occupation [2000] OJ L 303

Council Directive 2000/43/EC of 29 June 2000 implementing the principle of equal treatment between persons irrespective of racial or ethnic origin [2000] OJ L 180

Council Directive 2004/83/EC of 29 April 2004 on minimum standards for the qualification and status of third country nationals or stateless persons as refugees or as persons who otherwise need international protection and the content of the protection granted, [2004] OJ L 304/12

Council Directive 2004/113/EC of 13 December 2004 implementing the principle of equal treatment between men and women in the access to and supply of goods and services, [2004] OJ L 373; [2006] OJ L.153M

Directive 2006/54/EC of the European Parliament and of the Council of 5 July 2006 on the implementation of the principle of equal opportunities and equal treatment of men and women in matters of employment and occupation (recast), [2006] OJ L 204

Directive 2010/41/EU of the European Parliament and of the Council of 7 July 2010 on the application of the principle of equal treatment between men and women engaged in an activity in a self-employed capacity and repealing Council Directive 86/613/EEC [2010] OJ L 180

Council Directive 2000/78/EC of 27 November 2000 establishing a general framework for equal treatment in employment and occupation [2000] OJ L 303

Commission Recommendation (EU) 2018/951 of 22 June 2018 on standards for equality bodies, C/2018/3850, [2018] OJ L 167

European ParliamentSakharov Prize. (2022) "¡Basta Ya! – 2000, Spain". Retrieved 4 June, 2022, from: www.europarl.europa.eu/sakharovprize/en/-basta-ya-2000-spain/products-details/20200331CAN54182

European Parliament. (2016). *The book of Sakharov Prize Laureates 2016*. European Parliament, European Union

CJEU

Case C-472/13 Andre Lawrence Shepherd v Bundesrepublik Deutschland, [2015] EU:C:2015:117

Case C-472/13 *Andre Lawrence Shepherd v Bundesrepublik Deutschland* Opinion of AG Sharpston, EU:C:2014:2360

OSCE

OSCE "*Conference on Security and Co-operation in Europe (CSCE): Final Act of Helsinki*" (CSCE Helsinki 1 August 1975). Retrieved 26 May, 2022, from: www.osce.org/es/mc/39506

OAS

Inter-American Court of Human Rights
Case of the Mayagna (Sumo) Awas Tingni Community v. Nicaragua (Merits, Reparations and Costs) IACHR SeriesC No 79 (31 August, 2001)
Case Kawas Fernández vs. Honduras. Sentencia de 3 de abril de 2009 *(Fondo, Reparación y Costas)* IACHR Series C No. 196 (3 April 2009)
Inter-American Commission on Human Rights. *Informe sobre la situación de las defensoras y defensores de los derechos humanos en las Américas.* OEA/Ser.L/V/II.124. Doc. 5 rev. 1, 7 March 2006. Retrieved May 30, 2022, from: www.refworld.org.es/docid/5d7fc2bdd.html

Germany

Basic Law for the Federal Republic of Germany, 23 May 1949. *Last amended on 29 September 2020.* Retrieved 29 May, 2022, from: www.btg-bestellservice.de/pdf/80201000.pdf

NGOs and others

Cara. (2022) "*Cara. A lifeline to academics in risk*". Retrieved May 30, 2022, from: www.cara.ngo/
United StatesHolocaust Museum. (2022) "*Varian Fry*". Retrieved May 30, 2022, from: www.ushmm.org/collections/bibliography/varian-fry
Day of the endangered lawyer. (2022). "*Backgrounds. Establishing the Foundation*". Retrieved May 30, 2022, from: http://dayoftheendangeredlawyer.eu/backgrounds/#EstablishingThe Foundation.

6 The right to promote and protect human rights

The Declaration on human rights defenders has built a new paradigm of international and constitutional law where the principle of sovereignty and the legal entitlement of rights has been displaced by the principles of the human condition and universal plural exercise. The UDHR (1948) framework set up after the Second World War was based on human dignity (Carrillo Salcedo, 1999). The tension between these two principles—sovereignty and the human condition—was a constant issue in the debates held for 13 years within the working group to draft the Declaration on human rights defenders. However, after the disappearance of the two power blocs, the fall of the Berlin Wall and the disintegration of the Soviet Union, it was possible to draft the Declaration on Human Rights Defenders with a consensus. The debate regarding these controversial aspects converged in a wider principle based on the human condition. The final Declaration on Human Rights Defenders and the legal framework on the right to promote and protect human rights synthesizes this tension. The UN consensus opens the door to a legal paradigm that surpasses human dignity: the human condition.

In 1998, when the DHRD was adopted, the first effects of globalization were just emerging. It is not only by chance that the International Criminal Court Statute was adopted and Protocol No. 11 to the European Convention on Human Rights came into force. These three main legal changes widened the legal paradigm on dignity stemming from World War II, and opening the door to the process of individualization in international law, as pointed out by Peters (Peters, 2016). However, a challenging characteristic of the right to promote and protect human rights is its very nature: the right is established by its exercise more than by entitlement. Thus, it is a challenge not only for international law but for constitutional law as well. New scenarios require new actors. Individualism and legal pluralism are emerging as new trends in constitutional and international law. Both states and individuals are entitled to submit and fulfil international complaints, and to have duties. As in the International Court of Justice (ICJ Opinion, 11 April 1949), these are almost the mandatory conditions required to become an international legal subject. But maybe, as Peters reminds (2016), a constitutional approach to the individualization of international law is necessary, particularly, in order to understand this change from the traditional paradigm of the nation-state.

DOI: 10.4324/9780429264016-6

In this sense, the Declaration on human rights defenders goes even further. The individual is recognized not only as a victim or a passive subject of rights, or even as a complainant, but also as a driving force for human rights protection, recognizing in individuals the right not just to protect, but also to "strive" for human rights, in the article 1 of the DHRD (1998). From a theoretical point of view, there is a connection with the conception of human rights as not just an abstract axiological subject, but as one that is historical social, and even political. This is theoretically connected with Arendt's "Right to have rights" (1951), and with Bobbio's historical perspective on the struggle for rights (1991); it is also reminiscent of Aristotelean political theory. Individuals are neither bare life, nor only political and legal subjects built on a connection with citizenship and nationality. We are individuals capable of possessing, creating and striving for rights. Hence, there is a particular entitlement to rights based on the rights' exercise, and it depends on the individual's will to enforce it.

The emergence of human rights defenders: a new paradigm of constitutional and international law?

Consequently, the recognition of one's decision and will as a force for rights' entitlement is a particular conception of the right to promote and protect human rights, replacing the constitutional paradigm based purely on one's nation or peoples, which is now more inclusive of human beings as individuals. It does not imply a privatization of the constitutional function of the state or the international sphere. The individual's will not be omnipotent. The individual's will and exercise shall be inserted into domestic constitutional law and international human rights obligations (article 2 DHRD). Hence, the paradox of citizenship spelled out by Arendt (1951) could be solved in this new way of attributing rights. The binomial theory of law and the individual is inherent to the legal paradigm of the human condition. This could possibly have a responsible effect on individuals. Unfortunately, it could also lead to the individual abuse of rights if the right to promote and to protect human rights is considered absolute. However, for other human rights, it is not an absolute right.

Bobbio's (1991) theory on human rights considers them to be historical. Rights are built during the fight for new freedoms against old powers (Bobbio, 1991, p. 18). Nevertheless, it is necessary to add to his theory: human rights are also built on the struggle of old freedoms against new powers in the contemporary moment. The maintenance of certain "classic" rights —even if they are built under a state paradigm—make it necessary to guarantee human rights. So, fundamental rights emerge as a constitutional paradigm that must be opened to include international law, but they must not be destroyed or replaced. However, what is absolutely necessary is to connect and to strengthen synergies between international and constitutional law, in order to guarantee the constitutional function of law, that is, the protection of fundamental individual rights. This constitutional function can be carried out inside borders as well as a function undertaken by a state or by an international organization (Kumm 2013, 2018) (Peters 2015,

2016) but never as a duty for individuals. Again, positive obligations always remain with the state, not with individuals (Gavara de Cara, 2007, pp. 277–278). In this sense, some constitutional examples are necessary. For instance, article 10.2 of the Spanish Constitution (1978) opens the constitution to international law by means of interpretation: in article 10 there is a twofold constitutional engagement, first with human dignity, and second, with the international framework of human rights' protection. In article 10, the Spanish Constitution establishes that fundamental rights must be interpreted in accordance with the Universal Declaration of Human Rights, and the human rights' treaties signed by Spain. This is quite consistent with the threshold in article 2 of the Declaration on human rights defenders (1998).

Hence, it makes sense to think globally about the effects of individualization on international law at the constitutional level in the case of human rights defenders. Even if the DHRD is not binding, it has an irradiation effect. The Declaration and the setting of the UN thematic mechanism on human rights defenders in 2000 has created a multilevel legal system, as reminded by Bennet et al. (2016).

Presently, the European Union policy on human rights defenders is ascendant. The primacy of European Law makes it necessary to consider the impact of the DHRD at the constitutional and international level. However, there is an apparent dichotomy. Internally, human rights defenders exist in the EU in the space of freedom, security and justice. Thus, theoretically, it makes no sense to give HRDs protection from one EU Member State to another, nor does it make sense to grant asylum. But there is a difference between the *ad intra* and *ad extra* EU policy on human rights defenders. Beyond their borders, EU foreign policy considers the protection and promotion of HRD as a part of its external action. This EU action on HRDs and the impact on the EU states often remains unknown, even by state judiciary authorities, and possible interplay with the ECJ is unknown as well.

Rovira Viñas points out the need to build new and effective guarantees to cope with new global challenges in the contemporary world (Rovira Viñas, 2013, p. 21). In this sense, according to the Declaration on human rights defenders, individuals, groups and even national human rights institutions (NHRIs) have leading roles in contributing to solutions to meet these new challenges. In the long struggle of humankind against power, the acknowledgment of rights, and the recognition of some new rights is yet necessary. Hence, it would be necessary to enact new human rights guarantees. However, the contribution of individuals to the promotion and protection of human rights is a real need in the global world. This contribution is recognized in the Preamble of the DHRD as "the valuable work of individuals, groups and associations in contributing to, the effective elimination of all violations of human rights".

From a theoretical perspective, this recognition challenges the nation-state conception of power. Different reasons converge to reinforce this idea. There is a displacement of the law-making power. According to Torres del Moral, when considering the meaning of "policy", two concepts must be examined: activity and power (Torres del Moral, 2015, p. 48). After the DHRD, the activity and power of individuals to protect and promote human rights has become not only a political issue, but also a legal right. This is a key aspect of the declaration and its main challenge. When a right to promote and protect human rights is enabled, a new barrier to power is built. Because the main purpose of the DHRD is not recognition of the power of abstract entities such as states, peoples or nations, but the power of individuals. In this case, this new right to promote and protect human rights creates a new legal subject: human rights defenders.

In classic democratic theory, the concept of people is based on two complementary aspects. According to Torres del Moral: a) people governed are the target of state power and rules; and b) people governing are able to create, rules, institutions and organs (Torres del Moral, 2015, p. 45). The sovereignty of the state and the people as a subject of power are the subsequent consequences of traditional democratic theory. The first rupture was brought about in 1948 by the UDHR and it introduced a limit to the state's power: the limit was found in international human rights. Under the constitutional continental theory, the sovereignty of the state was legitimized by the need to respect fundamental rights, finding its core expression in German Basic Law and the synthesis provided in article 1:

1 Human dignity shall be inviolable. To respect and protect it shall be the duty of all state authority.
2 The German people therefore acknowledge inviolable and inalienable human rights as the basis of every community, of peace and of justice in the world.
3 The following basic rights shall bind the legislature, the executive and the judiciary as directly applicable law. (Basic Law for the Federal Republic of Germany, 1949, article 1)

In the European regional area, the interaction of constitutional law and international law on fundamental rights emerges from two main trends:

a The European Convention on Human Rights and the protection offered by the European Court of Human Rights case law.
b The supranational level of the EU integration and its primacy effect, even with remaining tensions in the state-nation sovereignty paradigm.

Both systems connect democracy, rule of law, and human rights. Thus, this new subject—human rights defenders—must be considered inside the established framework, not only out of it. The challenge is that individuals striving for human rights must be considered within the constitutional framework of the EU states members. It is a presumption that comes from the criteria as members, not only of the EU, but of the Council of Europe as well. In case of a violation of an individual's rights, there are regional systems in the European Convention on Human Rights (ECHR) and the European Charter of Fundamental Rights (ECFR). But if there is a gross pattern of ongoing violations, there are other systems for responding within EU law, and even in the EU Member States' constitutional laws. Both systems guarantee that the actions of individuals to promote and protect human rights are rights and not duties. Hence, the right to promote and protect human rights is not an absolute right. It can be limited by the framework of domestic constitutional law, the primacy of EU law, the regional systems, ECHR, other state human rights' obligations, as well as, finally, the UN Charter, according to article 2 of the DHRD legal framework. However, there is not nearly enough awareness of this multilevel legal framework.

As previously mentioned, there are several closing clauses in the DHRD that lead the interaction between individuals and state. These closing clauses express the commitment achieved after 15 years of discussion in the UN working group to draft the Declaration on human rights defenders. Under these discussions, the proceedings remain history, and the history of the opposition among two blocs: between "western" and "not western" countries. This is why the DHRD opens the door to a possible agreement on human rights, and it could be considered a particular example of global constitutionalism.

In this sense, authors on global constitutionalism remark on four main aspects that come from constitutional law: "Four principles or 'fundamental norms' make manifest these limiting and enabling functions: the rule of law, a balance or separation of powers, constituent powers and rights" (Lang and Wiener, 2017, p. 2). Hence, maybe the Habermas' conception of constitutional democracy arises as a necessary consideration, but it still fails at the global international level. However, it makes sense to think about it in the European area, due to its constitutional processes.

I am referring to this theoretical perspective in order to set human rights defenders inside the constitutional framework opened by, and as a result of, international law. If not, how can we arrive with the unlimited power of an individual to challenge the state? This crucial question is unsolved if it is considered merely in theoretical terms, or even in terms of international law. Democracy is not just action as a result of power granted through an election. Terrible historical episodes have shown how elected power can be used to erase individuals' rights. Arendt's criticism of human rights dependence on state power and citizenship is the point of departure for a new conception of rights. Thus, rights are not based on the state, but on the human condition, where individuals have a "Right to have rights" (Arendt, 1951). However, Arendt's concept is also based on the responsibility of individuals.

Peters (2016) considers this a turning point in the individualization of international law. Accordingly, consider the individual criminal responsibility emerging from Nuremberg: "These war crimes trials postulated the criminal responsibility of individuals under international law and removed the perpetrators from the protective shield of the State, behind which they tried to hide" (Peters, 2016, p. 20). Before this, there was a precedent in the individualistic orientation of international lawyers from the 1920s and 1930s. These scholars were urged by a feeling against the rise of totalitarianism "and tried to protect the individual from it with the help of international law" (Peters, 2016, p. 20). Even if they were not successful, Peters insists that they created "a breeding ground for the later general recognition and codification of international human rights" (Peters, 2016, p. 20). Thus, in the interwar period emerged this thesis on "international individualism" (Peters, 2016):

> International individualism was the thesis advocated by international legal scholars, especially during the interwar period. This was not only a reaction to the horrors of the First World War; the thesis was also strongly supported by democratic thought and fear of the emergence of mass society. (Peters, 2016, p. 20)

In 1998, three international changes arose from the individualization of international law: the adoption of the Rome Statute of the International Criminal Court; the Declaration on human rights defenders; and the direct complaints of individuals to the European Court of Human Rights, when Protocol No. 11 entries into force, this being a coincidence considered from a theoretical perspective, not merely the historical.

If individuals have the freedom to strive for human rights, and they must have both international and constitutional protection, they must also be responsible for their acts too. Hence, the right to promote and protect human rights is not a *carte blanche* against the state and other individuals. Consequently, what are the limits to the right to promote and protect human rights?

The human condition is the axiological basis of the Declaration on human rights defenders. Law is a manifestation of power, but law is not only an issue of nations, states or peoples. It is a matter pertaining to individuals and their collective action as performed by groups of individuals. The subject is not an abstract collective political entity. Nor is it a private one: individuals are not considered in terms of liberal political revendications. On the contrary, there is not a privatization of law, but an international trend of constitutionalization that considers individuals to be public actors.

This is the radical change of paradigm carried out by the DHRD. For centuries, decades, and years, individuals were not allowed to operate under the law. They were obliged to endure unfair rules, violations of rights and unequal justice. But throughout history, the struggles suffered by individuals have built fundamental rights, human rights, and guarantees at both the constitutional and international levels. Individuals were absent from the legal paradigm because only the result of their struggle—for rights—was recognized, but not their right to strive for human rights. This individual right to strive is now recognized by law as the right to promote and protect human rights in the Declaration on Human Rights Defenders (1998).

The content of the right to promote and protect human rights: exercising instrumental human rights

After 13 years of work, on 9 December 1998 the General Assembly of the United Nations adopted the Declaration on human rights defenders. Article 1 is the cornerstone of the declaration framework. It is worthwhile to point out several aspects of this article. Article 1 of the Declaration on human rights defenders states that: "Everyone has the right, individually and in association with others, to promote and to strive for the protection and realization of human rights and fundamental freedoms at the national and international levels" (A/RES/53/144, 8 March 1999).

First, the right's content aims "to promote and to strive for the protection and realization of human rights". Second, if the content of the right is an activity, the right can be defined by this activity. Therefore, the activity defines the legal subject, not vice versa. Third, this right can be exercised individually or collectively— in association with others. This aspect reminds us that groups and associations of individuals are holders of the right to promote and protect human rights too, as a result of the collective exercise of this right. Fourth, this right is not connected to territory or a citizenship requirement. However, its exercise is permitted in multiple levels, which are "the national and international levels" (Lang and Wiener, 2017, p. 2). Fifth, the legitimate action to promote and to strive for the protection and realization of human rights and fundamental freedoms is restricted to "recognized" human rights, and new or emerging human rights are included under the umbrella of instrumental rights, recognized specifically in article 7 DHRD: "Everyone has the right, individually and in association with others, to develop and discuss new human rights ideas and principles and to advocate their acceptance" (A/RES/53/144, 8 March 1999).

The main focus of the 1998 Declaration on human rights defenders is on action, rather than on an abstract subject. It is the action that builds the subject, and due to the action of this subject, the promotion and protection of human rights is carried out. The recognition of human activity as a matter of law is connected with the conception of human rights as historical, pointed out by Arendt (1951) and Bobbio (1991). It is also related to the Habermas' perspective on the performative sense inherent to the auto constitution of community (Habermas, 1987, pp. 411–413). Community is built by legal societies and the constitution is historical. Consequently, individual activity can be performative and constitutive: "en tant que projet d'une société juste, une Constitution articule l'horizon d'attente d'un avenir chaque fois anticipé au present". (Habermas, 1987, pp. 411–413)

As Arendt theorized, the right to promote and protect human rights leads to active citizenship, which is expressed by the exercise of rights, not by the subjecthood of the rights' holders, universally. The human condition is hence the new paradigm of subjecthood. But how can this change be articulated at the international and constitutional levels?

The Declaration on human rights defenders constitutes a legal recognition that builds a new human rights' framework. This framework is only enunciated by a declaration; it does not have the binding force of a treaty. However, even an international declaration has an international value (Gómez Sánchez, 2006, p. 284). It is a consensual manifestation with legal effects, not merely a linguistic or theoretical construction. The Declaration on human rights defenders is constitutive of this new legal paradigm among individuals, law, and power. These three elements are different from the nation-state law: they are contemporary forces in a global world. The tension with power does not come exclusively from state actors, but also from non- state actors. The state is still the main one responsible for violating human rights. However, in contemporary times, human rights violations do not exist due to the state's action, or lack of action. New global scenarios are overcoming the framework of nation-state, pushing it in divergent directions. For instance, transnational agents can challenge the international system of rights, and supranational actors can be better guarantors of it, in some situations. The main challenge for human rights face is respect for the individuals' will, their rights and their life. Individuals should not shoulder the weight of public troubles. It is absolutely necessary to enforce the public system at the constitutional and international levels by using new global responses that will not eliminate the necessary coexistence of different centres of power. Thus, if individuals are subjects of these new and older rights, there must be correlative obligations. Positive obligations do not lie with the holders of these rights (Gavara de Cara, 2007, pp. 277–278). In states, international organizations and institutions perform a constitutional function that is not only related to the nation-state dimension. Maybe all of this is just the beginning of a new period of human rights where counterweights must be created.

In the case of human rights defenders, this relationship is based on a new universal legal paradigm on the human condition. But due to the lack of legal attention at constitutional and international levels, the protection of human rights defenders is built on security aspects, but insufficiently protects the public legal framework of rights and guarantees. Usually, non-state actors assume the weight of human rights defenders' protections. This is particularly relevant because of their knowledge of the situation in the field—its risks, threats, and dangers. Specialized INGOs, as in the case of the European Union, are managing the EU *ad extra* protection by means of a consortium of civil and EU actors in order to protect defenders: ProtectDefenders.eu. This is the EU's mechanism to protect defenders by being more helpful and realistic. However, it does not replace the need to think about the role of human rights defenders in light of the law, in order to ensure not only their physical protection and safety, but also their contribution, action, and relevance for protecting and promoting human rights. To do so, it is necessary to enforce the right to promote and protect human rights. It is necessary to give a legal answer at the constitutional and international levels to protect defenders' rights. Without a public enforcement of the defenders' framework, there will always be violations of their rights. However, it is obsolete to think only in terms of the states' responsibility without any other international involvement. This perspective comes from the broken paradigm of the Second World War, and is based on the paradox that states can be both guarantors and violators of human rights.

At present, individuals become agents and stakeholders in human rights, but they are not substitutes for the state, they are complementary. Considering them as actors of human rights does not mean to diminish the state's responsibility. It recognizes that emerging needs in the global world require global and individual responses without prejudice toward the axiological tension between the individual and power. This is why there is still a lack of effectiveness in defenders' rights. However, the focus is often placed more on the subject—human rights defenders—rather than action—promoting and protecting human rights. Of course, it is necessary to guarantee the security and the protection of human rights defenders. But it is worthwhile to recall that the real need is the legal recognition of human rights defenders' legitimate actions. If the actions of defenders are understood, then it is also possible to gain a better understanding of why they are threatened and endangered. They are the silent voice, the individual challenge to state power. If the action to promote and protect human rights is recognized by states and the international community as a binding right, there is a reciprocal duty to respect it. The effect of HRD action would then be easily achieved, they would not be alone.

Threats from state and non-state actors attempt to silence defenders. The real threat against human rights defenders is the lack of acceptance of human rights and the struggle to obtain them. The struggle for human rights is a struggle against power. Power is held by states and non-state actors, such as transnational companies, armed groups, etc., but power arises from international and supranational organizations and transnational civil society too, as formed by individuals and groups. This is a new global framework formed after the breakdown of the state-based law, due to the effects of globalization. However, there are still not enough answers to these new challenges. Therefore, recognition of the legitimate action of individuals, groups or even national independent institutions is a necessary step in order to fill these gaps with a new paradigm based on the human condition rather than national sovereignty. International and supranational organizations should empower individuals, but it is no substitute for public action. It means public action cannot depend purely on the leaders of sovereign states, as the human condition cannot depend on national sovereignty. Therefore it is important to avoid some trends on authoritarian presidentialism and struggle to reinforce parliamentarianism.

Human rights defenders are not only professionals—individuals or groups—focused on protecting and promoting human rights. In other words, a human rights activist working for an NGO is a human rights defender, but a doctor, nurse, teacher, scientist, mathematician, musician, artist, fireman, entrepreneur, trade union member, lawyer, philosopher, farmer, worker, indigenous leader, ecologist, gender and social worker, among numerous others, may also be HRDs. This is because the subject of human rights defenders is defined by their activities and the holder of the right is universal: the human being.

Bennet et al. (2016) state that there is neither any definition of human rights defenders present in the 1998 declaration, and nor a "standardized procedure" for defining them (Bennet, et al., 2016, p. 403). Hence, someone promoting, protecting and striving for human rights is performing an activity and can become a human rights defender. However, this is not automatic. In order to achieve this status, it is necessary to have a legitimate framework of action. This framework is based on the Declaration on human rights defenders. Therefore, as for the Special Rapporteur on human rights defenders, the right to promote and protect human rights is based on instrumental rights necessary for the defence of human rights:

> The Declaration reaffirms rights that are instrumental to the defence of human rights, including, inter alia, freedom of association, freedom of peaceful assembly, freedom of opinion and expression, and the right to gain access to information, to provide legal aid and to develop and discuss new ideas in the area of human rights. (A/66/203, 2011, para.2)

According to commentary by the Special Rapporteur on the situation of human rights defenders, under the basis of the former thematic mechanisms, the Special Representative of the Secretary General on the situation of human rights defenders—Hina Jilani (2000–2008)—and the first Special Rapporteur on the situation of human rights defenders—Margaret Sekaggya (2008–2014)— the main rights of the declaration are:

- The right to be protected
- The right to freedom of assembly
- The right to freedom of association
- The right to access and communicate with international bodies
- The right to freedom of opinion and expression
- The right to protest
- The right to develop and discuss new human rights ideas
- The right to an effective remedy
- The right to access funding. (SR HRD, 2011)

In 2018, the Special Rapporteur on human rights defenders keep these nine key rights articulated in the Declaration on human rights defenders, calling attention "to three of these rights in the context of the current challenges facing human rights defenders: the right to be protected; the right to develop and discuss new human rights ideas; and the right to access funding" (A/73/215, 2018, para.19). In 2020, with her first report, the new Special Rapporteur on human Rights Defenders—Mary Lawson—identified several priorities for her mandate, as recognizing the difficulties increased for defenders due to the pandemics of Covid-19.

These were the priorities for the future activities and work of the Special Rapporteur on human rights defenders:

a   Trends and challenges in relation to defenders, including in the context of the pandemic, with analysis to be carried out regularly;
b   Defenders most exposed to violent attacks and violations, with attention
c   paid to the most marginalized and vulnerable, (…).
d   Defenders at high risk of being killed;
e   Defenders sentenced to, and serving, long terms in prison;
f   Physical and mental integrity of defenders, including those whose wellbeing is threatened or damaged by online attacks;
g   Role of businesses and financial institutions in both harming and protecting the work of defenders;

h Reprisals against defenders who have cooperated with the mandate holder and/or other human rights mechanisms and offices of the United Nations and other regional and intergovernmental organizations;
i Strengthening of follow-up to individual cases brought to her attention, inparticular by enhancing collaboration with stakeholders, (…).
j How the universal periodic review mechanism is being used, and how it can be better used, to improve the situation of defenders;
k Strengthening of cooperation with other mandate holders, regional mechanisms and other stakeholders. (A/75/165, 2020, para. 7).

Bennet et al. (2015) analyzed the security and protection of human rights defenders while considering the multilevel regime of protection mechanisms that have emerged. All this led to a multilevel system for defenders' rights: "Over time, a multilevel, multi-actor international protection regime for the rights of human rights defenders has emerged, derived from the international human rights regime" (Bennet et al., 2015, p. 884). In the same sense, when I analyzed the right to the freedom of expression and the right to promote and protect human rights, in my previous book (2015), and in my PhD thesis (2016), I also concluded that there is a multilevel system for instrumental rights. However, as for the main right to promote and to protect human rights, and striving for them, I now think it is necessary to reinforce the constitutional dimension of this right, both in domestic and international law.

To arrive at this conclusion, I decided to develop a multilevel method analyzing several instrumental rights of defenders in order to research about the dimensions of the right to promote and protect human rights. In my view, this multilevel system of rights is still incomplete. The defender's rights' guarantees are built by focusing more on the physical protection of the legal subject—human rights defenders—than on defenders' rights and reinforcing the human rights public framework. It is therefore necessary to adopt an approach that reaffirms the right to promote and protect human rights, but not only considering the subject of these rights: human rights defenders. Thus, there could be confusion between the right to be protected, as just an instrumental right, established in the Declaration on human rights defenders among other rights. The primary right to promote and protect human rights is composed of several instrumental rights, not only a right of protection. Thus, it is important to build a multilevel system reinforcing other instrumental rights too.

The right to promote and protect human rights: multilevel guarantees

The risks and threats to human rights defenders are only the tip of the iceberg in an examination of the erosion of the traditional legal guarantees of states. Consequently, a global approach is necessary in order to protect the legal subject—human rights defenders—but more specifically to protect the main right: the right to promote and protect human rights. Protecting the civil population and vulnerable groups of people is not something new in international or constitutional law, but it is particularly characteristic of international humanitarian law (IHL). For instance, in the case of IHL the obligations are placed not on states, but on combatants; thus, non-state actors, such as individuals. Due to the nature of armed conflicts, individuals are both victims while remaining responsible for the very worst crimes. Hence, human rights defenders' protection can come, mainly, from states, but it is important to remember the role of non-state actors: companies, armed groups, lobbies, and other actors that are outside the control of the state-based framework.

Individuals do not have a duty to protect other individuals, nor must they enforce human rights or the positive obligations of fundamentals rights, according to Gavara de Cara (2007). But this does not eliminate individuals' responsibility to respect the rights of other individuals and the existence of some horizontal effect.

The most interesting contribution of the Declaration on human rights defenders is not the right for protection, but the right to promote and *strive* for human rights. In order to protect and promote human rights, it is necessary to grant instrumental rights such as the freedoms of opinion and expression. This can only be accomplished through a change in paradigm of international and constitutional law, thus moving toward a real multilevel system of human rights and HRDs rights, based not only on physical protection. This change of paradigm begins with a change in the paradigm of legal subjecthood. However, if human rights defenders' rights are only set up, but the content of the rights is not reinforced, there would always be a lack of protection leading to a feeble subject that will ultimately need physical protection.

All this indicates an erosion of the right to promote and protect human rights. For this and other reasons explained thus far, I am focusing on an analysis of the multilevel protection of some instrumental rights from the Declaration on human rights defenders. By means of this analysis, I try to conclude if the right to promote and protect human rights could be considered a new human right, present not only in the United Nations' system, but in different regional and supranational human rights' systems as well.

I ultimately reached the conclusion that the right to promote and protect human rights is a new right, not merely an emerging right although it requires stronger legal recognition and guarantees. After the process of codification in the UN Declaration on human rights defenders (1998), the right to promote and protect human rights has extended institutional and judiciary guarantees, particularly with Rapporteurships at local, national, regional, supranational, and international levels. But its presence has increased in the case law of international courts. Hence, the constitutional dimension of this right is more urgent with regard to constitutional and international laws.

According to Gómez Sánchez, the United Nations' Declaration on Human Rights Defenders, enforced in 1998, has legal and social effects, even though it is not a binding instrument (Gómez Sánchez, 2006, p. 284). Even when treaties, as law, cannot be applied, the declaration has legal value as a legal agreement, even if it is not binding. Thus, according to Gómez Sánchez, it is important to distinguish between the "legal value" of the declaration and its "internal legal effectiveness"

(Gómez Sánchez, 2006, p. 284). Furthermore, "in the United Nations practice a declaration is a formal and solemn instrument suitable for rare occasions when principles of great and lasting importance are being enunciated, such as the Declaration of Human Rights" (Hodgson, 2003, p. 87). In this context, the DHRD is more than a legitimate claim, but it is not yet a binding international instrument. The reciprocal system of guarantees established remains feeble, as evidenced by continuous threats to human rights defenders.

Therefore, it is necessary to rethink the international human rights system and fundamental rights at the constitutional level in order to integrate the right to promote and protect human rights at the international and constitutional levels. Only with the requirement of a real multilevel perspective from cities, states, and regions, up to supranational and international levels, can the global constitutional function of the right to promote and protect human rights be achieved. It is time to think globally, providing global answers to global troubles. Consequently, this is not just a question that may be resolved by adopting a treaty or a local plan to protect human rights defenders. It concerns a deeper crisis in the human rights system that requires better supranational and international guarantees in connection with constitutional systems. These new guarantees should take into account new threats to human rights from both state and non-state actors. According to this new paradigm, state sovereignty must give way to the human condition as the leading principle in international and constitutional law, and not vice versa. Human dignity applies to not just the protection of HRDs physical integrity. It recognizes the individual as an active subject of rights, going further than human dignity, creating a paradigm of the human condition necessary for the twenty-first century.

Human dignity remains the driving force behind the system of human rights and it is necessary as a complementary axiological principle. But the Second World War human rights paradigm was broken after globalization. Now it is slightly different. The recognition of the constitutional function of international and constitutional law is not just based in the dignity paradigm. It is now time for the human condition paradigm. In this sense, Peters theorizes that it is important to be reminded of the humanism behind international law, to go further than a mere postmodern approach (Peters, 2019). In my view, it is necessary to achieve this constitutional perspective for human rights defenders, based on the human condition, both at the international and constitutional levels. HRDs are the tip of the iceberg in the crisis of the public system. They recall the weakness of public guarantees eroded by globalization and nationalist interests that fail to respond to global challenges.

Hence, the newly born right to promote and protect human rights must be analyzed by examining instrumental HRD rights. For several reasons, it is not possible to draw conclusions based only on the right to promote and protect, in abstract. The legal recognition in the Declaration on human rights defenders possesses a complementary irradiation effect (Bennet et al. 2015, 2016) at the regional, supranational, and national levels, but not only in terms of institutional guarantees. After analyzing multilevel instrumental rights, it will be possible to reach some well-founded conclusions. Nonetheless, it is worthwhile to point out that exhaustive research is impossible. At present, the changing nature of rights, case law, and policies at the international, regional, and supranational levels is an impediment to exhaustive research. However, multilevel analysis is a legal research method that might offer some conclusions from a global constitutionalism perspective on dimensions of the right to promote and protect human rights through instrumental rights. The second reason underlying the necessity for adopting a multilevel method of analysis is the interconnection between international law and constitutional law. In the case of human rights defenders, convergence can be found in this new area. As previously stated, a change of paradigm in international law has consequences for constitutional law. Constitutionalism cannot ignore human rights defenders any longer. Frequently, there are violations of HRD's rights because national systems do not recognize them and their rights. The Special Rapporteur on the situation of human rights defenders expressed her concern on the use of national legislation to regulate the activities of human rights defenders:

> the Special Rapporteur focuses on the use of legislation to regulate the activities of human rights defenders, in the light of considerable concern about legislation being adopted and/or enforced in ways that restrict the activities of human rights defenders in various countries, across continents and in diverse political and social contexts. (A/67/292, 2012, para. 2)

Nevertheless, the DHRD

> contains provisions protecting defenders against arbitrary use of legislation to restrict their activities. Notably, article 2 holds that each state is to adopt such legislative, administrative and other steps as may be necessary to ensure that the rights and freedoms referred to in the declaration are effectively guaranteed. (A/67/292, para. 8)

Principles of legality, necessity and proportionality, non-discrimination, and the limited nature of the derogation clauses must be respected and guaranteed. Hence, international guarantees and constitutional clauses are related. The Special Rapporteur on human rights defenders specifically appeals to constitutional safeguards (A/67/292, 2012, para. 77). Constitutional safeguards provide human rights defenders with instrumental rights such as the rights to the freedom of assembly, freedom of association, freedom of opinion and expression, freedom from arbitrary arrest, detention, torture, degrading treatment, and the right to an effective remedy and a fair trial. Consequently, constitutional safeguards are a guarantee for human rights defenders too. Even more, constitutional safeguards are guarantees against repressive legislation. The threats to HRDs' activities emerge when fake constitutional principles are used to enable oppressive laws in dictatorial contexts. This is why challenging oppressive and unconstitutional laws in constitutional courts is a strong guarantee for human rights defenders:

The Special Rapporteur notes that, in some cases, defenders have successfully challenged the constitutionality of oppressive laws, notably in national constitutional courts, often rooted in the argument that the applicable law infringed basic human rights guaranteed in a country's constitution. Such avenues of recourse should be easily accessible to individuals and associations seeking to defend human rights. These procedures being an integral part of the rule of law, States should do their utmost to make them easily accessible to ordinary citizens and their legal representatives. (A/67/292, 2012, para. 78)

Therefore, bearing in mind the multilevel nature of the guarantees of HRDs rights—local, legislative, constitutional, regional, supranational, and international—a feasible approach to examining the right to promote and protect human rights may be developed. As a result, by means of accepting and reinforcing these new multilevel paradigms on international and constitutional law, HRDs rights may be guaranteed, and the right to promote and protect human rights may be effective. However, it is still too early to assert that the right to promote and protect human rights is fully recognized and protected within the global constitutional system because many guarantees are aimed at instrumental rights, but do not protect and guarantee the main right of the declaration. Moreover, the protective mechanisms and guarantees are asymmetric among states, depending on legislation, constitutions and the international ratification of treaties and their guarantees. Nevertheless, this rising multilevel system for the protection of human rights defenders is a first step to achieve enhanced protection, not only of the physical security of human rights defenders, but of their rights and human rights in general, with a wider global constitutional perspective.

Human rights defenders: instrumental rights and asymmetric enforcement

The legal recognition of the right to promote and protect human rights is a challenge for the coming years. It represents a conflict between state sovereignty and the human condition. Providing legal protection for the promotion and protection of human rights held by non-state actors is a new paradigm of law that is necessary in a global world. International and constitutional human rights law requires individuals, groups and INHR to be able to do their work. Without individual claims regional courts cannot operate; reports and information from NGOs are key requirements for fact-finding; and constitutional courts make no sense without individual claims.

Even so, we are talking about something that is more far-ranging, *stricto sensu*. Any human activity can contribute to the protection and promotion of human rights according to the Declaration on human rights defenders. This is why the individuals' will and methods become crucial for this right and the paradigm of constitutional and international law. Hence, being a necessary resource in a global world with evolving and changing risks for human rights. States cannot face these new challenges to human rights alone. Marrani's (2012) analysis of a second modernity, following Beck (1992), recognizes current trends toward the dissolution of nations into a cosmopolitan society. The essence of this change is the change of the law paradigm based on the state's monopoly to create rules: "Concepts such as sovereignty and nation-state are fading" (Marrani, 2012, pp. 34–35). The second modernity, according to this author, is "a time of pluralism, generally speaking, which has permeated the legal field through normative pluralism" (Marrani, 2012, pp. 34–35). In this new scenario, the state's monopoly to create rules is under attack: "These attacks come from official and non-official rules, created both within and outside the State" (Marrani, 2012, p. 35). New challenges and multiple difficulties arise from these changes, brought about by globalization effects on the legal field. First, according to Marrani, the distinction between legal and non-legal phenomena is vanishing. Second, the distinctions between legal orders, systems, traditions, and cultures are no longer clear. Third, systems become incomplete in the global world: "They are characterized by internal dynamics and tensions, and lack fixed borders" (Marrani, 2012). Interconnection between systems and culture is difficult: "What seems to be certain, however, is that legal pluralism is associated to this era of the second modernity" (Marrani, 2012, p. 35).

There are different scenarios because repeatedly, even when recognizing human rights and HRD rights, states are incapable of guaranteeing them. In this case another paradox arises: sometimes human rights defenders are forced to protect HRD rights. This is why national institutions on human rights are also considered human rights defenders, constituting the explicit acknowledgement that there are violations of human rights coming from both states and non-state actors.

Pérez Luño uses the category "change of paradigm" when analyzing different generations of rights (Pérez Luño, 1996, p. 15). I consider this categorization helpful for two reasons: first, the change of legal subject introduced by the DHRD implies a change of legal paradigm. Second, this legal openness reflects the idea that the catalogue of freedoms is never closed and finished. Pérez Luño (1996) thinks that an open society must always be sensitive and ready for new needs because they can be the foundation of new rights (Pérez Luño, 1996, p. 15). In the author's view, as long as these rights are not recognized in the national and international legal order, they still act as protesting, pre-normative and axiological categories (Pérez Luño, 1996, p. 15). However, human rights are a "must be". Of course, according to the author, there is a utopian dimension providing legitimacy, but also a historical dimension that is reinforced by historical forms of freedoms (Pérez Luño, 1996, p. 15).

The main right to promote and protect human rights uses different instrumental rights. These instrumental rights have asymmetric enforcement, recognition and guarantees at the local, national, regional, supranational, and international levels. The annual reports of the Special Rapporteur on human rights defenders serves as an expert legal opinion on the main trends and issues concerning defenders from an international point of view. However, it is also useful to examine the reports from regional systems for the protection of human rights defenders, such as the African Union system or the Inter-American system. Both human rights systems chose to put into practice a Rapporteurship for human rights defenders. These procedures are complementary to the jurisdictional or quasi-jurisdictional guarantees of instrumental rights provided by the case law of the Inter-American and the African system. Of course, when these bodies apply the law, they are applying their own human rights treaties and not the Declaration on human rights defenders. However, by means of the human rights treaties' protection, the instrumental HRD rights are protected too. In the European regional human rights system, the Commissioner for Human Rights protects human rights defenders institutionally, while the European Court of Human Rights protects them as a judiciary body through its case law. Human rights defenders are key actors, and are essential for achieving the Council of Europe's goals:

The work of human rights defenders is essential for the advancement of human rights, democracy and the rule of law. Human rights defenders play a central role in making state policies human rights compliant and authorities accountable. Human rights defenders are also instrumental in defending victims of human rights violations and ensuring their access to redress and remedy. Human rights defenders are key partners of the Council of Europe Commissioner for Human Rights. (Council of Europe Commissioner for Human Rights, 2022)

The European Union set the policy on human rights defenders. Axiologically, the European Union "is founded on the values of respect for human dignity, freedom, democracy, equality, the rule of law and respect for human rights, including the rights of persons belonging to minorities", according to the Treaty on European Union (TEU), (Consolidated version of the Treaty on European Union, 7 June 2016, art. 2). These values should be upheld and promoted in the European Union's relations with the world at large (TEU, art. 3.5). This policy must contribute to the protection of human rights and to the strict observance and development of international law, including respect for the principles of the United Nations Charter (art. 21.1. TEU). In the international arena, the European Union action must also be guided by the same principles that have inspired its own creation, development, and enlargement. Human rights are part of those principles:

The Union's action on the international scene shall be guided by the principles which have inspired its own creation, development, and enlargement, and which it seeks to advance in the wider world: democracy, the rule of law, the universality and indivisibility of human rights and fundamental freedoms, respect for human dignity, the principles of equality and solidarity, and respect for the principles of the United Nations Charter and international law. (art. 21.1 TEU)

Article 21 TEU opens the door to cooperation between the supranational and international levels, including "multilateral solutions to common problems, in particular in the framework of United Nations". According to these guiding principles at the international level, the European Union shall define and pursue common policies and actions to consolidate human rights and the principles of international law (art. 21. 2. b TEU). For these reasons the European Union's action concerning human rights defenders is focused more on external aspects. However, the European Union is bound by the Charter of Fundamental Rights. Since the entry into the Treaty of Lisbon (article 6), the European Charter of Fundamental Rights is a binding law in the EU, "which shall have the same legal value as the Treaties". By means of the application of the Charter of Fundamental

Rights, the case law of the European Court of Justice, the constitutional traditions common to the European members, and the ECHR as general principles of EU law, there are instrumental rights for human rights defenders, including a higher protection, such as the right to the freedom of assembly, or freedom of expression.

Within the wider framework for the protection of fundamental rights, the EU applies its own rules *ad intra* based on the Charter of Fundamental Rights. In the EU context, the rights established in the DHRD are implemented through the application of the Charter of Fundamental Rights. But the case law of the ECtHR is also converging. Protection in the EU has supranational aspects that are characteristic of the system. This may be observed, for instance, in the link between the right to free movement and the protection of fundamental rights. A crucial aspect in the European Union is the creation of an area of freedom, security, and justice. This area is intrinsically linked to the free movement of persons and the elimination of internal borders, as Piçarra noted (Piçarra, 2013). Only exceptional reasons admit the suspension of these rights. Freedom of movement is an aspect with federal implications (Piçarra, 2013, p. 141) and implies developing the participation in a supranational framework of community and the European citizenship (Piçarra, 2013, p. 141). Freedom of movement is typical of the EU system and is linked, among other things, to the multilevel protection of fundamental rights. The need to reinforce some social and economic rights, such as the right to health can be a challenge to the EU. But if there is a stronger harmonization among countries, it would be possible to face and cope with the challenge of exceptional situations, like pandemics. National solutions, in the short-term, can produce results, but supranational European responses are long-term solutions necessary to all countries. Interdependence between economic, social and cultural rights, and civil, political rights is behind the defence of human rights, as established at the Vienna Conference in 1993. The UN included this interdependence as a criterion to become human rights defenders. Behind this division remains this dark past of the two blocs, which hopefully disappeared after the fall of the Berlin Wall.

Freedom of movement has facilitated the creation of European social movements. The case law of the ECJ has examined cases in which the right to protest entered into conflict with the right to free movement. In the well-known *Schmidberger* case (ECJ 12 June 2003), the ECJ recognized that the protection of fundamental rights, such as the right to assembly, may constitute a legitimate interest in EU law, admitting the restriction of the right to free movement of goods.

References

Arendt, H. (1951). *The Origins of Totalitarianism*. New York: Brace, Harcourt.
Bennet, K., Ingleton, D., Nah, M. A., and Savage, J. (2016). *Critical Perspectives on the Security and Protection of Human Rights Defenders*. Oxon & New York: Routledge.
Bennett, K., Ingleton, D., Nah, A. M., and Savage, J. (2015). "Critical perspectives on the security and protection of human rights defenders". *International Journal of Human Rights*, 19(7), 883–895. https://doi.org/10.1080/13642987.2015.1075301.
Bobbio, N. (1991). *El tiempo de los derechos*. Madrid: Sistema.

Gavara de Cara, J. C. (2007). "La vinculación positiva de los poderes públicos a los derechos fundamentales". *Teoría y Realidad Constitucional*, 20, 277–320.

Carrillo Salcedo, J. A. (1999). *Dignidad frente a barbarie. La Declaración Universal de Derechos Humanos cincuenta años después*. Madrid: Trotta.

Gomez Sanchez, Y. and Gros Espiell, H. (2006). *La Declaración Universal sobre Bioética y Derechos Humanos de la UNESCO*. Granada: Comares.

Habermas, J. (1987). *Théorie de l'agir constitutionnel*. Paris: Fayard.

Hodgson, D. (2003). *Individual duty within a human rights discourse*. Surrey: Ashgate.

Kumm, M. (2013). "The cosmopolitan turn in constitutionalism: An integrated conception of public law". *Indiana Journal of Global Legal Studies*, 20(4).

Kumm, M. (2018). "Global constitutionalism and the rule of law". In *Handbook on Global Constitutionalism*. Cheltenham: Edward Elgar.

Lang, A. F. and Wiener, A. (2017). *Handbook on Global Constitutionalism*. Cheltenham: Edward Elgar Publishing.

Marrani, D. (2012). "'Mission Impossible': Interconnecting the common law legal culture and civil law legal systems in the European integration". In T. Freixes, J. C. Remotti, D. Marrani, J. Bombin, and L. Vanin-Verna (Eds), *La gouvernance multi-level. Penser l'enchevêtrement* (pp. 33–55). Bruxelles: E.M.E.

Pérez Luño, A. E. (1996). "Derechos humanos y constitucionalismo en la actualidad ¿continuidad o cambio de paradigma?" In Pérez Luño (Ed.), *Derechos Humanos y Constitucionalismo ante el tercer milenio*. Madrid: Marcial Pons.

Peters, A. (2015). *Global Constitutionalism Strands of Global Constitutionalism*. https://doi.org/10.1002/9781118474396.wbept0421.

Peters, A. (2016). *Beyond Human Rights: The Legal Status of the Individual in International Law*. Cambridge: Cambridge University Press.

Peters, A. (2019). *Humanisme, constitutionnalisme, universalisme. Etude de droit international et comparé*. Paris: Pedone

Piçarra, N. (2013). "Direito à liberdade e à segurança". In A. Silveira and M. Canotilho (Eds), *Carta dos Direitos Fundamentales da Uniao Europeia Comentada*. Coimbra: Almedina.

Rovira Viñas, A. (2013). "Gobernanza y Derechos Humanos". In A. Rovira Viñas (Ed.), *Gobernanza Democrática*. Madrid: Marcial Pons.

Saura Freixes, N. (2016). *Human Rights Defenders. El derecho a promover y proteger los derechos humanos*. Madrid: UNED.

Saura-Freixes, N. (2015). *Libertad de expresión y derecho a promover y proteger los derechos humanos*. Barcelona: J.M. Bosch Editor.

Suami, T., Peters, A., Kumm, M., and Vanoverbeke. (2018). *Global Constitutionalism from European and East Asian Perspectives*. Cambridge: Cambridge University Press.

Torres del Moral, A. (2015). *Estado de Derecho y Democracia de Partidos*. Madrid: Universitas

Documents

Treaties

American Convention on Human Rights (adopted 22 November, 1969, entered into force 18 July 1978) 1144 U.N.T.S.123; O.A.S.T.S. No. 36 ("Pact of San Jose, Costa Rica", ACHR)

Charter of the United Nations (adopted 24 October 1945) 1 UNTS XVI

Convention for the Protection of Human Rights and Fundamental Freedoms, as amended, (adopted 4 November 1950, *entered into force 3 September 1953) ETS No.* 005 (ECHR)
Consolidated Version of the Treaty on European Union [2012] OJ C 326/13
International Covenant on Civil and Political Rights (adopted 16 December 1966, entered into force 23 March 1976) 999 UNTS 171 (ICCPR)
International Covenant on Economic, Social and Cultural Rights (adopted 16 December 1966, entered into force 3 January 1976) 993 UNTS 3 (ICESCR)
Protocol no.11 to the Convention for the Protection of Human Rights and Fundamental Freedoms Restructuring the Control Machinery Established Thereby (adopted 11 May 1994, entered into force 1 November 1998) ETS No.155
Rome Statute of the International Criminal Court (adopted 17 July 1998, entered into force 1 July 2002) 2187 UNTS 3

UN

Universal Declaration of Human Rights UNGA Res. 217A (III) (10 December 1948)
Declaration on the Right and Responsibility of Individuals, Groups and Organs of Society to Promote and Protect UniversallyRecognized HumanRights and Fundamental Freedoms UNGA A/RES/53/144 (8 March 1999)
UNGA "Human rights defenders. *Note by the Secretary-General.* Report of the Special Rapporteur on the situation of human rights defenders" (28 July 2011) *UN Doc A/66/203.* Retrieved 4 June, 2022, from: https://digitallibrary.un.org/record/709670?ln=es
UNGA "*Situation of human rights defenders. Note by the Secretary-General. Report of the Special Rapporteur on the situation of human rights defenders*" (23 July 2008) UN Doc A/73/215. Retrieved 29 May, 2022, from: https://digitallibrary.un.org/record/1639412?ln=es
UNGA "*Situation of human rights defenders. Note by the Secretary General. Report of the Special Rapporteur on the situation of human rights defenders*" (10 August 2012) UN Doc A/67/292. Retrieved June 6, 2022, from: https://documents-dds-ny.un.org/doc/UNDOC/GEN/N12/459/42/PDF/N1245942.pdf?OpenElement
UNGA "*Situation of human rights defenders. Note by the Secretary General. Report of the Special Rapporteur on the situation of human rights defenders*" (16 July 2020) UN Doc A/75/165. Retrieved June 6, 2022, from: https://documents-dds-ny.un.org/doc/UNDOC/GEN/N20/185/66/PDF/N2018566.pdf?OpenElement
World Conference on Human Rights in Vienna. Vienna Declaration and Programme of Action (25 June 1993). *Retrieved 3 June*, from: www.ohchr.org/sites/default/files/vienna.pdf

ICJ

Reparation for Injuries Suffered in the Service of the United Nations (Advisory Opinion) [1949]. ICJ Rep 1949, p. 174. Retrieved 29 May, 2022, from: www.icj-cij.org/en/case/4

COE

COE Commissioner for Human Rights (2022). "Human Rights Defenders". Retrieved May 30, 2022, from: www.coe.int/en/web/commissioner/human-rights-defenders#:~:text=The%20work%20of%20human%20rights,rights%20compliant%20and%20authorities%20accountable

EU

Charter of Fundamental Rights of the European Union [2012] OJ C 326

Case C-112/00 *Eugen Schmidberger, Internationale Transporte und Planzüge v Republik Österreich. Reference for a preliminary ruling: Oberlandesgericht Innsbruck - Austria.* [2003] EU:C:2003:333

Spain

The Spanish Constitution. BOE 29 December 1978, *no* 311, p. 29313–29424 www.boe.es/legislacion/documentos/ConstitucionINGLES.pdf

Germany

Basic Law for the Federal Republic of Germany, 23 May 1949. Last amended on 29 September 2020. Retrieved 29 May, 2022, from: www.btg-bestellservice.de/pdf/80201000.pdf

7 Instrumental rights for the promotion and protection of human rights

I have chosen to deliberately focus on the main rights of the Declaration on human rights defenders due to their larger impact on the multilevel system of protection, and for the higher degree of consolidation at different levels. Other reasons guiding my choice were their social and collective impact on politics, democracy, and power. This is why I did not focus on more procedural rights, or newer emerging rights. However, this is a decision to limit my academic investigation in order to arrive at well-founded conclusions. It does not mean that the Declaration on human rights defenders has established a hierarchical framework of rights. Rather, all rights in the DHRD are instrumental to the right to promote and protect human rights. This right is built on all the different instrumental rights.

The Declaration on human rights defenders establishes several instrumental rights along with the main right to promote and protect human rights. Before going into a deeper analysis of the rights selected for this multilevel research, a schematic analysis of the Declaration on human rights defenders' rights is necessary.

With regards to exceptional legal regimes and restrictions on the activities of defenders, the Special Rapporteur on human rights defenders highlighted the need to avoid undue restrictions in conflict or wide emergency situations, when only are allowed derogations in limited cases, if they comply with the legal criteria and conditions of necessity and proportionality:

The Special Rapporteur stressed that no circumstances can account for the suspension or sidelining of protections and rights enshrined in the Declaration on Human Rights Defenders, which is based on binding norms. In the limited cases where derogations are permissible, these must be prescribed in law, be in accordance with international law and meet both substantive and procedural conditions, including those of necessity and proportionality (A/HRC/43/51, 2019, para. 21).

The Special Rapporteur on human rights, at the 20th anniversary of the Declaration on human rights defenders, reminded us of the nine key rights to promote and protect human rights, present in the previous analytical report of 2011 to map out the rights provided in the DHRD (A/66/203):

> the right to be protected; the right to freedom of assembly; the right to freedom of association; the right to access and communicate with international bodies; the right to freedom of opinion and expression; the right to protest; the right to

DOI: 10.4324/9780429264016-7

develop and discuss new human rights ideas; the right to a remedy; and the right to access funding (A/66/203, 2011) (A/73/215, 2018).

The Special Rapporteur on human rights defenders highlighted that there are no new rights created by the DHRD, they come from human rights already enshrined in binding instruments (A/73/215, 2018, para. 18).

The right to be protected (art. 2, 9, 12 DHRD)

The right to be protected refers to the state's obligation to protect human rights defenders against any violation of their rights when promoting, protecting and striving for human rights (Saura-Freixes, 2015, p. 94). This state obligation is from the main duty and responsibility of states to protect human rights as enshrined in article 2 of the International Covenant on Civil and Political Rights (A/66/203, 2011, para. 9). This obligation of protection applies against violations of human rights from state actors, but also from non-state actors as well. Furthermore, obligations to protection are twofold, positive and negative: "On the one hand, States must refrain from violating human rights. On the other hand, States should act with due diligence to prevent, investigate and punish any violation of the rights enshrined in the Declaration" (A/66/203, 2011, para. 10). The right to be protected is crucial for human rights defenders. In 2020, the Special Rapporteur on human rights defenders sent in her report a final warning and raised alarm on the "prevalence of killings of human rights defenders in many areas of the world", being Latin America the most affected area (A/HRC/46/35, 2020): "In the period from 1 January 2019 to 30 June 2020 alone, the Special Rapporteur sent communications to 10 Member States on the killing of 100 human rights defenders, including 17 women human rights defenders" (A/HRC/46/35, 2020, para. 3).

The state holds the prime responsibility for protecting human rights and HRDs: "Each State shall adopt such legislative, administrative and other steps as may be necessary to ensure that the rights and freedoms referred to in the present Declaration are effectively guaranteed" (art. 2. DHRD). The obligation to protect, therefore, has different dimensions. First, the security of human rights defenders must be guaranteed. If a state cannot guarantee the security of human rights defenders', the international community and other states must protect them. There are different responses, the EU supports a system of urgent aid, the Inter-American system promotes national programs of security for HRD and interim measures with protective aims. Nevertheless, the protection of human rights defenders covers the exercise of human rights, including the promotion and protection of human rights (art. 9 DHRD). Consequently, protection should refer not only to physical security but also to secure the exercise of other rights.

Therefore, according to article 12, authorities shall take all necessary measures to ensure individual HRDs protection and in association with others without arbitrary arrest or detention, "against any violence, threats, retaliation, de facto or de jure adverse discrimination, pressure or any other arbitrary action as a consequence of his or her legitimate exercise of the rights referred to in the present Declaration" (A/RES/53/144, 8 March 1999). This right leads to a subsequent right, which is laid out in art. 12. 3 DHRD:

> to be protected effectively *under national law* in reacting against or opposing, through peaceful means, activities and acts, including those by omission, attributable to States that result in violations of human rights and fundamental freedoms, as well as acts of violence perpetrated by groups or individuals that affect the enjoyment of human rights and fundamental freedoms. (A/RES/53/144, 8 March 1999)

Hence, to be protected "under national law" leads to a multilevel system of protection with referrals between regional, international and supranational legal systems of protection and national law. The constitutional framework opens to a multilevel system by the synergies from constitutional to international law as well as by the legislative measures, both national and regional, in order to give local protection on human rights defenders. However, security has always been a state competence because it is inherent to sovereignty (Guillen, 2012, p. 38). In a global world security cannot be only enforced at the national level. Rather, according to Guillen, supranational challenges have been primarily addressed by intergovernmental cooperation, not by supranational means where states assume obligations in order to face international security issues (Guillen, 2012, p. 38). HRDs' security requires at least a supranational approach in a multilevel legal framework in order to effectively deal with HRDs' threats. However, the security and protection of HRDs leads to establishing human rights and HRDs' rights in a multilevel legal framework. Thus, international law, and also constitutionalism, must pay attention to the protection of human rights defenders.

In the EU area, the right to be protected is intrinsically linked in the EU to the freedom and security guaranteed by the EU Charter of Fundamental Rights (ECFR) in article 6. The creation of an area of security and freedom in the EU has also led to an area of freedom and security for HRDs, who have been able to find refuge in the EU thanks to the external action of the Union. Security as a concept, as Piçarra points out, may be defined in different ways. In the first place it may be defined as the prohibition of arbitrary imprisonment or detention; second, as a right of public order intended to protect persons and goods; and third, as a right to know what may or may not be done (Piçarra, 2013, p. 91). This last definition entails a prohibition of arbitrariness. It is arbitrary decisions by state or judicial authorities which constitute a worldwide risk for HRDs. However, the right to promote and protect human rights is not absolute and must be exercised according to the framework of the Declaration on Human Rights Defenders. The legal and ethical exigence of strict compliance with the criteria to possess the status of human rights defenders minimizes the trend of criminalization with regard to human rights defenders. This is why, *intra* EU, there is a presumption of each state's compliance with human rights, a criterion for being member of the EU, without the need for setting secondary judiciary control by the other state members. The right to freedom as a fundamental right in the EU also implies protection from arbitrary detention and custody. On the other hand, as Piçarra notes, it traditionally implies a monopoly on legitimate violence of the state for the purpose of combating crime and guaranteeing public order and security (Piçarra, 2013, p. 91). However, as a result of the process of European integration, supranational measures must be taken in response to new transnational threats. The right guaranteed by art. 6 ECFR is also protected under art. 3 of the DHRD, which recognizes the right to life, as well as under art. 9 ICCPR and art. 5 ECHR. However, an interpretation derived from art. 52.3 ECFR shows that the restrictions that may be imposed in the EU on the right to freedom and security may not exceed the limits established by the ECHR (Piçarra, 2013, p. 94). The principles of referral and interconnection between the different legal levels, aimed at achieving maximum guarantees and the protection of rights, are essential for building a multilevel legal system and guaranteeing freedom and security.

The right to freedom of assembly (art. 5.a and art. 12 DHRD)

The right to freedom of assembly is necessary to the promotion and protection of human rights. Without the right to freedom of assembly, it is not possible to carry out actions that defend human rights. Hence, this right allows for the collective exercise of the right to promote, to protect, and to strive for human rights and the articulation in the public and private sphere of individual and social claims for human rights (Saura-Freixes, 2015, p. 95). It is a twofold right within the framework of the Declaration on Human Rights Defenders:

> In articles 5 and 12 the Declaration on human rights defenders recognizes the right to freedom of assembly and the legitimacy of participation in peaceful activities to protest against violations of human rights. The right to peaceful assembly is essential for human rights defenders; without the guarantee of this right and the protection against its violation by State officials and non-State entities, the ability of defenders to fulfil their role in the protection and promotion of human rights and fundamental freedoms is severely restricted. (A/66/203, 2011, para. 21)

Rights are protected against violations coming both from state and non-state actors. This right is not absolute. To be entitled to this right it is necessary to fulfil the following criteria: peaceful activities and respect of the universality and interdependence of human rights. The universality of human rights require that the individual not use the right to freedom of assembly for destroying the rights of others or abusing rights. The abuse of rights is characterized by the abusive exercise of a right, against the nature of this right, being exercised for an illegitimate goal, under human rights law (Rovira Viñas, 1983). Under the DHRD framework several activities of protest such as challenging actions against power are possible "from meetings inside private residences to conferences in public places, demonstrations, vigils, marches, picket lines and other kinds of assemblies" (A/66/203,

2011, para. 23). However, assemblies must be non-violent. Even more so, they must be peaceful; this is the criterion set up by DHRD. In article 5, "To meet or assemble peacefully" does not imply a lower degree of protest, it just means that violence is not a legitimate method to promote and protect human rights. Gillion considers protest to be effective according to its impact (Gillion, 2013, p. 10). Thus, massive demonstrations may be more effective if they are peaceful rather than violent. Violence, however, implies not only explicit physical violence, but coaction, or the threat of force. Freedom of assembly is inherent to "social movements", which may also exist as subjects of the right to promote and protect human rights, according to the Declaration on human rights defenders. However, the assemblies can be organized by groups or by individual defenders: "The assemblies can be organized by an NGO, a trade union, an ad hoc group, a social movement, or by individual defenders seeking to raise an issue for debate or protesting against human rights violations of different kinds" (A/61/312, 2006, para. 32).

Tilly and Wood have characterized social movements, from 1750 to the present, according to these three aspects:

A sustained, organized public effort making collective claims on target authorities (let us call it a *campaign*);

Employment of combinations form among the following forms of political action: creation of special-purpose associations and coalitions, public meetings, solemn processions, vigils, rallies, demonstrations, petition drives, statements to and in public media, and pamphleteering (call the variable ensemble of performances the *social movement repertoire);* and

Participants' concerted public representatives of WUNC: worthiness, unity, numbers, and commitment on the part of themselves and/or their constituencies (call them WUNC displays). (Tilly and Wood, 2016)

Thus, freedom of assembly and social movements dovetail. Restrictions on the freedom of assembly must be balanced and limited by international standards. Nevertheless, by limiting freedom of assembly the right to promote and protect human rights may be restricted in a legitimate manner, according to the art. 2 DHRD. Limitation clauses are present in different human rights systems. But article 21 of the International Covenant on Civil and Political Rights is a point of departure for the DHRD framework (A/66/203, 2011, para. 25). Following the ICCPR, three requirements must be fulfilled to be considered a legitimate restriction on the freedom of assembly: first, restrictions must be imposed by law; second, restrictions must be necessary in a democratic society; and, finally, they must be justified on legitimate grounds of national security or public safety, public order, the protection of public health or morals, or the protection of the rights and freedoms of others (A/66/203, 2011, para. 25). Regional treaties set up similar clauses too. Using unjustified restrictions, or an excessive use of force, is not allowed under the DHRD or the main human rights treaties. There must therefore be a reciprocal commitment in national law at the constitutional, legislative and local levels to respect this framework, including the constitutional reference and function of the UN Charter and the human rights obligations set in art. 2 DHRD. In 2004, the Special Rapporteur on human rights defenders in Africa was created by the African Commission on Human's and People's Rights and "has developed with human rights defenders themselves, important guidelines on freedom of association and assembly" (A/73/215, 2018, para. 49).

The right to freedom of association (art. 5. DHRD)

The right to the freedom of association is an indispensable tool for the promotion and protection of human rights. By means of the freedom of association, non-state agents such as NGOs can perform activities for the defence of human rights without unjustified obstacles (Saura-Freixes, 2015, p. 95). But this is a right not only of registered associations and organizations, because groups are included within the scope of the DHRD. There are two criteria to be fulfilled to have this right: respect the principle of universality of human rights and the principle of non-violence (A/66/203, 2011, para. 29). This right is directly linked with participation in the public domain. However, non-violence it is not just by abstention, it is required to comply with the DHRD framework, thus it must be peaceful. Over time, human rights claims have been conducted by means of collective action. Hence, Boyle considers how "freedom of association is the freedom to pursue collective action" (Boyle, 2010 p. 272). This collective action is carried out by three different types of organizations within the scope of freedom of association: political parties, trade unions and civil organizations such as NGOs (Boyle, 2010, p. 272). Under the position of the Special Rapporteur on human rights defenders (2021), dealing with many cases of undue long-term detention for the founders and members of associations acting as human rights defenders:

> Arrest or detention as punishment for the legitimate exercise of the rights guaranteed in the International Covenant on Civil and Political Rights is arbitrary, including rights to freedom of opinion and expression (art. 19), freedom of assembly (art. 21), freedom of association (art. 22) and the right to privacy (art. 17). (A/76/143, 2021, para. 51)

Civil organizations can become human rights defenders. This new subject is necessary to the international human rights system. Fact-finding depends on NGOs since they usually participate in international standard-setting, and international and local advocacy (Ladmann and Abraham, 2004, p. 1). They are entitled to lodge individual complaints in the ECtHR, for instance. More than 2500 NGOs have a consultative status on the United Nations (Kamminga, 2005, p. 97), where NGOs can also participate in the Universal Periodic Review. Finally, under a Statute of the International Criminal Court (art. 15.2), the Prosecutor may seek additional information from intergovernmental or non-governmental organizations.

This right has both a negative and a positive dimension. On the one hand, it has the right to adhere to an association; while, on the other hand, it has the right to not adhere. Therefore freedom of association is also linked with ideological freedom, as well as with freedom of expression. The negative dimension of this right is related to the wider scope of article 19.1 ICCPR.

Freedom of association is a right recognized in international and regional human rights treaties, and by the European Charter on Fundamental Rights. In the DHRD framework, no more restrictions to the freedom of assembly are accepted other than those established by human rights treaties, but this is not an absolute right and it must be exercised with respect to the domestic law, if it is consistent with human rights (A/66/203 2011, para. 32). This is the constitutional function done by the human rights treaties, according to article 3 DHRD. In this sense, what is allowed under domestic law is particularly sensitive. However, respecting democracy and fundamental rights seem to be sensible criteria.

This right is tempered by the terms of limitative clauses in human rights treaties, which are not absolute, as in art. 11.2 ECHR. Domestic law can have stricter terms to avoid promotion or the repetition of historical backgrounds of dictatorship or totalitarianism (with strong differences between countries), as well as the limitation of illegal activities, like violence, hate or racism. Limits based on the abuse of rights are important to consider too. The associations' actions, not their ideas, are definitive in considering their status, or lack of status, as a human rights defender.

To conclude, there is a connection under the DHRD with other instrumental rights. The freedom of association is linked with the freedom of expression and the right to access and to communicate with international bodies. The Special Rapporteur on the situation of human rights defenders considers the following:

> By referring explicitly to this right under two separate provisions, the Declaration recognizes that accessing and communicating with international bodies are essential for human rights defenders to carry out their work and to alert the international community to human rights problems and bring key cases to the attention of regional and international human rights mechanisms. (A/66/203, 2011, para. 32)

The right to freedom of opinion and expression (art. 6 DHRD)

The right to freedom of opinion and expression is recognized in article 6 DHRD. It is an important tool to promote and protect human rights. This right is construed as an instrumental right enabling social participation and the expression of public opinion. The individual exercise of this right leads to active citizenship (SR HRD 28 July 2011, para. 43). Thanks mainly to the right of freedom of opinion and expression, there are claims for human rights. Action for the promotion of human rights is possible because of the freedom to opinion and expression. The Special Rapporteur on human rights defenders highlights the universal dimension of this right: "all individuals are entitled to freedom of expression and opinion". Thus, what is relevant is the exercise of this right. The DHRD includes "the right to develop and discuss new human rights ideas, allowing all people to be part of the progressive development of human rights ideas" (A/73/215, para. 21). Hence, it is a right with a clear double dimension: social and individual. These two dimensions are recognized by the Inter-American Court of Human Rights (*Baruch Ichver Bronstein v. Peru*, 2001, paras. 146–149) and by the European Court of Human Rights (*Soulas et autres v. France*, 2008) in their case law (A/66/203, para. 44). The DHRD does not apply only the US paradigm on the right to freedom of speech. In terms of interdictions based on opinions and freedom of thought, it is close to art. 19.1. International Covenant Civil Political Rights (ICCPR), but it is not absolute. Human rights defenders have this right, but they must respect two criteria. They have to accept and apply the principles of universality and non-violence according to the Special Rapporteur on the situation of human rights defenders. The right to freedom of opinion and expression must be exercised under the DHRD framework—domestic law and human rights treaties' obligations—and the interdiction of the abuse of rights.

Under the Declaration of Human Rights Defenders there are three different aspects on article 6:

> a) the right to hold opinions without interference; (b) the right of access to information; and (c) the right to impart information and ideas of all kinds. With regard to the first aspect, the right to hold opinions, no restrictions are permitted. (SR HRD, 28 July 2011, para. 44)

Restrictions on the right to freedom of opinion and expression can be accepted only under the international human rights framework:

> Art. 19.3 of the International Covenant on Human Rights sets up three conditions to be fulfilled: restrictions must be "provided by law" and must be justified as being "necessary" for one of the following purposes: (a) respect of the rights or reputations of others; and (b) the protection of national security or of public order (*ordre public*), or of public health or morals. (SR HRD, 28 July 2011, para. 44)

Due to its social dimension, freedom of opinion and expression concerns individuals' duties and responsibilities. Limitative clauses of this right are present in regional human rights' treaties. However, according to the Special Rapporteur on the freedom of opinion and expression, Frank LaRue (11 August 2010, para. 35), these limitative clauses cannot be used as grounds to restrict freedom of opinion more than necessary. It is important to remember two criteria: proportionality and public interest. Journalists, with lawyers and labour leaders are among human rights defenders in long-term undue detention (A/76/143, 2021, para. 12).

The social dimension of this right is present in the case law of the European Court of Human Rights. Oetheimer contends that political discourse is placed in the centre of ECtHR protection (Oetheimer, 2007, p. 64). The ECtHR admits fewer restrictions on political discourse for this reason (Oetheimer, 2007, p. 64). The social function of this individual right is a consistent doctrine for ECtHR case law. However, the Special Rapporteur on human rights defenders pointed out that the national legislation and framework may be inconsistent with the freedoms of opinion and expression (A/67/292, 2012). It is important to guarantee this right because "without this right, defenders would not be able to perform their monitoring and advocacy work to promote and protect human rights" (A/66/203, 2011, para. 43). In conflict and post-conflict areas "Attacks and human rights violations perpetrated against journalists, limit access to independent and reliable information" (A/HRC/43/51, 2019, para.33). Nevertheless, journalists and human rights defenders that speak out publicly become targets for attacks and threats (A/HRC/46/35, 2020). They are one of the most vulnerable collective groups of human rights defenders (A/HRC/19/55, 21 December 2011).

Female human rights defenders often challenge the division between public and private space. In some contexts, claiming human rights in the public sphere can be grounds for the persecution and stigmatization of female human rights defenders. It is therefore important that the national and constitutional framework are respectful of human rights and the freedoms of opinion and expression. Freedom of expression, as Tenorio Sánchez explains, has been given a preferential status in contemporary societies, but it is not an absolute right (Tenorio Sánchez, 2014, p. 19). One of the challenges faced by such rights is their application in multicultural societies (Tenorio Sánchez, 2014), in which their social function continues to be vital, but the social context is significantly less homogeneous.

The right to protest (art. 5 and art. 12.1 DHRD)

The right to protest is related to the right to assembly and freedom of expression. It makes the defence of human rights possible in the public sphere as a mechanism of legal and social change, as well as democratic participation (Saura-Freixes, 2015, p. 96).

The right to protest is a right which, seen as a part of the multilevel system of human rights, derives from other pre-existing rights such as the right to freedom of expression, or the right of assembly and association. There are no human rights treaties that contain an independent definition of this right, but it might be argued that the right to protest has certain particularities that have allowed it to find a place in the international system of human rights. Thus, the declaration on the right and responsibility to protect human rights does not include the right to protest as an independent right, but rather refers to pre-existing rights, as pointed out by the Special Rapporteur on the situation of human rights defenders (SR HRD, Sekaggya, 28 July 2011, para. 53). However, in the official UN Commentary of the Declaration on Human Rights Defenders (2011), it is considered an instrumental right, *per se,* to the right to promote and protect human rights; and I must agree with this perspective.

A standard characteristic of protest in the multilevel system of human rights is that it must be peaceful. The insistence on admitting its legitimacy according to the different systems of human rights is not so much related to its content, considering that even radical demonstrations of protest are allowed in terms of opinions, but rather to the non-violent character or method of protest. Unfortunately, there are often persistent patterns of human rights defenders doing legitimate peaceful protest charged with long-term detention, in the case-studies highlighted by the Special Rapporteur on human rights defenders (A/76/143, 2021).

In the regional systems of human rights, reference must be made to the case law of the ECtHR which, on the one hand, excludes any liberticidal discourse from the protection of the convention, admitting the application of limitations regarding hate speech. On the other hand, the ECtHR case-law is a binding ruling while preserving the possibility of dissidence and protest as a driving force for change, including the possibility of questioning the established constitutional system provided it does not attack democracy (Gargarella, 2009, p. 64). Thus, in democracy, pluralism, tolerance, and a spirit of openness must be guaranteed (*Handyside v. United Kingdom*, 1976, para. 49), as well as debate on political programs: "It is of the essence of democracy to allow diverse political programs to be proposed and debated, even those that call into question the way a State is currently organised, provided that they do not harm democracy itself" (*Socialist Party of Turkey v. Turkey*, ECtHR, 12 November 2003, para. 43).

One of the inherent characteristics of the right to protest, and which may generate legal complications, is that it is a right of revindication that may enter into conflict with other rights. Maina Kiai, former Special Rapporteur on the rights to the freedom of peaceful assembly and of association, he considers, however, that peaceful protest is necessary and constitutes an alternative to violence, which does not deserve human rights protection as a method for advocating change:

> That right was indeed at the heart of any democratic society, for that was how ordinary citizens could peacefully influence and alert their Governments on their issues. Importantly, participating in peaceful protests was an alternative to violence and armed force as a means of expression and change, which should be supported. Peaceful protest must thus be protected, and protected robustly. (A/HRC/19/40, 2011, para. 13)

Even so, protest may lead to a "clash of rights" (Gargarella, 2009). The right to protest may conflict, for instance, with the right to the free movement of a whole community. The existence of a possible clash of rights does not eliminate the right to protest, which instead should be legally balanced against other rights because it is a fundamental right in a democratic society. This means a balance must be struck that allows for the right to protest to be exercised with a minimum impact on other rights. However, it is important to recall the closing clauses of the DHRD art. 3, and the interdiction of the abuse of rights:

> Nothing in the present Declaration shall be interpreted as implying for any individual, group or organ of society or any State the right to engage in any activity or to perform any act aimed at the destruction of the rights and freedoms referred to in the present Declaration. (art. 19 DHRD)

Finally, there is a last constitutional check with the Charter of the United Nations: "Nothing in the present Declaration shall be interpreted as permitting States to support and promote activities of individuals, groups of individuals, institutions or non-governmental organizations contrary to the provisions of the Charter of the United Nations".

The right to protest is a right that may be exercised individually or collectively. This is important for two reasons. First, the right to protest may be exercised individually by a human rights defender. Even so, the protest may be initiated by an isolated individual and subsequently be taken up by a group. Second, the right of protest may be exercised collectively, precipitating the formation a social movement.

In this respect the recommendations of the OSCE in the Guidelines on the Freedom of Peaceful Assembly are quite useful as they may provide guidance in case rights that must be weighed against each other. As the Special Rapporteur to the Secretary General on the situation of human rights defenders pointed out in her Report on the right to peaceful protest (A/62/225, 2007, para. 34), the guidelines contain the following recommendations:

a   presumption in favour of holding assemblies
b   the State's duty to protect peaceful assembly
c   legality
d   proportionality
e   good administration
f   non-discrimination (OSCE Guidelines on Freedom of Peaceful Assembly, 2010).

The right to develop and discuss new human rights ideas (art. 7 DHRD)

Rights are not static and experience changes in the course of history, often as a result of long years of struggle. The possibility to debate and develop new ideas on human rights is inherent to the history of law and permits a drive to legislative change and the adaptation of new social realities while providing a response to social claims (Saura-Freixes, 2015, p. 96).

Article 7 of the Declaration on human rights defenders guarantees this right: "Everyone has the right, individually and in association with others, to develop and discuss new human rights ideas and principles and to advocate their acceptance" (A/RES/53/144, 8 March 1999). The Special Rapporteur on human rights defenders reminds the freedom of thought allowing discussion of new ideas, even if controversial:

> This right recognizes that some of these new ideas may be culturally, religiously or politically controversial; it is precisely this potential for controversy that demands space for free and open discussion and debate. In recent years, human rights defenders seeking further discussion on sexual orientation and

gender identity have faced repression in violation of this right (A/73/215, 2018, para. 21).

Bobbio observed that human rights are historical and the result of long social struggle against power (Bobbio, 1991, p. 18). At the constitutional level, the evolution of constitutional case law and constitutional reform are a response to new ideas, debates and social demands, showing that there is synergy between civil society and constitutional change. During this process, as Gordon Lauren describes it, changes of major legal importance are achieved thanks to the near visionary actions of individuals such as human rights defenders (Lauren, 1998, p. 282). Nonetheless, the road is not easy because, as the author remarks, those who are currently getting involved in this unfinished revolution in the field of human rights should be aware that those who preceded them encountered: "resistance, conflict, uncertainty, cynicism and frustration caused by gaps between normative aspirations and behavioral reality" (Lauren, 2013, p. 314).

According to Wildhaber, the ECtHR itself considered that with regard to the European Convention of Human Rights, an evolutionary interpretation must be used, given that:

> it is precisely the genius of the Convention that it is indeed a dynamic and a living instrument. It has shown a capacity to evolve in the light of social and technological developments that its drafters, however far-sighted, could never have imagined. (Wildhaber, 2004, p. 84).

This is why one of the most relevant principles in the case law of the ECtHR is that the ECHR must be interpreted "in the light of present-day conditions".

This right, which is recognized by art. 7 DHRD, even though it is still an emerging right recognized for the first time, is a key element for the social construction of the law. It also influences the relationship between human rights and civil society because, as Rodley indicates, "human rights achievements are only as secure as the determination of civil society to defend them is maintained or recovered" (Rodley, 2008, p. 6).

However, it is important to remember that it is a right to develop and discuss new human rights, ideas, and principles to advocate for their acceptance (art. 7 DHRD). Strictly, according to the title and framework of the Declaration on Human Rights Defenders, what the Declaration on Human Rights Defenders' guarantees are all "Recognized Human Rights and Fundamental Freedoms", not enforcing all the emerging rights, that should fall under scope of a specific instrumental right, according to article 7 DHRD.

The right to access and communicate with international bodies (art. 9.4 and 5.c DHRD)

In contemporary global society, many transnational activities for the defence of human rights are being developed beyond the framework of the state. This means that acting in the defence of human rights requires access, without obstacles at the national level, to international bodies in order to provide them with information and communication (Saura-Freixes, 2015, pp. 95–96).

The DHRD recognizes this right, both in relation to communication with civil society's organizations: "For the purpose of promoting and protecting human rights and fundamental freedoms, everyone has the right, individually and in association with others, at the national and international levels: To communicate with non-governmental or intergovernmental organizations" (art.5. DHRD) and to international bodies with general or special competence in the field of human rights:

> To the same end, and in accordance with applicable international instruments and procedures, everyone has the right, individually and in association with others, to unhindered access to and communication with international bodies with general or special competence to receive and consider communications on matters of human rights and fundamental freedoms. (A/RES/53/144, 8 March 1999, art. 9.4)

In conflict and post-conflict situations this right is particularly harmed due to the fear of reprisals in civil populations:

> In post-conflict contexts, intimidation of defenders perpetuates mistrust vis-à-vis institutions and transitional justice efforts. United Nations field presences also report on how their fact-finding, peacekeeping and humanitarian work is affected when local communities avoid cooperating for fear of reprisals. These downward spirals must be stopped (A/HRC/43/51, 2019, para. 33).

This is a right that has also been recognized in optional protocols to treaties in order to try and guarantee that attempts to communicate with treaty bodies do not lead to reprisals or harm to human rights defenders.

This right is contained in the Optional Protocol to the Convention on the Elimination of All Forms of Discrimination against Women (art. 11), the Optional Protocol to the Convention against Torture and Other Cruel, Inhuman or Degrading Treatment or Punishment (art. 15), and the Optional Protocol to the International Covenant on Economic, Social and Cultural Rights (art. 13) (A/66/203, 2011).

In the case of the DHRD, this right must be considered in connection with article 12, which establishes the right to protection when exercising rights under the DHRD. In practice, there have been numerous cases of individuals and organizations that have suffered reprisals for their cooperation with the United Nations. This has even been the case within the European Union.

Measures to guarantee the security of persons contacting international organizations or collaborating with them are not sufficient because security measures still depend, to a large extent, on the collaboration of states. No parallel security mechanisms have yet been developed to complement existing legal guarantees, even though they are becoming increasingly necessary.

As Brotat observes, in global society, states which traditionally exercised authority have experienced a loss of power. However, in spite of this loss of authority: "States have not been able to develop a supranational authority controlling or regulating the consequences of globalisation" (Brotat, 2014, p. 158, author's translation). This has had direct repercussions on the security and protection of human rights defenders because even though legal guarantees have been established, no mechanisms for human security have been developed. Brotat points out that, paradoxically, now that state power is in decline, the demands for security are increasing (Saura-Freixes, 2015, p. 96).

This fact does not undermine the validity of this right, on the contrary, it only shows the imperative need for its effective implementation. The interconnection between international bodies and organizations, as well as with international NGOs has become vital for the international system for the protection of human rights and reflects the complexity of a multilevel legal system that emerges in response to the effects of globalization.

The right to an effective remedy (art. 9 DHRD)

The right to an effective remedy obligates states to investigate, review and redress violations of the human rights of HRDs (Saura-Freixes, 2015, p. 158). As stated by the Special Rapporteur on the situation of human rights defenders: "Ending impunity is a necessary condition to ensure the security of defenders" (A/66/203, 2011, para. 67). This right has found extensive multilevel legal expression and is present in the majority of human rights instruments:

- The Universal Declaration of Human Rights (Article 8).
- The International Covenant on Civil and Political Rights (Articles 2(3) and 9(5)).
- Convention against Torture and other Cruel, Inhuman, or Degrading Treatment or Punishment (Article 13 and 14).
- The International Convention on the Elimination of All Forms of Racial Discrimination (Article 6).
- The European Convention on Human Rights (Article 13).
- The African Charter on Human and Peoples' Rights (Article 7).
- The American Convention on Human Rights (Article 25).
- The Inter-American Convention on Violence against Women (Article 4(g)).

This right is generally developed using the principles of investigation, punishment, and redress. However, the DHRD contains a series of procedural guarantees that apply to this right, which seek to satisfy the need for justice for human rights defenders. In the first place, there is a right to protection and to an effective remedy in human rights cases if the rights of HRDs are violated. Second, a right is established to complain to a judicial authority with the necessary guarantees to avoid arbitrariness. Art. 9.2 DHRD defines this as a right:

to complain to and have that complaint promptly reviewed in a public hearing before an independent, impartial and competent judicial or other authority established by law and to obtain from such an authority a decision, in accordance with law, providing redress. (art. 9.2 DHRD)

The scope of the right includes a specific reference to the right to report action to the public authorities: "to complain about the policies and actions of individual officials and governmental bodies with regard to violations of human rights and fundamental freedoms" (art. 9.3. a DHRD). In these procedures, no undue delay is allowed; an adequate response must be given in accordance with the law, without delay. Particular attention must be paid to the whistleblowers's special regime under measures set in the new EU Directive (EU) 2019/1937 of the European Parliament and of the Council of 23 October 2019 on the protection of persons who report breaches of Union law.

In this respect, the DHRD also includes an innovative right that answers to the petitions of international NGOs that act as international observers during hearings in order to guarantee that proceedings are made public, leaving less room for arbitrariness. This is the right "to attend public hearings, proceedings and trials so as to form an opinion on their compliance with national law and applicable international obligations and commitments" (art. 9.3 b).

Finally, protection is also provided for lawyers who act in cases of human rights violations and in defence of the rights of HRDs. They are often victims of pressure, threats and intimidation. In this respect, it is important to recognize the work done by lawyers to facilitate the protection of human rights, and thus, human rights defenders. Art. 9. 3.c. DHRD recognizes the right: "To offer and provide professionally qualified legal assistance or other relevant advice and assistance in defending human rights and fundamental freedoms". It must be pointed out that the right to an effective remedy also has an international dimension and is not limited to the national sphere because it is directly related to the right to access and communicate with international bodies.

This right is, for the Special Rapporteur on human rights defenders, related to the interdiction of arbitrariness in detention without periodic review or fair trial, even in times when temporary derogation is allowed under article 4 of the ICCPR, this is "only possible in times of public emergency which threatens the life of the nation" and "to the extent strictly required by the exigencies of the situation". Persons with deprivation of liberty are entitled "to a prompt trial or release, and in cases of arbitrary detention they are entitled to compensation" (A/76/143, 2021, para. 53). In the human rights defenders' cases related to business impact on human rights, "ensuring access to effective remedy for victims is a central part of the State duty to protect" (A/72/170, 2017, para. 47).

The right to access funding (art. 13 DHRD)

Article 13 of the DHRD recognizes the right to access funding for the purpose of promoting and protecting human rights:

> Everyone has the right, individually and in association with others, to solicit, receive and utilize resources for the express purpose of promoting and protecting human rights and fundamental freedoms through peaceful means, in accordance with article 3 of the present Declaration.

This right has proven controversial. During the 13 years that the Declaration on human rights defenders was debated, it was very difficult to reach a consensus on this issue. Even so, it is a necessary right, especially for human rights' organizations and associations. Without it, they might struggle to achieve their objectives.

Therefore, even though no specific provisions exist in the treaty-based instruments on human rights, this aspect should be recognized "as an inherent element of the right to freedom of association" (A/66/203, 2011, para. 68). The right to the freedom of association as such, and as we have seen throughout this entire study, is recognized in almost all systems for the protection of human rights, including at the constitutional level. For individual cases, it is particularly relevant the need of adequate funding for an effective remedy and private law claims (A/72/170, para. 47). Some practices of intermediary lending have damaged activities and safety of defenders and created confusion "regarding where remedy can be sought" (A/72/170, para.77).

Perhaps the right to access funding is one of the rights that very clearly demonstrates the existing dichotomy between domestic and international law. Many states have legislation that limits the possibilities for funding NGOs and associations in the field of human rights, particularly in the case of foreign funding (SR HRD, 4 August 2009, para. 94). As the Special Rapporteur on the situation of human rights defenders stated: "According to the provisions of the Declaration, States are under obligation to permit individuals and organizations to solicit, receive and utilize funding. However, one or several of the three phases of the funding cycle are very often curtailed" (4 August 2003, para. 93). Article 13 itself refers to article 3, which considers domestic law a legal framework in which this right must be exercised. More specifically, article 3 establishes that:

> Domestic law consistent with the Charter of the United Nations and other international obligations of the State in the field of human rights and fundamental freedoms is the juridical framework within which human rights and fundamental freedoms should be implemented and enjoyed and within which all activities referred to in the present Declaration for the promotion, protection and effective realization of those rights and freedoms should be conducted. Consequently, only domestic legislation that is consistent with international human rights norms can be considered an appropriate legal framework for the enjoyment of the right of access to funding. (SR HRD, 2011, para. 94)

Therefore, domestic law is the framework which determines how the rights established in the DHRD are to be exercised, which includes the right to access funding. Nonetheless, it also makes reference to the Charter of the United

Nations and other obligations of the state in the field of human rights. This means domestic law, as such, is not sufficient. The framework required by the article 3 DHRD consists of: "Domestic law consistent with the Charter of the United Nations and other international obligations of the State in the field of human rights and fundamental freedoms". This is a clear example of the constitutionalisation process in international law, and the internationalisation of constitutional law.

All in all, we are experiencing the effects of the process of globalization. According to Tajadura and De Miguel Bárcena, the effects lead to "the fragmentation of the subjects with decision-making capacity" (Tajadura and de Miguel Bárcena, 2014, p. 83, author's translation). Therefore, the emergence of new subjects must be accompanied by the emergence of new guarantees. Individual and group action for the protection and promotion of rights, however, is not just a phenomenon of the twenty-first century. Over the course of history, many people did not hesitate to fight against the abuse of power or authority. They contributed to the creation of rights by claiming recognition, guarantees, protection, and promotion. The struggle for human rights is also the history of individuals who, anonymously or often without any social recognition, dedicated their lives to the defence of their own human rights and those of others. All of them are human rights defenders. Providing legal guarantees for rights does not fall within their scope of action, as it is the obligation of state institutions or international bodies. Their actions are limited to the protection and promotion of human rights, not as an obligation but as a right. They therefore have no obligation to expose themselves to retaliations and the abuse of power. Consequently, new kinds of legal guarantees must be part of a multilevel system. In this system, international law and constitutional law are interconnected, while supranational bodies and spheres may be created. The principle of human dignity is not limited by the principle of sovereignty. These new kinds of guarantees also require new kinds of multilevel governance where decisions are not made in situations with legal gaps that facilitate the abuse of power, or where the protection of rights and decision-making procedures are not properly aligned. Recognition of the importance of the right to promote and protect human rights and the activities of human rights defenders responds to a historical reality and necessity that ties in with the "right to have rights", according to Hannah Arendt (1951). The human condition is a paradigm of law.

Dissent, democracy, and the right to promote and protect human rights

The right to promote and to strive for human rights contains a challenge: activity is the essential component of a right defined more for the exercise than for the subject.

Hence, to strive for human rights is what defines human rights defenders. There is no prior status of human rights defenders that allows for a right's exercise—the subjecthood is universal. Thus, it leads to an open question: is whoever considers himself or herself a human rights defender, a human rights defender?

The necessary conditions to be a human rights defender are not in the DHRD under a closed definition or enumeration. These criteria are set by the doctrine created at the United Nations by the Special Procedure (former Special Representative of the Secretary General) on human rights defenders. Peaceful means is the main criteria to become a human rights defender, but also activity for promotion and protection of human rights, as well as acceptance of human rights' universality and interdependence. All these criteria fall under the umbrella of the Declaration on Human Rights Defenders and the framework set up in 1998.

The European Union provides the sole definition on human rights defenders at the international level, although it is by means of a *soft law* instrument in the EU Guidelines on human rights defenders:

> Human rights defenders are those individuals, groups and organs of society that promote and protect universally recognised human rights and fundamental freedoms. Human rights defenders seek the promotion and protection of civil and political rights as well as the promotion, protection and realisation of economic, social and cultural rights. Human rights defenders also promote and protect the rights of members of groups such as indigenous communities. The definition does not include those individuals or groups who commit or propagate violence. (EU Guidelines on human rights defenders, 2008, para. 3)

What is worthwhile to consider is the last sentence: "The definition does not include those individuals or groups who commit or propagate violence" (EU Guidelines on human rights defenders, 2008, para. 3). But what does this mean? It is not an easy question to answer.

When considering the individualization of international law, Peters considers the international criminal responsibility arising from Nuremberg Trials and the previous intellectual commitment by individuals from the International Scholars during the inter-war period as a failed attempt to counteract the rise of totalitarianism (Peters, 2016, p. 20).

Since the Second World War, we have known about the dangers of the state, but we must also be aware of the dangers of political parties, or groups of individuals who abused state political power. Thus, it is worthwhile to recall the constitutional framework of fundamental rights when thinking about human rights defenders and subjecthood.

Eguren Fernández and Patel point out some interesting aspects with regard to this question (Eguren Fernández and Patel, 2015). However, I disagree with their approach in relational terms. The United Nations requires "practice" more than "entitlement" to comply with the main requirement for recognition as a human rights defender, in order to promote and protect human rights, and to strive for them. The Special Rapporteur on the situation of human rights defenders has introduced the interpretation criteria of the "special effort" to promote and protect human rights (Special Rapporteur on the situation of human rights defenders, 2022).

This action cannot be considered outside of the constitutional framework, only in terms of international law. Why? Because, from the DHRD, the individual's action must be executed first under the domestic legal framework consistent with human rights and the UN Charter. Thus, it is an individual right, but not a duty. The state is still the main one responsible for protecting and promoting fundamental and human rights: this is the constitutional function and the final legitimation of the state, but it can be shared with other international bodies. Thus, let us analyze the implications of the criteria to be considered human rights defenders.

First, the action of promoting and protecting human rights is accomplished by means of several instrumental rights to the right to promote and protect human rights. But it is important not to forget that each of these rights has internal constraints in the different instruments on human rights. Below, I will develop ideas on the freedom of expression and the right to protest and dissent; having due attention to the "special effort" done to protect and promote human rights (Special Rapporteur on the situation of human rights defenders, 2022).

Second, peaceful action is not the only an external legal commitment to be fulfilled before becoming a human rights defender, or to have the right to be protected under international and constitutional law. Peaceful action is an internal criterion. It is one part of the core content of the right to promote and protect human rights. Which is the correct political response to a situation of oppression is another question outside of the scope of this right. In democracy and the rule of law framework, there is no legitimate use of force, except in cases of legitimate defence accepted and on rule by criminal law, not by the DHRD. In the case of oppressive situations, the use of violence needs another legal ruling and basis that is outside the right to promote and protect human rights; mainly in the right of resistance, but that is another legal figure and situation to consider. This peaceful commitment, while it might seem to be a hard commitment, is at the root of why human rights defenders possess a different status than mere activists, or even guerrillas. This is why it is so important to go back to the precedent of dissenters: in order to understand the lines in differing law from politics, ideas, discourse, and actions. Hence, it could be interesting to think about the concept of non-violence in order to delimitate it.

Third, Eguren Fernández and Patel point out that it is necessary to think about the question of "who is right and who is wrong" (Eguren Fernández and Patel, 2015, p. 21). According to the Fact Sheet No. 29 of the United Nations, what is relevant is not only who is right or wrong. Thus, what is relevant since their origins, is not ideology, but the rights they defend:

> It is not essential for a human rights defender to be correct in his or her arguments in order to be a genuine defender. The critical test is whether or not the person is defending a human right. Human rights defenders must be defined and accepted according to the rights they are defending and according to their own right to do so. (OHCHR, 2004, p. 9)

Hence, the "right-wrong" question on human rights defenders must be related with democracy. What, then, is right or wrong?

For the Special Rapporteur on human rights defenders (2022), the relevant is not who is right or who is wrong but "A second important issue concerns the validity of the arguments being presented. It is not essential for a human rights defender to be correct in his or her arguments in order to be a genuine defender. [...] The key issue is whether or not their concerns fall within the scope of human rights" (OHCHR, SR on human rights defenders, 2022). As a right based on exercise, the exercise of the right to promote and to protect human rights must be free, in terms of opinion, but not in method or action. Accepting the exercise of the right only depends on content or proposals; it would be a counterweight to the necessary freedom of exercise. Then, it is necessary to examine carefully how to exercise instrumental rights, such as the right to freedom of association, assembly, protest, etc., under the rule of law and human rights. I will focus on freedom of expression as a mean for dissent. Any undue restriction can bias the exercise of the right to promote and protect human rights and reciprocally undermine the new paradigm of this legal subject. In the case of the EU, it would be connected with the new-born paradigm of citizenship.

Then, the democratic dimension is necessary for understanding what is behind this right to promote and protect human rights. Von Bogdandy and Venzke establish a necessary theoretical distinction on the holistic or communitarian approach and the individualistic paradigm (von Bogdandy and Venzke, 2014, p. 140). This is clear in terms of EU citizenship, as built on the individualistic paradigm. It lessens pressure on the necessity to find—the people—behind the legitimacy of the courts and the political and legal system. Without this identarian foundational constraint, citizenship can be built in terms of a system of individual decisions and rights. According to von Bogdandy and Venzke, it opens the door for consideration of a cosmopolitan or transnational citizenship, where, in the Habermasian approach, "the *political* dimension is essential" (von Bogdandy and Venzke, 2014, p. 143). In this sense, it is interesting to accept that even if there is not an international legal framework for citizenship, there are grounds "to interpret provisions of international law in their light" (von Bogdandy and Venzke, 2014, p. 143).

In considering the connection between human rights defenders as legal subjects and democracy: if we go deeper into the requisite of peaceful means there is a worthwhile assumption to recall. According to Peters: "Furthermore, the idea of a legal community means that the relationships are governed by law, and not by force" (Peters, 2011 p. 153). The idea of governance by law and not by force is essential. Law is what gives strength, or even the force of law, but not violence. Never violence.

Human rights defenders are actors and stakeholders of the promotion and protection of human rights. That is, they are individuals, not states or international organizations, but necessary subjects in the international system. Thus, I will follow the constitutionalist paradigm according to Peters and Kumm. For Peters, constitutionalism gives us a sense of the ultimate legal subject in international law: individuals. Hence, constitutions are not abstract rules without a foundation. Rather, they are grounded in the constituent power, but the legitimate will is not mediated by the people without limits, under cosmopolitan or multilevel governance and plural societies. Contemporary constitutions should not be grounded in abstract obsolete entities like nation or people, with obsolete *jus sanguinis* or uniformity on identity as criteria, but on individuals and jurisdiction leading to democracy across borders. Following globalization, people and nations were fractured due to increased mobility, shared and coexisting cultures under state frameworks. Constitutions are not legitimated by uniformist identity, but on the function to protect all fundamental and human rights under state jurisdiction, even beyond borders, as in the extraterritorial application of the ECHR. Peters considers this in the following:

> Constitutionalism, as I understand it, postulates that natural persons are the ultimate unit of legal concern. Global constitutionalists abandon the idea that sovereign states are the material source of international norms. In consequence, the ultimate normative source of international law is—from a constitutionalist perspective—humanity, not sovereignty. (Peters, 2011, p. 155)

This displacement from sovereignty to humanity is the paradigm behind the Declaration on human rights defenders too. By accepting the legal recognition of an individuals' right to contest, or even to challenge or to push the state under a clash of rights, the DHRD gives birth to the active paradigm of citizenship and to a new trend in legal personhood. However, this legal paradigm does not set an absolute right. This individual force and recognition prevent the return of totalitarianism.

According to Peters, individuals are "the basic axiom" of the international legal order, and "the individual is the ultimate unit of all law, international and municipal" (Peters, 2011, p. 158). I agree that it does not mean to eliminate the Parliamentarism in the law-making process: "The reason is that civil society actors need to stay outside the formal political and legal process in order to fulfil their watchdog and opposition function" (Peters, 2011, p. 156).

Thus, it is important to refer to the axiological possibility to have rights, in the Arendtian sense, of "the right to have rights". From a constitutionalist perspective, it is related with the oppression of opponents emerging from the denial of rights: "Historically, these codifications responded to the practice of totalitarian regimes to divest political opponents of their rights ('civil death')" (Peters, 2011, p. 159).

However, following this constitutional approach, there emerges a two-edged subject. If individuals are the subject of international and constitutional rights which are not merely passive, as in the case of human rights defenders, they are subjects of international and constitutional obligations too. In consideration of criminal law, we should refer to the axis set up by the Nuremberg background on individual responsibility, and never forget it:

> That international law imposes duties and liabilities upon individuals as well as upon States has long been recognized. [...] Crimes against international law are committed by men, not by abstract entities, and only by punishing

individuals who commit such crimes can the provisions of international law be enforced. [...] The very essence of the Charter is that individuals have international duties which transcend the national obligations of obedience imposed by the individual State. (NMT, Nuremberg, 1947)

The main responsibility pertaining to human rights remains, and should remain, with states. Individuals are not a substitute for public power but are the basis of it at the constitutional and international levels. When an individual exercises, solely or collectively, the instrumental right to promote, protect, and strive for human rights, their action is driven by a constitutional paradigm (even at the international level), not by an international "state-paradigm".

Article 10.2 ECHR sets a restrictive clause with specific criteria to be fulfilled: the legality and the legitimate aim of any restrictive measure of the right to freedom of expression, and according to the case law of the ECtHR it must be "necessary in a democratic society". This restrictive clause set in paragraph 2 is also present in other rights: art. 8.2, art. 9.2, art. 10.2, art. 11.2 ECHR, with slight differences, but the same structure. Because of this conception a twofold and reciprocal notion of the freedom of expression arises. It is an individual right, but it has a social function (*Soulas et autres v. France*, ECHR, 10 July 2008). Due to public interest, this is why political discourse is highly protected in the ECHR case law (Oetheimer, 2007). However, in some particular cases, the ECtHR refers not to art. 10.2 ECHR but to art. 17 ECHR on the abuse of rights to directly dismiss the application.

These cases are then outside of the jurisdiction without being a part of the judiciary case law and analysis. They do not have any legal basis for consideration and there is no need to apply a restrictive clause since it is an abuse of rights. These are for instance the cases of negationism, considered at the light of article 17 ECtHR: "Nothing in [the] Convention may be interpreted as implying for any State, group or person any right to engage in any activity or perform any act aimed at the destruction of any of the rights and freedoms set forth herein or at their limitation to a greater extent than is provided for in the Convention". Article 17 ECHR is used as an interpretive tool in some cases on hate of speech.

This clearly differs from the US conception of freedom of expression. According to the First Amendment of the US Constitution:

> Congress shall make no law respecting an establishment of religion, or prohibiting the free exercise thereof; or abridging the freedom of speech, or of the press; or the right of the people peaceably to assemble, and to petition the Government for a redress of grievances. (US Constitution, amend. I, 1791)

Hence, in the US legal framework it is not possible to enforce legal constraints on the freedom of expression, but it remains limited by certain case law. However, doctrines of the "content-based test" and "fighting words" from the US system are particularly interesting. Thus, limits on freedom of expression cannot only come from the discourse of ideas, it is necessary to consider effects, as well as context and intention.

This is often forgotten in discourse that supports the absolute freedom of expression. A dilemma arises when freedom of expression, as an individual right, counteracts another individual right, or a legitimate social goal. If it is with another right, the test is valid because it can be balanced. However, when there is a limit based on its effects and a social goal, the continental perspective can suffer from some biased effect. Hence, it has sense to recall this case law construction of "fighting words", coming from the US supreme Court, that even the ECHR has taken into account in some cases on freedom of expression and hate speech (Oetheimer, 2007).

When Peters recalls the other side to the individualization of rights, they are counteracted under the rule of law, criminal responsibility and the individual paradigm on international responsibility that emerged after Nuremberg. None of this is by chance. Recent historical episodes can show the effects of mere "words" on the violation of human rights and criminal responsibility, which can even lead to a genocide. This was the case with *Médias de la haine* (2007) in Rwanda, as analyzed earlier in this book.

The abuse of rights is relevant because, according to Rovira Viñas, its basis can be found in the exercise of rights (Rovira Viñas, 1980). Thus, this legal framework is not mere words, but the conditions and intentions behind the exercise of the right to freedom of expression. Rovira Viñas began studying this question in Spain, considering the abuse of rights to be based on private doctrine and the influence of the French Revolution and the German legal framework (Rovira Viñas, 1980). There are intrinsic and extrinsic limits to the rights. Extrinsic limits are ineffective, so some preventive measures are necessary. In this case, what is more relevant is the will of the individual and how they exercise these rights (Rovira Viñas, 1980, pp. 171–172). These two aspects are coincident with the core content of the right to promote and to protect human rights.

In this sense, Sánchez-Molina makes a distinction on the criteria for the limitation of rights. Firstly, intrinsic limitations on rights refer to the impossibility of applying an international human rights instrument with the aim of limiting or suppressing rights recognized by it (Sánchez Molina, 2018). So, there is no coverage under international human rights treaties for destroying human rights on behalf of human rights. The abuse of rights is present in several human rights instruments: articles 30 UDHR, 54 ECFR, 17 ECHR, and art. 5.1 ICCR (Sánchez Molina, 2018). Abuse of rights is a closing clause in the system of human rights that differs, according to Sanchez-Molina, from the extrinsic limits to human rights. Due to extrinsic limits, it is not possible to apply a lower level of protection to an external right with (Sánchez Molina, 2018). This is usually forbidden by means of the clause toward a higher standard of protection of rights, for instance, art. 53 ECFR:

> Nothing in this Charter shall be interpreted as restricting or adversely affecting human rights and fundamental freedoms as recognised, in their respective fields of application, by Union law and international law and by international agreements to which the Union or all the Member States are party, including

the European Convention for the Protection of Human Rights and Fundamental Freedoms, and by the Member States' constitutions.

Under freedom of expression, there remains a balance between the individual, freedom, and society. Limits can become constitutional commitments for the future of Europe. It is worthwhile to mention that human rights do not depend on a mediator, such as people, or even a nation. In the twenty-first century, fundamental rights emerge from the human condition. This is why it is inherent to individual rights that they cannot be biased by other individuals because they have all equality on rights—if not, it would be legitimizing discrimination. Positive obligations are the state's duty. So, states, even under the umbrella of the ECHR, must guarantee individual rights, such as freedom of expression, with positive obligations. From a legally comparative point of view, this is both remarkable and helpful in strengthening the position of the right to promote and protect human rights. It has a constitutional function rather than physical protection for the subject of rights: human rights defenders. It is necessary to point out that the ECtHR has developed a case law in order to put on the table several controversial questions emerging from dissent and instrumental freedoms.

The construction of dissent is not a banal question. Using human rights—such as freedom of expression, freedom of association, freedom of assembly or the right to protest—is necessary to dissent against the state, and against other actors in the international community. Dissent is not directly related to legal compliance, but mostly with democracy. Consequently, the rule of law and dissent respect the option for disagreement, but with the obligation of compliance with the law. This is present in the article 3 DHRD, which states that domestic law must be respected, setting a constitutional check with human rights treaties and the UN Charter.

In considering dissent, what is the most interesting is the framework of the freedom of expression and its connection with the freedoms of association and assembly as rights of collective expression. This is a slightly different framework from the right to protest. Protest and dissent are part of the notion of a "Vigilant citizenry", to borrow the expression from Arendt's theory, as explained by Pogge (Parekh, 2007). Parekh claims a popular dimension of human rights. I consider it essential to recall the collective exercise of individual rights not done by intermediation of other abstract entities, such as peoples or nations.

The Declaration on Human Rights Defenders refers to groups and the collective exercise of rights. Groups are a complex subject of rights due to their mutability and non-entitlement, but it is possible to consider them by using a constitutional approach. It is necessary to refer to this new challenging paradigm for the exercise of rights, instead of entitlement.

Finally, article 12 DHRD establishes the right to protest: "Everyone has the right, individually and in association with others, to participate in peaceful activities against violations of human rights and fundamental freedoms". Historically, protest has been a driving force for human rights.

The European Guidelines on human rights defenders encourages criticism as a driving force for human rights. However, it is interesting that value is found not only in social action, but also in individual intellectual dissent and the "independence of mind and free debate". Thus, social action is a key role for defenders:

> The work of human rights defenders often involves criticism of government's policies and actions. However, governments should not see this as a negative. The principle of allowing room for independence of mind and free debate on a government's policies and actions is fundamental, and is a tried and tested way of establishing a better level of protection of human rights. Human rights defenders can assist governments in promoting and protecting human rights. As part of consultation processes they can play a key role in helping to draft appropriate legislation, and in helping to draw up national plans and strategies on human rights. This role too should be recognised and supported. (EU Guidelines on human rights defenders, 2008, para. 59)

"Independence of mind" and "free debate" are at the core of the right of protest in the EU framework on human rights defenders. But in my view, they are consistent with the UN Declaration on human rights defenders that come from Soviet dissent as historical precedent. Thus, the social and individual dimension of freedom of thought is the cornerstone of the UN Declaration, which is not merely based on the collective, social pressure or clash of rights, that lead in the past to individual's oppression. This is why it is important to remember that protecting or striving for human rights it is not only a "physical" action, but an intellectual one too. According to Quinn and Levine's work on intellectual human rights defenders, these might be:

- Academics, researchers and lecturers working in areas directly related to human rights
- Academics, researchers and lecturers targeted due to the content of their work in the human rights domain, even if they do not recognize themselves as human rights defenders
- Prominent professors of a particular ethnic, religious or geographic group (Quinn and Levine, 2014, pp. 210–211)

Academic freedom is not often one of the claims of human rights defenders, but there is a real lack of academic freedom and it is an oxymoron to separate collective action from individual freedom of the mind.

Even if legal dissent is accepted, there are some groups of defenders that must cope with social stigma. For instance, this is often the case with sexual and reproductive rights defenders:

> Despite recognition of sexual and reproductive rights under international law, these rights remain socially and politically contested in many places. Discrimination and stigma persist against those protecting, enforcing, and effectuating these rights. Stigma can both lead to, and be reinforced by,

government laws and policies that discriminate against individuals or certain reproductive or sexual choices or entities. (Sohoo and Hortsch, 2011, p. 991)

Sometimes we forget that social trouble is still present behind the legal recognition of human rights and enforcement. In many cases, human rights defenders live with stigma, threats, killings, and harassment. Behind individual persecution is the hidden will that to silence a human rights defender is to silence the public's interest. Something similar happens to journalists in armed conflicts. Crimes against them are one way to keep armed conflicts outside of international concern.

This is why a multilevel system of protection is necessary. The dissent of human rights defenders against the state, public power, and non-state actors is essential and necessary for any democracy, and it is not the same as forcing democracy by violence, including coercion, threats or the threat of force.

This approach is present in the ECtHR case law, let us look at some leading cases on it. The court case law makes an interpretation of collective rights—freedom of assembly or even freedom of association—in light of the individual right to the freedom of expression (art. 10 ECHR). Freedom of assembly has been considered a collective expression of the right to freedom of expression in the system of the European Convention on Human Rights. There are two characteristic elements to this system:

As Fabre-Alibert points out, the reference to a democratic society is the cornerstone of the European system of human rights (Fabre-Alibert, 1998, p. 468). Sudre considered that, even if it is not defined by the ECHR, it is the central value of European public order (Sudre, 2006, p. 214). Oetheimer (2007) reminds us that there is a reinforced protection on political discourse. Political discourse is placed at the center of protection, and few restrictions of it are accepted. Then, this discourse can be defined as: "Celui qui contribue de façon significative à un échange d'informations et d'idées au sein de la société démocratique, au center de son œuvre protectrice" (Oetheimer, 2007, p. 64). Byoy (2012) considers public assemblies in open spaces to be connected with freedom of expression, but the most interesting and challenging part of his opinion, is that it does not depend on the content of opinions expressed in a demonstration. All this leads to the application of a horizontal effect and positive obligations (Byoy, 2012, p. 743–745).

These collective rights can be challenged by exceptional measures. In some countries, this leads to the suspension of the European Convention on Human Rights. The ECtHR refers explicitly to the connection between art. 10 and art. 11 ECHR in the case law. Therefore sometimes the freedom of association and assembly must be interpreted in light of the freedom of expression:

> Notwithstanding its autonomous role and particular sphere of application, Article 11 (art. 11) must, in the present case, also be considered in the light of Article 10 (art. 10) (*Young, James and Webster v. the United Kingdom*, judgment of 13 August 1981, para. 57). The protection of personal opinions, secured by Article 10, is one of the objectives of freedom of peaceful assembly as enshrined in Article 11 (art. 11). (*Ezelin v. France*, 26 April 1991, para. 37)

Hence, in public demonstration, pluralism, and respect for minorities must be guaranteed as a collective exhibition of the individual's freedom of expression. It is obvious that the freedom of assembly or association can never be compulsory or controlled. The position of the ECtHR can be summarized in this principle: article 10 is to be regarded as *lex generalis* in relation to article 11, which is considered *lex specialis* (*Ezelin v. France*, 26 April 1991, para. 35). Article 11 is interpreted reciprocally in light of article 10 ECHR: "However, notwithstanding its autonomous role and particular sphere of application, Article 11 must, in the present case, also be considered in the light of Article 10", because "the protection of personal opinions, secured by Article 10, is one of the objectives of freedom of peaceful assembly enshrined in article 11" (*Ezelyn v. France*, 26 April 1991, para. 23). It is worthwhile to point out the clear mention of the peaceful character of assembly. It is in this framework that the right to protest must be understood.

In the case of *Navalnyy and Yashin v. Russia* (4 December 2014, para. 51), the ECtHR sets two interesting views on freedom of assembly and protest. A reprisal for peaceful march hold after a demonstration was considered in this case, leading to the violation of article 11 and article 5.1 for unlawful arbitrary detention. However, it is important to keep in mind that these are individual rights exercised collectively. The Court considers in this case article 11, at the light of article 10, with a consistent practice in this sense.

This is quite different from statist public bodies involved in protest. In my opinion, there is a strong difference in the terms of human rights defenders, between institutions and individuals. Institutions are not only considered under the terms of human rights defenders, because they are part of the state. They fall beneath the umbrella of public responsibility or the public interest in institutions and the state. Law has a performative nature, as explained by Austin, constitutive of enforcement (Austin, 1975). It is important to recall that the problems to limitations of protest is not a "content-based" choice of ideas. Legal trouble arises from abuse of the exercise of the right of political representation, assembly, or association. It could be closer to an abuse of rights if the right of political representation is used to destroy others' political representation and opinions. But limiting opposition without proportion or necessity is not according to human rights standards and the Declaration on human rights defenders. Even if action is taken by the majority, democratic parliamentary rules and constitutional control are a guarantee of the respect of fundamental rights, minority, and political representation in democracy. Hence, trying to explain protest solely in political terms does not explain anything real, because in terms of political ideas, everything is valid in a democracy, as the ECtHR set out, but not when it comes to the loss of fundamental rights.

If the axiological point on the right to promote and protect human rights is the exercise of the right, maybe it is important to think that even intellectual activity is an activity, exercised by the individual or collectively, as a mode of protest related to freedom of thought. But to determine who is a human rights defender will depend only on individual will?

Of course, state and political powers cannot decide who is or not a human right defender. But since it is a legal concept, there are some legal criteria that must be met. It is not a restriction of individual will; it is a guarantee of human rights. If we forget that individuals are also responsible for their acts, this would lead to non-compliance with human rights' limits or toward abuse of rights. Human rights are part of instrumental rights. They are built with limitative clauses, such as art. 10.2 ECHR or the articles 19.2 or 20 ICCPR, *lex specialis*, with exceptions only accepted in a democratic society, under the conditions of proportionality and necessity. So maybe, on the one hand, it does not sound very idealistic or utopian to admit this restriction, but on the other hand, there is a necessary distinction: to avoid the abuse of power by individuals and without any constraint. It is not against democracy. The interdiction of the abuse of rights by majorities or individuals is part of the democratic heritage against totalitarianism. This opens the door to some questions, such as the distinction between human rights defenders, the limits on democracy, and the legal commitments of militant democracy.

References

Arendt, H. (1951). *The Origins of Totalitarianism*. New York: Brace, Harcourt.
Arendt, H. (2018). *The Human Condition*. Chicago & London: The University of Chicago Press.
Austin, J. L. (1975). *How to Do Things With Words: The William James Lectures delivered at Harvard University in 1955*. Harvard: Harvard University Press.
Bobbio, N. (1991). *El tiempo de los derechos*. Madrid: Sistema.
Boyle, K. (2010). "Thought, expression, association, assembly". In D. Moeckli, S. Sangeeta, & S. Sivakumaran, *International Human Rights Law*. Oxford: Oxford University Press.
Brotat, R. (2014). *La seguridad urbana: entre la seguridad ciudadana, el civismo y la convivencia en espacios públicos*. Barcelona: Universitat Autònoma de Barcelona.
Byoy, X. (2012). "La protection renforcée de la liberté d'expression politique dans le contexte de la Convention européenne des droits de l'homme". *Les Cahiers de droit*, vol. 53.
Eguren Fernández, L.E. and Patel, C. (2015). "Towards developing a critical and ethical approach for better recognising and protecting human rights defenders". *The International Journal of Human Rights*, 2019(7).
Fabre-Alibert, V. (1998). "La notion de 'société démocratique' dans la jurisprudence de la Cour Européenne des Droits de l'Homme". *Revue trimestrielle des droits de l'homme*, 9, 465–496.
Gargarella, R. (2009). "A dialogue on law and social protest". In A. Sajó, (Ed.). *Free to Protest: Constituent Power and Street Demonstration*. Utrecht: Eleven International Publishing.
Gillion, D. Q. (2013). *The Political Power of Protest: Minority Activism and Shifts in Public Policy*. Cambridge: Cambridge University Press.
Guillen, F. (2012). *Policia i Seguretat*. Universitat Autònoma de Barcelona: Departament de Publicacions.
Ladmann, T. and Abraham, M. (2004). "Evaluation of nine non-governmental human rights organisations", IOB Working Document. Retrieved 30 October 2022, from: www.pointk.org/resources/files/9orgs_evaluation.pdf
Kamminga, M. T. (2005). "The evolving status of NGOs under international law: A threat to the inter-state system?". In P. Alston, *Non-State Actors and Human Rights*. Oxford: Oxford University Press.

Parekh, S. (2007). "Resisting dull and torpid assent: Returning to the debate over the foundations of human rights". *Human Rights Quarterly*, 29(3), 754–778.
Lauren, G. (1998). *The Evolution of International Human Rights: Visions Seen.* Philadelphia: University of Pennsylvania Press.
Oetheimer, M. (2007). "La cour européenne des droits de l'homme face au discours de haine". *Revue Trimestrielle des droits de l'homme*, 69.
Peters, A. (2016). *Beyond Human Rights: The Legal Status of the Individual in International Law.* Cambridge: Cambridge University Press.
Peters, A. (2011). "Membership in the global constitutional community". In A. Peters, J. Klabbers, & G. Ulfstein, *The Constitutionalization of International Law.* Oxford: Oxford University Press.
Peters, A., Klabbers, J., and Ulfstein, G. (2009). *The Constitutionalization of International Law.* Oxford: Oxford University Press.
Piçarra, N. (2013). "Direito à liberdade e à segurança". In A. Silveira & M. Canotilho (Eds), *Carta dos Direitos Fundamentales da Uniao Europeia Comentada.* Coimbra: Almedina.
Quinn, R. and Levine, J. (2014). "Intellectual-HRDs and claims for academic freedom under human rights law". *The International Journal of Human Rights*, 18(7–8), 898–920.
Rodley, N. (2008). "The Universal Declaration of Human Rights: Learning from experience". *Essex Human Rights Review*, 5(1).
Rovira Viñas, A. (1983). *El abuso de los derechos fundamentales.* Madrid: Península.
Saura-Freixes, N. (2015). *Libertad de expresión y derecho a promover y proteger los derechos humanos.* Barcelona: J.M. Bosch Editor.
Saura-Freixes, N. (2016) *Human Rights Defenders. El derecho a promover y proteger los derechos humanos.* Madrid: UNED.
Sohoo, C. and Hortsch, D. (2011). "Who is a human rights defender? An essay on sexual and reproductive rights defenders". *University of Miami Law Review*, 65(3).
Sudre, F. (2006). *Droit européen et international des droits de l'homme.* Paris: Presses Universitaires de France.
Tajadura, J. and de Miguel Bárcena, J. (Eds) (2014). *Federalismos del s.XXI.* Madrid: Centro de Estudios Políticos y Constitucionales.
Tenorio Sánchez, P. J. (Ed.) (2014). *La libertad de expresión. Su posición preferente en un entorno multicultural.* Madrid: Walter Kluwers.
Tilly, C. and Wood, L. J. (2016). *Social Movements. 1768–2012.* New York: Routledge.
von Bogdandy, A. and Venzke, I. (2014). *In Whose Name? A Public Law Theory of International Adjudication.* Oxford: Oxford University Press.
Wildhaber, L. (2004). "The European Court of Human Rights in action". *Ritsumeikan Law Review*, 21.

Documents

Treaties

African Charter on Human and Peoples' Rights (adopted 27 June 1981, entered into force 21 October 1986) (1982) 21ILM, (African Charter)
American Convention on Human Rights (adopted 22 November, 1969, entered into force 18 July 1978) 1144 UNTS 123, OASTS. No. 36 ("Pact of San Jose, Costa Rica", ACHR)
Charter of the United Nations, (adopted 24 October 1945) 1 UNTS XVI
Consolidated Version of the Treaty on European Union [2012] OJ C 326/13

Convention against Torture and Other Cruel, Inhuman or Degrading Treatment or Punishment (adopted 10 December 1984, entered into force 26 June 1987) 1465 UNTS 85

Convention for the Protection of Human Rights and Fundamental Freedoms, as amended (adopted 4 November 1950, entered into force 3 September 1953) ETS No. 005 (ECHR)

Inter-American Convention on the Prevention, Punishment and Eradication of Violence against Women (adopted 9 June 1994, entered into force 5 March 1995) ("Convention of Bélem do Pará")

International Convention on the Elimination of All Forms of Racial Discrimination (adopted 7 March 1966, entered into force 4 January 1969) 660 UNTS 195

International Covenant on Civil and Political Rights (adopted 16 December 1966, entered into force 23 March 1976) 999 UNTS 171 (ICCPR)

International Covenant on Economic, Social and Cultural Rights (adopted 16 December 1966, entered into force 3 January 1976) 993 UNTS 3 (ICESCR)

Optional Protocol to the Convention against Torture and Other Cruel, Inhuman or Degrading Treatment or Punishment (adopted 18 December 2002, entered into force 22 June 2006) 2375 UNTS 237 (OPCAT)

Optional Protocol to the Convention on the Elimination of All Forms of Discrimination against Women (adopted 6 October 1999, entered into force 22 December 2000) 2131 UNTS 83

Optional Protocol to the International Covenant on Economic, Social and Cultural Rights (adopted 10 December 2008, entered into force 5 May 2013) Doc. A/63/435; C. N.869.2009

Protocol no.11 to the Convention for the Protection of Human Rights and Fundamental Freedoms Restructuring the Control Machinery Established Thereby (adopted 11 May 1994, entered into force 1 November 1998) ETS. No.155

Rome Statute of the International Criminal Court (adopted 17 July 1998, entered into force 1 July 2002) 2187 UNTS 3

UN

Universal Declaration of Human Rights UNGA Res. 217A (III) (10 December 1948)

Declaration on the Right and Responsibility of Individuals, Groups and Organs of Society to Promote and Protect Universally Recognized Human Rights and Fundamental Freedoms UNGA A/RES/53/144 (8 March 1999)

UNGA "Situation of human rights defenders. Note by the Secretary General. Report of the Special Rapporteur on the situation of human rights defenders" (5 September 2006) A/61/312. Retrieved May 31, 2022, from: https://documents-dds-ny.un.org/doc/UNDOC/GEN/N06/488/07/PDF/N0648807.pdf?OpenElement

UNGA "Situation of human rights defenders. Note by the Secretary General. Report of the Special Rapporteur on the situation of human rights defenders" (13 August 2007) A/62/225. Retrieved May 31, 2022, from: https://documents-dds-ny.un.org/doc/UNDOC/GEN/N07/457/26/PDF/N0745726.pdf?OpenElement

UNGA "Human rights defenders. Note by the Secretary-General. Report of the Special Rapporteur on the situation of human rights defenders" (28 July 2011) UN Doc A/66/203. Retrieved 4 June, 2022, from: https://digitallibrary.un.org/record/709670?ln=es

UNGA "Situation of human rights defenders. Note by the Secretary General. Report of the Special Rapporteur on the situation of human rights defenders" (10 August 2012) UN

Doc A/67/292. Retrieved May 31, 2022, from: https://documents-dds-ny.un.org/doc/UNDOC/GEN/N12/459/42/PDF/N1245942.pdf?OpenElement
UNGA "Situation of human rights defenders. Note by the Secretary General. Report of the Special Rapporteur on the situation of human rights defenders" (19 July 2017) UN Doc A/72/170. Retrieved May 31, 2022, from: https://documents-dds-ny.un.org/doc/UNDOC/GEN/N17/220/75/PDF/N1722075.pdf?OpenElement
UNGA "Situation of human rights defenders. Note by the Secretary General. Report of the Special Rapporteur on the situation of human rights defenders" (23 July 2018) UN Doc A/73/215. Retrieved May 31, 2022, from: https://documents-dds-ny.un.org/doc/UNDOC/GEN/N18/234/82/PDF/N1823482.pdf?OpenElement
UNGA "Situation of human rights defenders. Note by the Secretary General. Report of the Special Rapporteur on the situation of human rights defenders, Mary Lawlor. States in denial: the long-term detention of human rights defenders. Trends and patterns in the use of long-term detention against human rights defenders" (19 July 2021) UN Doc A/76/143. Retrieved June 6, 2022, from: https://documents-dds-ny.un.org/doc/UNDOC/GEN/N21/196/67/PDF/N2119667.pdf?OpenElement
HRC "Report of the Special Rapporteur on the situation of human rights defenders, Margaret Sekaggya" (21 December 2011) UN Doc A/HRC/19/55. Retrieved June 6, 2022, from: https://documents-dds-ny.un.org/doc/UNDOC/GEN/G11/175/06/PDF/G1117506.pdf?OpenElement
HRC "Human rights defenders operating in conflict and post-conflict situations. Report of the Special Rapporteur on the situation of human rights defenders" (30 December 2019) UN Doc A/HRC/43/51. Retrieved June 6, 2022, from: https://documents-dds-ny.un.org/doc/UNDOC/GEN/G19/355/08/PDF/G1935508.pdf?OpenElement
HRC "Final warning: death threats and killings of human rights Defenders. Report of the Special Rapporteur on the situation of human rights defenders, Mary Lawlor" (24 December 2020) UN Doc A/HRC/46/35. Retrieved June 6, 2022, from: https://documents-dds-ny.un.org/doc/UNDOC/GEN/G20/355/11/PDF/G2035511.pdf?OpenElement
HRC "Summary of the Human Rights Council panel discussion on the promotion and protection of human rights in the context of peaceful protests prepared by the Office of the United Nations High Commissioner for Human Rights" (19 December 2011) UN Doc A/HRC/19/40. Retrieved May 31, 2022, from: https://documents-dds-ny.un.org/doc/UNDOC/GEN/G11/174/57/PDF/G1117457.pdf?OpenElement
Special Rapporteur on human rights defenders. (2022) "About human rights defenders". Retrieved June 6, 2022, from: www.ohchr.org/en/special-procedures/sr-human-rights-defenders/about-human-rights-defenders
OHCHR (2004). Fact Sheet No. 29, Human Rights Defenders: Protecting the Right to Defend Human Rights, No. 29. Retrieved June 6, 2022, from: www.refworld.org/docid/479477470.html
World Conference on Human Rights in Vienna. Vienna Declaration and Programme of Action (25 June 1993). Retrieved 3 June, from: www.ohchr.org/sites/default/files/vienna.pdf

Nuremberg Military Tribunals

NMT Case 3, the Justice Case (*USA v. Josef Altstoetter et al. 1947*). Retrieved June 6, 2022, from: http://nuremberg.law.harvard.edu/transcripts/3-transcript-for-nmt-3-justice-case?seq=10890.

EU

Charter of Fundamental Rights of the European Union [2012] OJ C 326
Council of the EU (Foreign Affairs). Ensuring protection. European Union Guidelines on human rights defenders [2008]. Retrieved 4 June, 2022, from: www.eeas.europa.eu/sites/default/files/eu_guidelines_hrd_en.pdf

ICTR

The Prosecutor v. Ferdinand Nahimana, Jean-Bosco Barayagwiza, Hassan Ngeze (Appeal Judgment), ICTR-99–52-A (28 November 2007). Retrieved 4 June, 2022, from: www.refworld.org/cases,ICTR,48b5271d2.html

OAS

Baruch Ivcher Bronstein v. Peru, IACHR Series C No. 74, (6 February 2001)

COE

Ezelin v. France, App no 11800/85 (ECtHR, 26 April 1991)
Handyside v. the United Kingdom App no 5493/72 (ECtHR, 7 December 1976)
Navalnyy and Yashin v. Russia App no 76204/11 (ECtHR, 4 December 2014)
Parti Socialiste de Turquie (STP) et autres v. Turquie, App no 26482/95 (ECtHR, 12 November 2003)
Soulas et autres v. France App no 15948/03 (ECtHR, 10 July 2008)

OSCE

Guidelines on Freedom of Peaceful Assembly, 2nd edition. Warsaw, Strasbourg, OSCE Office for Democratic Institutions and Human Rights (ODIHR), 2010

US

US Constitution, amend. I, December 15, 1791

8 Human rights defenders
The European multilevel framework

After the DHRD in 1998 and the creation of a thematic mechanism on the situation of human rights defenders in 2000, new regional, supranational, and even national mechanisms have been created for the implementation of DHRD in a multilevel system (Bennet et al., 2016). However, this multilevel system is still imperfect: first, the focus on the protection should not only be on the physical safety and protection of the legal subject, i.e., human rights defenders. Protection and security are necessary conditions for exercising human defenders' rights, but the state's positive obligations extend beyond this. They must guarantee all the instrumental rights, not only the right to protection. The instrumental rights established by the DHRD are based on rights having a binding effect as they are based on treaties: these are human rights.

Second, there is insufficient development of the mechanisms for guaranteeing the exercise of the right to promote and protect human rights. This is directly related to the previous compliance of positive and negative state obligations regarding human rights. Hence, the creation of new guarantees is necessary to address the challenges brought about by globalization.

Third, regarding the change in the paradigm of legal subjects following the legal recognition of human rights defenders: the connections and referrals between international and constitutional law must be defined and improved so that the promotion and protection of human rights becomes a right instead of a duty of individuals and groups. This duty is not legal. It is the assumption of a forced obligation caused mainly by the ineffectiveness and paralysis of international, regional, and constitutional mechanisms. This change in paradigm shows that for human rights to be effective, it is important and absolutely necessary to be able to count on the collaboration of civil society, but not on the assumption of positive obligations by individuals (Gavara de Cara, 2007).

The multilevel effect of the UN thematic mechanism on the situation of human rights defenders in regional human rights systems in Europe

Even though we may say that there is a multilevel system for the protection of human rights defenders (Bennet et al., 2016; Saura-Freixes 2016), the system is

DOI: 10.4324/9780429264016-8

imperfect despite its existence as a trend or part of the constitutionalization of international law. This aspect is not strengthened enough yet. I consider the constitutionalization of international law as theorized by the works of Anne Peters (Peters, 2016, 2017). As for the internationalization of constitutional law, I began to work on my analysis by using the conceptions of Chang and Yeh (2012). The development of this multilevel system on human rights defenders is a trend coincident with processes under global constitutionalism. My analysis follows the conception of global constitutionalism laid out before by Peters and Kumm. However, I consider the multilevel system of human rights defenders according to Bennet in 2016, but with some differences in the axiological and theoretical basis. In my perspective, at present this multilevel system on human rights defenders is evolving accordingly with global constitutionalism, even if it is imperfect. The other main difference is my focus on instrumental rights rather than the subject of rights. After analyzing rights, my conclusions focus on the changing paradigm of the subject; the focus is not on the protection of subjects, but the protection of rights. This is closer to the EU's perspective. However, I must assume and point out that, to be honest, it is difficult to achieve.

The reasons for the development of this multilevel system on human rights defenders can be summarized as follows: thanks to the thematic instrument of the United Nations, they have an institutional guarantee. By means of the reports of both the Special Representative, and later the Special Rapporteurs on the situation of human rights defenders, a doctrine on the rights contained in the DHRD exists. This thematic instrument allows for individual communications to be received, even without the previous consent of the concerned state. The Special Procedures of the United Nations are thematic mechanisms and, unlike treaty bodies, they do not require previous state acceptance. They have been created to precisely overcome the reservations of states as the subject of international investigations due to human rights violations. This is another example of the process of individualization in international law, where, as Carrillo Salcedo observed, the principle of human dignity prevails over the principle of sovereignty (Carrillo Salcedo, 1999). In spite of this, the binding character of these mechanisms are still considerably more limited than judicial or treaty-based systems. This, however, does not lessen their importance. At times, the international visibility of a dissident or human rights defender may contribute to ensuring his or her safety. In other cases, it may sadly add to their persecution.

Mention should be made of the effects generated by the creation of this thematic mechanism. The appointment of an UN Rapporteur on the situation of human rights defenders has had a spin-off effect on the regional mechanisms for the protection of human rights. Similar institutions have been recently created, such as Rapporteurships, at the Inter-American and African level. In other cases, previously existing organizations, such as the Council of Europe, have incorporated the protection of human rights defenders and the DHRD's rights using the protection of the European Convention from ECHR case law at the judiciary level, and the COE Commissioner for Human Rights. At the supranational level, the European Union has not created a similar institution, like Rapporteurships.

Instead, the EU has developed a twofold support policy *ad intra*, under the ECFR and the areas of freedom, security, and justice; and *ad extra*, considering human rights defenders as within the context of Common Foreign Policy, more specifically under the Union's external action. The EU Global Strategy on Foreign and Security Policy in 2016–2019 considered that: "The EU will invest in pivotal non-state actors. We will sharpen the means to protect and empower civic actors, notably human rights defenders, sustaining a vibrant civil society worldwide" (Questionnaire human rights defenders, EEAS, 2020). Particularly, the guidelines on human rights defenders, set in 2004 and revised in 2008, were strengthened by the Council Conclusion in June 2014; this was a turning point. For their implementation, the EU delegations and the embassies of Member States were necessary, even just for translation. An EU Liaison Officer on human rights defenders must be appointed by EU delegations abroad. The EU Guidelines on human rights defenders were integrated in the EU Human Rights and Democracy Country Strategies in 2012–2016 and in 2016–2020 (Questionnaire human rights defenders EEAS, OHCHR 2020).

This EU system on human rights defenders set a consortium of NGO–ProtectDefenders.eu–with 12 specialized NGOs able to work from the field, advocacy, campaigning on behalf of HRD, according to the principles set by article 21 TEU (ProtectDefenders.eu, 2022). This is a good example of cooperation between civil society and EU institutions. This system finally connects *ad intra* with the legal and constitutional framework of EU states, and even with local bodies. EU regions and cities that give shelter to human rights defenders rely on a particular system of temporal relocation that is not exactly the same as the EU asylum framework, since it is more complicated to operate.

The EU system characteristics *ad extra* differ from the EU system *ad intra*. The protection of fundamental rights in the EU *ad intra* provides for the indirect protection of the rights of human rights defenders under the DHRD by means of a supranational process based not on a specific policy on human rights defenders, but mostly on the system of EU fundamental rights. The EU *ad intra* system on defenders is based on the legal framework set up by the EU Charter of Fundamental Rights. This *ad intra* system and the EU policy on defenders is coherent with the requisites set by the Copenhagen Criteria (1993) and the framework of the EU area of freedom, security, and justice. Hence the EU, despite its existence an international organization, has an inherent constitutional function executed by means of three convergent core aspects: fundamental rights, democracy, and the rule of law.

This is why it would be apparently inconsistent, from a certain perspective, to set a specific EU institution or policy *ad intra* on human rights defenders. It would not be coherent with the Copenhagen Criteria to be part of the EU—or to continue to be in—to accept that the EU can have intra-state patterns of individuals persecuted inside the EU simply for the promotion or protection of human rights. In this case, the state should operate under the exclusionary system of progressive sanctions, even the exclusion of voting rights. But this is, and would be, an increasingly sensitive issue. It could be used by political interests of *ad intra* state movements, whose leaders could claim to be human rights defenders when they do not comply with the necessary criteria, or by EU Member States in order to enforce their frameworks on nationalistic terms when such an action is unnecessary.

Again, the protection and promotion of human rights is the exercise of an activity. But it must be respectful of the twofold system; the UN framework of the DHRD and the different regional systems set up later. In the EU there is primacy with EU law and the particularities of a stronger process of integration and constitutionalization. The connections and referrals between international and constitutional law must be defined and improved so that the promotion and protection of human rights becomes a right instead of the duty of individuals and groups, caused by the ineffectiveness and paralysis of international and constitutional mechanisms. This change in paradigm also shows that for human rights to be effective, it is important and necessary to be able to count on collaboration with civil society.

In this sense, the increasing relevance of non-state actors must be pointed out. The negative aspects of non-state actors are their responsibility for violations of human rights, and reciprocally, violations of the right to promote and protect human rights too. It is not only state actors who are behind the attacks and threats to human rights defenders. In this sense, the system of human rights protection is still imperfect.

Vulnerable groups of defenders are, however, part of the EU's problem. This is why, for instance, defenders of social and economic rights are often threatened or harassed by non-state actors in relation to business dealings. This is especially relevant to whistleblowers, requiring even the passing of the Directive (EU) 2019/1937 of the European Parliament and of the Council of 23 October 2019 on the protection of persons who report breaches of Union law. The UN Working Group on Business and Human rights "highlights the need for addressing the adverse impact of business activities on human rights defenders" (A/HRC/47/39/Add.2, 2021). In 2021, this UN Working Group set the "The Guiding Principles on Business and Human Rights: guidance on ensuring respect for human rights defenders", what is a remarkable effort to address the increasing responsibility of business as non state actors and to rise awareness on their action, without erasing the public responsibility of the state.

However, this is still an EU problem, for defenders are more exposed outside of the framework of trade unions. In the case of intellectual human rights defenders, they are not often visible as defenders, even in the EU, under the assumption that civil and political rights, such as freedom of thought, are not endangered. This problem mainly stems from a lack of complaints on academic freedom and the further invisibility of their work and risks in the academic domain (Quinn and Levine, 2014). LGBT human rights defenders are always among the most vulnerable groups, also *ad intra* the EU. Gender perspectives are another prism to keep in mind, particularly because there is not nearly enough data on it. This is why one of the next objectives of the Fundamental Rights Agency of the EU is to collect more data on the subject. Even in the cases of those working in international organizations, such as the UN system, they always have a more complicated action as vulnerable group (Mulé, 2018). Journalists are human rights defenders, that due to their public actions or claims become targets of threats, harassments, and even legal consequences that can vary depending on the region and the intensity of the physical danger against them. Lawyers have to cope with complicated patterns even in complaints to European institutions such as the European Court of Human Rights. Lastly, hate speech is a threat against anyone who dares to challenge a violation of human rights. Another outrageous practice is weaponizing fake news to defeat dissidents and human rights defenders. But we are living an underpinning trend on the system of freedom of expression around the world, even inside the EU or the ECHR system of human rights and fundamental rights, where freedom of expression undertakes a twofold individual and social function.

Human rights defenders and the Council of Europe

Cassese reminds us that 1945 is the constitutive year of the system of international law after the Second World War (Cassese, 2005). 1998 is, from my perspective, the turning point in the system of human rights, giving birth to the twenty-first century for international law. 1998 is a year of transition, marking the beginning of some of the main challenges of globalization. Three main events converge: the entry into force of the Protocol 11 to the European Convention on Human Rights; the adoption of the Rome Statute of the International Criminal Court on the 17 July 1998; and finally, the setting of the Declaration on the Right and Responsibility of Individuals, Groups and Organs of Society to Promote and Protect Universally Recognized Human Rights and Fundamental Freedoms, on 9 December 1998. What these three events have in common is that they are a step further toward the "individualization" of international law being consolidated in the present, as theorized by Peters (2016). In 1999, just one year after these three events, Tomuschat pointed out this rising trend in international law, "progressively moving from a sovereignty-centred to a ... individual-oriented system" (Tomuschat, 1999, cited in Peters, 2016, p. 2). However, in 1999 this trend was not yet enough consolidated, according to Peters (Peters, 2016, pp. 3–4) and Tomuschat (1999). In the 1999 General Course on Public International Law at the Hague Academy of International Law, Tomuschat considered that "The transformation from international law as a State-centered system to an individual-centered system has not yet found a definitive new equilibrium" (Tomuschat, 1999, cited in Peters, 2016, p. 3). Peters' theory on the Individualization of international law is present in her work *Beyond human rights* (2014, 2016). Peters states that there is a changing paradigm shift from state sovereignty to the individual. There are two main aspects from her theoretical essay that we are going to consider; thus, the use of the term "individual" as concept, and not just "human being" as an abstract entity, or "human dignity" as an axiological principle or value. This is not a mere subtle difference. It is maybe the symptomatic change from the paradigm of human rights set after the Second World War, and the changing paradigm of globalization, that can be related to the three main events previously highlighted. One is the entry into force of Protocol No. 11 to the European Convention of Human Rights, in 1998. It is not by hazard, when considered today, that we find this "revolutionary" heading on the famous article 34 on "Individual applications". It is reproduced below:

> Article 34 – Individual applications
> The Court may receive applications from any person, non-governmental organisation or group of individuals claiming to be the victim of a violation by one of the High Contracting Parties of the rights set forth in the Convention or the protocols thereto. The High Contracting Parties undertake not to hinder in any way the effective exercise of this right.

This trend on the individualization of international law (Peters, 2016) is related to the changing paradigm of legal personhood in international law, conforming to it:

> Individuals not only have numerous "subjective" international rights (in the plural) but also are further entitled to international legal subjectivity (international legal personality) in virtue of their personhood on the basis of customary international law and general principles of law and as an aspect of their human right to legal personality. (Peters, 2016, p. 8)

The development of the European framework on human rights defenders is part of the process of the individualization of international law.

Human rights defenders and the European Court of Human Rights

With Protocol No. 11, individuals acquired direct access to an international court, complying then with one of the requisites for personhood in international law. This led to correlative changes at the constitutional level, with the transfer of more constitutional functions to international institutions and organizations. Almost a decade later, Wildhaber, the first President of the European Court of Human Rights after the change (1998–2007) made a comparison of the new situation with the beginning of the twentieth century when states were "only sovereign actors" entitled to "treat citizens and foreigners alike as objects, whose legal status and whose human rights were defined solely by national law" (Wildhaber, 2007, p. 522). Conversely, the legal status of individuals at the beginning of the twenty-first century was quite different:

> We end the 20th and begin the 21st century with individuals who have become subjects of international law and a European Court of Human Rights which is the most spectacular illustration of this change in paradigms. In the same vein, modern sovereignty should be understood as requiring respect for, rather than the breach of human rights, minority rights, democracy, and the rule of law. (Wildhaber, 2007, p. 522)

The process of human rights building in Europe is not only related to the Council of Europe. More and more, the EU must be a prominent actor on human rights. After the adoption of the EU Charter of Fundamental Rights and the Treaty of Lisbon, entered into force in 2009, the EU promised to adhere to the European Convention of Human Rights. Enrich insists that behind the final adhesion there is not merely an institutional strategy. In this process of convergence, we find men and women, citizens and politicians, that share the common will for human rights in Europe in their two main organizations, the European Union and the Council of Europe:

> Elle sera vraisemblablement l'aboutissement d'un long processus grâce aux efforts de nombreux femmes ethommes politiques et citoyens européens, qui ont mis leurs espoirs dans une protection uniforme des droits de l'homme en Europe. Elle sera aussi le début d'une nouvelle histoire, que nous souhaitons longue etfructueuse, fondée sur la coopération entre les deux organisations internationales européennes plus représentatives: l'Union européenne et le Conseil de l'Europe, et leurs respectives Cours, la Cour de Justice de l'Union européenne et la Cour européenne des droits de l'homme, si différenciés à leurs débuts dans les années 50 et si proches aujourd'hui. (Enrich, 2011, pp. 227–228)

Article 34 opened the door for individuals to submit direct complaints on human rights to an international body. In present times, subjects are allowed, under article 34, to submit complaints: "any person, non-governmental organization or group of individuals claiming to be the victim of a violation". Thus, they are correlative to subjects that can potentially be considered human rights defenders, as recognized in the title of the DHRD: Individuals and groups. Organs of society means national human rights institutions. But NHRI are not allowed, by article 34 ECHR, as governmental organization, to submit complaints due to their hybrid "statist" nature. It does not mean that they do not act as human rights defenders. Inversely, the Venice Commission in 2019 adopted the "Principles on the protection and promotion of the ombudsman institution" ("The Venice Principles"). According to these principles, if an ombudsman, in a single or collective formation, complies with the criteria of impartiality, they shall not follow any order of authorities, and their mandate must cover public administration and the protection of human rights and fundamental freedoms can be considered a human rights defender. This is why, reciprocally, they and their staff-office must have a guarantee of immunity, and "States shall refrain from taking any action aiming at or resulting in the suppression of the Ombudsman Institution or in any hurdles to its effective functioning, and shall effectively protect it from any such threats" (Venice Commission, Strasbourg, 18 March 2019).

Thus, by means of the procedural article 34, it was possible to open the ECHR to a judiciary dimension where citizenship and sovereignty were not the most relevant aspect: "The right to apply to the Court is absolute and admits of no hindrance. This principle implies freedom to communicate with the organs of the

ECHR" (ECHR, 2022). Consequently, the relevant criterion to apply to the ECHR is not citizenship, but jurisdiction, accepting that the ECHR is an "instrument of European Public order" (*Al Skeini and others v. the United Kingdom*, 2011, para. 141). It can be applied even to cases out of boundaries, as in the case of *Al-skeini and others v. the United Kingdom*, 7 July 2011. In this case, the ECHR has an extraterritorial application based on the control of the state executive, or judicial functions in accordance with international law:

> the Court has recognised the exercise of extra-territorial jurisdiction by a Contracting State when, through the consent, invitation or acquiescence of the Government of that territory, it exercises all or some of the public powers normally to be exercised by that Government (Banković, cited above, § 71). Thus where, in accordance with custom, treaty or other agreement, authorities of the Contracting State carry out executive or judicial functions on the territory of another State, the Contracting State may be responsible for breaches of the Convention thereby incurred, as long as the acts in question are attributable to it rather than to the territorial State. (*Al-skeini and others v. the United Kingdom*, 2011, para. 134)

The extraterritorial application of the European Convention of Human Rights is related with the structure and extension of the right to a fair remedy for human rights defenders, as set by articles 9.4 and 9.5 DHRD. Article 9.4 sets "the unhindered right to have access to international bodies" and article 9.5 DHRD builds the 1998 state responsibility to conduct a prompt and impartial investigation on human rights using this jurisdictional criterion:

> The State shall conduct a prompt and impartial investigation or ensure that an inquiry takes place whenever there is reasonable ground to believe that a violation of human rights and fundamental freedoms has occurred in any territory under its jurisdiction. (article 9.5 DHRD 1998)

However, more and more, human rights defenders can fall under the framework of ECHR individuals, NGOs or associations claiming the violation of their human rights, or even lawyers applying to the ECHR, particularly in rising cases of some eastern countries. This is why in May 2017, the COE Secretary General launched a mechanism to "assist human rights defenders who believe that they have been subject to reprisals for their interaction with the Council of Europe" (COE Secretary General, 21 December 2018). This mechanism was created with the designation of a Private Office procedure as a Focal point to coordinate measures to be able to report directly on them. But in 2019 it was reformed after interaction with the Council of Europe. The Procedure:

- Allows external direct reporting (e.g. by human rights defenders and non-governmental organisations) in addition to Council of Europe entities;
- Is triggered by information provided to the Secretary General's Private Office focal point;

- Seeks to determine the accuracy of the allegation and define follow-up action, considering whether the reprisal, or risk of reprisal, meets a minimum level of severity, upon which it will warrant consideration. The assessment of this minimum level will depend on the circumstances of the case; there should be a reasonable degree of causality between the interaction or the intention to interact and the alleged reprisal; a submission that is too vague or general, contains misleading information, makes use of offensive language, is based on inaccurate facts or spurious allegations, or is in any other way unsubstantiated, will not be considered;
- Continues to include the assessment and the proposals for follow-up action being submitted to the Secretary General;
- Results in a report on the types of cases which will be presented annually to the Committee of Ministers (or more regularly, if circumstances require). (COE Secretary General, 2022)

However, the revised private office procedure to investigate reprisals against human rights defenders is different from those of the European Court of Human Rights, the Council of Europe Commissioner of Human Rights, and the Commission of Venice. All of them have distinct functions to undertake on behalf of human rights defenders under the COE framework. The European Court of Human Rights is the key actor, but this does not mean that all of the other non-judicial measures that apply to human rights defenders are not necessary, and even complementary.

According to Oetheimer, a harmonization of rights emerged from the case law of the European Court of Human Rights in the domain of civil and political rights, and the margin of appreciation (2001). The margin of appreciation plays a particular function for key rights of the ECHR, such as freedom of expression, which challenges internal legal systems, creating a dialogue between courts, and even the cultural and legal backgrounds of different countries (Oetheimer, 2001). For social rights the situation is slightly different. De Carreras reminds us that the most relevant change to emerge at the end of the twentieth century in Europe was the external dimension of rules for constitutional social states under the rule of law (De Carreras, 1991, p. 46). The social dimension of the state would be more often challenged, as the COVID-19 pandemic unfortunately reminded us. During the last economic crisis in the twenty-first century, criticism is merited due to the progressive European dismantlement of the social state's pillars.

In the last report by the Secretary General of the Council of Europe, Thorbjørn Jagland stated that "Since 2009, the Council of Europe has emphasized that the economic crisis and the austerity measures should not result in the deterioration of protection for social rights" (Secretary General of the Council of Europe, Thorbjørn Jagland, 2019, p.19). The constitutional function of the state is extended to the guarantee of fundamental rights, including social rights as well. The two main basic rights are education and health, and both have been diminished in Europe. There is a lesson to learn from the 2020 global pandemic, especially in European countries. The dismantlement of the social state contributes to the dismantlement of the rule of law. The European Convention on Human Rights traditionally covers civil and political rights—but health can fall under the umbrella of articles 2 or 8 ECHR—and the European Social Charter is more specifically associated with social rights, like the health of workers (COE 2019). Thus, there is a twofold dimension to rights required by the United Nations Vienna Declaration of 1993, which established the interdependence of human rights at the end of Cold War (para.5): "All human rights are universal, indivisible and interdependent and interrelated". The interdependence between rights that are civil, political, economic, cultural, and social are a requisite for human rights defenders. They must accept the interdependence of rights. This is a backlash to the division that was common after the Second World War, and in the aftermath of the Cold War. The COE body charged with the guarantee of social rights is the European Committee of Social Rights (ECtSR). However, the ECSR do not have the same system as the ECtHR for filing individual complaints, because the ECSR cannot accept individual applications. The European Committee of Social Rights has different systems of guarantee for the Social Rights of the 1961 Charter, revised in 1996, structured by the collective complaints procedure and the reporting system. The reporting system is based on reports written by state parties. The Collective Complaints Procedure is enacted when collective complaints are submitted by collective actors, as for the accepting state parties of the Protocol 158. The European collective actors are the European Trade Union Confederation (ETUC) for employees, and the "Business Europe and International Organisation of Employers (OIE), for employers" (COE, 2022). The INGOs accepted by the Council of Europe holding participatory status (COE, 2022) can have a role too given that their task is to promote and protect human rights.

National human rights institutions can be active actors for economic and social rights, but they are outside of the Collective Complaints Procedure due to their hybrid statist status. Hence, individuals, as human rights defenders, can complain to the European Court of Human Rights, but they cannot complaint to the European Committee of Social Rights. This creates an unbalanced system for human rights defenders depending on their defence of civil and political rights, or economic and social rights. The economic and social rights can be submitted to the ECtHR, but always under the umbrella of some of the other rights extended by the criterion of interpretation in "present times". At the same time, this leads to a lack of control regarding the compliance of the European Social Charter. Finally, all this can have a secondary effect: the reduction of the social constitutional state in Europe. In this situation, the destinatary of social measures and the bearers of social rights cannot complain about it as an individual. Particularly, for the individuals the right to a fair remedy granted by article 9 of the Declaration on Human Rights Defenders could be incomplete if the clause in paragraph 9.4 is not fulfilled for economic and social rights, and not accessible in terms of individual complaints:

> To the same end, and in accordance with applicable international instruments and procedures, everyone has the right, individually and in association with others, to unhindered access to and communication with international bodies

with general or special competence to receive and consider communications on matters of human rights and fundamental freedoms. (A/RES/53/144, 8 March 1999, art.9.4)

Global experience shows how the reduction, or the lack of constitutional function by the states, assuming the constitutional guarantee of rights, including social rights, is sometimes replaced by the action (not by the will) of individuals. They must promote and protect human rights to enforce them, because neither the state nor an international body, neglecting their constitutional function, can guarantee them. But the paradoxical and perverse effect of the privatization of constitutional functions is what Gavara de Cara calls the undesirable assumption of positive obligations by individuals (Gavara de Cara, 2007). This is not acceptable under the constitutional framework on the fundamental rights of the state, because the function of states is to protect and guarantee human and fundamental rights, not only to protect the physical integrity of individuals. This is at the basis of the Basic Law of Bonn, article 1: "Human dignity shall be inviolable. To respect and protect it shall be the duty of all state authority".

If we can observe a process of "constitutionalization" of civil and political rights at the international level, which are strongly present in the COE framework, it is less clear in the case of the social and economic rights in Europe. Balaguer Callejón reminds us that since economic interpretation of the fundamental rights are part of the European public debate, it can erode not only social and economic rights but also pluralism, democracy and citizenship. Europe and the EU constitutional function are being pressured by the economic crisis and the economic functional interpretation of the EU (Balaguer Callejón, 2013).

Another paradox in the COE system is the lack of possibility for accessing different instrumental rights of the Declaration on human rights defenders, because if there is the possibility to claim the European Court of Human Rights, then there is no possibility to claim another international body, with less international repercussions. Even if another international body, like the UN Special Procedure on the situation of human rights defenders, has no judiciary competence, its function is to enable a constructive dialogue with governments by using allegation letters or an urgent appeal as the result of a violation of the Declaration on human rights defenders. But despite the Special Procedures are without judiciary power, simultaneous complaints are not allowed. Then, even in this case, the criteria followed by the ECHR is more restrictive than in the Inter-American Court. It seems, from my perspective, too extensive an interpretation of art. 35 ECHR "of the criteria of admissibility for individual complaints and the requisite of the interdiction of international ne bis in idem".

With the exhaustion of domestic remedies and strict limited exceptions, the main requisite of art. 35 ECHR is domestic jurisdiction. The second worthwhile requisite reminds us that the interdiction of international *ne bis in idem*, which has a particular impact on human rights defenders, limiting their access to the UN Special Procedure on the situation of human rights defenders. The consequence is that human rights defenders could face a dilemma: to choose between claiming the ECtHR or accessing the UN Special Procedure, with an international reporting impact. This criterion was set to avoid the duplication of procedures, and what is called "forum shopping" (Pizarro Sotomayor, 2009, p. 77). Pizarro Sotomayor (2009, p. 7) recalls that the only UN Human rights treaty body that does not require this criterion is the Committee on the Elimination of Racial Discrimination (CERD). This criterion could seem quite reasonable in the case of the Treaty Bodies, such as the UN Committee of Human Rights, as the body of guarantee for the ICCPR, but this was not very consistent for all the Special Procedures.

However, in the case *Kavala v. Turkey*, 10 December 2019, the court accepted a previous intervention and the urgent appeal procedure of the UN Working Group on Arbitrary Detention. The UN Working Group developed this "urgent action" procedure for cases in which there are sufficiently reliable allegations that a person may be detained arbitrarily, and that the continuation of the detention may entail a serious threat for his or her health, physical or mental integrity or life. The court dismissed the objection on art. 35.2. ECHR by the government, because there was no evidence of the personal lodging of the application to the UN Working Group. The complaint was not exactly the same:

> The Court further observes that it has not been established that the applicant or his close relatives lodged any appeal before the United Nations bodies (compare Peraldi (dec.), cited above, where the applicant's brother had submitted a request to the working group, asking it to examine the applicant's situation rather than his own), or that they had actively participated in any proceedings before them. In this connection, it reiterates that, under its case-law, if the complainants before the two institutions are not identical (see Folgerø and Others v. Norway (dec.), no. 15472/02, 14 February 2006), the "application" to the Court cannot be considered as being "substantially the same as a matter that has … been submitted". (*Kavala v. Turkey*, 10 December 2019, para. 94)

In the case of Special Procedures, like the UN Special Rapporteur on the situation of human rights defenders, art. 35.2 ECHR, from my perspective, should not be applied using a strict interpretation because the nature of this charter-based mechanism differs from that of a judiciary forum. In the case of the UN Special Procedures, there is no binding decision, nor a quasi-judiciary function, their task is just to set a "constructive dialogue". The UN Special Procedure on the situation of human rights defenders exchanges letters or communications with the UN delegation of the concerned state about the situation and rights of human rights defenders. These are later made public in a report. This is why, in my opinion, Special Procedures should not be considered under the prism of the duplication of procedures—the function of an international court and the function of Special Rapporteur are not the same.

To eliminate the possibility for HRD of sending a communication could be hindering the legal system on human rights defenders and the international dimension of their appeal. This lesser possibility of complaining could challenge article 9.4 of the Declaration on human rights defenders and the right to communicate with international bodies.

Human rights defenders and the COE Commissioner of Human Rights

In Europe, neither the EU, nor the ECHR developed a Rapporteurship on human rights defenders. This is the main difference between the UN and other regional systems. In the COE, human rights defenders' protection is enforced by means of the case law of the ECHR, the European Committee on Economic and Social Rights and the Commissioner of Human Rights. However, the functions of each body are different. In the case of the Commissioner of Human Rights, the mandate is clear and direct, but not judicial or quasi-judiciary. In this case, if the COE Commissioner for Human Rights had institutional character, the role would be similar to that of a Rapporteurship. The COE Commissioner for Human Rights "has a specific duty concerning the support of human rights defenders, their protection and the development of an enabling environment for their activities" (CommDH(2019)10, 2019, para. 2).

This specific role comes from the adoption of a Declaration by the Committee of Ministers on 6 February 2008 (CommDH(2019)10, 2019). In this regard, it is the Commissioner's task to provide advice and recommendations to member states with a view to assisting them in fulfilling their obligations vis-à-vis defenders, raising issues about defenders' working environment, risks and cases related to, in a dialogue with authorities and to let it known for public interest (CommDH (2019) 10, para. 2) and to undertake regularly consultations with human rights defenders.

The power to intervene before the ECtHR is particularly relevant in cases related to human rights defenders. The COE Commissioner for Human Rights Dunja Mijatovic intervened before the Strasbourg case as a third party in *Kavala v. Turkey* (10 December 2019). The ECtHR considered the extended detention of a human rights defender, with the ulterior purpose of reducing him to silence. This situation had a chilling effect on civil society. The ECtHR ruled in violation of article 5 § 1 of the convention on account of the lack of reasonable suspicion that the applicant had committed an offence.

The most relevant contemporary cases and applications with third-party intervention of the COE Commissioner for Human Rights are:

- *Kavala v. Turkey* (Application No. 28749/18)
- *Huseynov v. Azerbaijan* (Application No. 1/16)
- *EcoDefence and others v. the Russian Federation* (Application No. 9988/13)
- *Estemirova v. the Russian Federation* (Application No. 42705/11)
- *Yunusova and Yunusov v. Azerbaijan* (Application No. 68817/14)
- *Jafarov v. Azerbaijan* (Application No. 69981/14)
- *Mammadli v. Azerbaijan* (Application No. 47145/14)
- *Intigam Aliyev v. Azerbaijan* (Application No. 68762/14)
- *Hilal Mammadov v. Azerbaijan* (Application No. 81553/12)b (Commissioner for Human Rights, 2022)

In the leading case of the ECHR, *Aliyev v. Azerbayan*, 20 September 2018, there is a specific use of the term "human rights defenders" to identify a lawyer. It is worthwhile to recognize the role of human rights defenders in the system of COE human rights:

> Firstly, as regards the applicant's status, the Court notes that it is not disputed between the parties that the applicant is a human-rights defender and, more specifically, a human-rights lawyer. [...] In line with the international materials cited above (see paragraphs 88–92 above) ... the Court attaches particular importance to the special role of human-rights defenders in promoting and defending human rights, including in close cooperation with the Council of Europe, and their contribution to the protection of human rights in the member States. (*Aliyev v. Azerbayan*, 2018, para. 208)

This dual system is different in the EU. The EU has a twofold system based on the protection *ad intra* and *ad extra* of human rights defenders, as is developed below. But the COE legal framework on human rights defenders has a twofold system based on the existence of two different institutions of protection for defenders with two main notable aspects: the judiciary ECtHR case law; and the protection of human rights defenders by the COE Commissioner for Human Rights. In this sense, despite not having a Special Rapporteurship on human rights defenders, the double system of COE is based on a judiciary guarantee with the ECtHR *fora*, and another institutional guarantee, the Commissioner for Human Rights.

The COE Commissioner for Human Rights can undertake visits to specific countries of the ECHR area, write reports, make statements on human rights defenders, and consider them in their Human Rights Comments. In some countries it is quite relevant to be in dialogue with national human rights institutions, that must comply the Paris Principles. In 2018, human rights defenders were explicitly recognized as "key partners of the Council of Europe Commissioner for Human Rights (hereinafter the Commissioner) and her Office" (CommDH(2019)10, para. 2).

The COE Commissioner for Human Rights has a specific duty concerning the support of human rights defenders, their protection, and the development of an enabling environment for their activities. This body provides advice and recommendations to Member States with a view toward assisting them in fulfilling their obligations vis-à-vis defenders; The COE Commissioner for human rights rises awareness related to the working environment of human rights defenders and cases of those who are at risk, both through her dialogue with authorities and publicly. The Commissioner intervenes as third party before the European Court of Human Rights in cases concerning human rights defenders. The COE Commissioner must be in contact with human rights defenders and organize regular consultations with them (CommDH(2019)10).

The OSCE Guidelines on human rights defenders

The OSCE is a relevant international organization in the field of human rights. It is, historically, an organization with precedent for human rights defenders. This is why it is necessary to mention it along with the OSCE's work in the European area. The Helsinki Final Act (1975) gave birth to the "right to know and to act". It is considered a precedent to the right to promote and protect human rights. After the evolution of the organization, it is now relevant for human rights defenders in the OSCE area, the Office for Democratic Institutions and Human Rights (ODIHR). This is the OSCE body located in Warsaw (Poland) which through tasks and actions supports human rights defenders. Since 2016, the ODIHR has been training and providing workshops for human rights defenders, focusing on the education, promotion, and security for human rights defenders in their countries and the OSCE area:

> In line with its mandate to assist OSCE participating States to implement their commitments, ODIHR has long been engaged in promoting the protection of human rights defenders. This is done through regular monitoring and reporting on the situation of defenders across the OSCE region, provision of expert advice and legislative reviews, raising of OSCE participating States' awareness about their obligations to protect defenders, and facilitating dialogue between participating States and civil society on issues related to human rights defenders' work. ODIHR also supports national human rights institutions (NHRIs) and other defenders through different activities, building their capacity to conduct human rights monitoring and reporting in a safe and secure manner, including using new technologies (OSCE, ODIHR, 2021).

The setting of the OSCE Guidelines on human rights defenders (2014) created a tool to guide countries in the implementation and development of the commitments achieved in this area. In 1990, during the Copenhagen Meeting of the Conference on the Human Dimension of the CSCE, the countries of the OSCE area reaffirmed:

> Their commitment to ensure effectively the rights of the individual to know and act upon human rights and fundamental freedoms, and to contribute actively, individually or in association with others, to their promotion and protection.
> (CSCE, Copenhagen, 1990)

The year 1992 was particularly important for the rights of NGOs and their increasing involvement in the CSCE's (later OSCE) activities. In 1994, the commitment achieved by the Budapest Summit Declaration improved the Human Dimension in OSCE activities with a specific mention of human rights defenders under the rule of law: "The participating States emphasize (…) the need for protection of human rights defenders (para.18)". The use of this term is remarkable, even before the UN Declaration on Human Rights Defenders in 1998. The 2010 Astana Commemorative Declaration Towards a Security Community highlighted, for OSCE countries to: "value the important role played by civil society and free media in helping us to ensure full respect for human rights, fundamental freedoms, democracy, including free and fair elections, and the rule of law" (OSCE, 2010).

However, as highlighted by Steinbrück Platise, Mosser and Peters, the work of the OSCE does not usually have the same binding character as other international organizations. These commitments are supposed to be considered political commitments, more than having a real strong binding legal effect (Steinbrück Platise et al., 2019).

References

Balaguer Callejón, F. (2013). "Una interpretación constitucional de la crisis económica". *ReDCE*, 19.
Bennet, K., Ingleton, D., Nah, M. A., and Savage, J. (2016). *Critical Perspectives on the Security and Protection of Human Rights Defenders*. Oxon & New York: Routledge.
Gavara de Cara, J.C. (2007). "La vinculación positiva de los poderes públicos a los derechos fundamentales". *Teoría y Realidad Constitucional*, 20, 277–320.
Carrillo Salcedo, J. A. (1999). *Dignidad frente a Barbarie, La Declaración Universal de Derechos Humanos, cincuenta años después*. Madrid: Trotta.
Cassese, A. (2005). *International Law*. Oxford: Oxford University Press.
COE Secretary General (2018). "Private Office procedure on Human Rights Defenders". *News 2018*.
De Carreras, F. (1991). "Norma y ordenamiento jurídico en la Constitución Española". *Revista Del Centro de Estudios Constitucionales*, May-August.
Enrich, M. (2011). "L'adhésion de l'Union européenne à la Convention européenne des droits de l'homme". In M. Sales (Ed.), *El sistema multinivel de los derechos fundamentales en Europa*. Bellaterra: Universitat Autònoma de Barcelona.
Mulé, N. J. (2018). "LGBTQI-identified human rights defenders: courage in the face of adversity at the United Nations". *Gender & Development*, 26(1).
Oetheimer, M. (2001). *L'harmonisation de la liberté d'expression en Europe: Contribution à l'étude de l'article 10 de la Convention européenne des droits de l'homme et de son application en Autriche et au Royaume-Uni*. Paris: Pedone.
Peters, A. (2016). *Beyond Human Rights: The Legal Status of the Individual in International Law*. Cambridge: Cambridge University Press.
Peters, A. (2017). "Constitutionalisation". *MPIL Research Paper Series 8*, 8.
Peters, A. (2017). "Proportionality as a global constitutional principle". In F. A. Lang & A. Wiener (Eds), *Handbook on Global Constitutionalism*. Cheltenham: Edward Elgar.
Pizarro Sotomayor, A. (2009). "The rule of the duplication of procedures in the regional systems of human rights". *Revista Panameña de Política*, 8.
Quinn, R. and Levine, J. (2014). "Intellectual-HRDs and claims for academic freedom under human rights law". *The International Journal of Human Rights*, 18(7–8), 898–920.
Saura-Freixes, N. (2016) *Human Rights Defenders: el derecho a promover y proteger los derechos humanos*. Madrid: UNED.
Steinbrück Platise, M., Mosser, C., and Peters, A. (2019). *The Legal Framework of the OSCE*. Cambridge: Cambridge University Press.
Tomuschat, C. (1999). "International law: Ensuring the survival of mankind on the eve of a new century: General course on public international law". *Recueil Des Cours*.
Wildhaber, L. (2007). "The European Court of Human Rights: The past, the present, the future". *American University International Law Review*, 22(4), 521–538.

The European multilevel framework 195

Documents

Treaties

Additional Protocol to the European Social Charter Providing for a System of Collective Complaints, Strasbourg (adopted 9 November 1995, entered into force 9 November 1995) ETS No. 158

American Convention on Human Rights (adopted 22 November, 1969, entered into force 18 July 1978) 1144 UNTS 123, OASTS No. 36 ("Pact of San Jose, Costa Rica", ACHR)

Charter of the United Nations, (adopted 24 October 1945) 1 UNTS XVI

Consolidated Version of the Treaty on European Union [2012] OJ C 326/13

Convention for the Protection of Human Rights and Fundamental Freedoms, as amended, (adopted 4 November 1950, entered into force 3 September 1953) ETS No. 005 (ECHR)

European Social Charter (adopted 18 October 1961, entered into force 26 february 1965) ETS No.035

European Social Charter (revised) (adopted 3 May 1996, entered into force 1 July 1999) ETS. No. 163

International Convention on the Elimination of All Forms of Racial Discrimination (adopted 7 March 1966, entered into force 4 January 1969) 660 UNTS 195

International Covenant on Civil and Political Rights (adopted 16 December 1966, entered into force 23 March 1976) 999 UNTS 171 (ICCPR)

International Covenant on Economic, Social and Cultural Rights (adopted 16 December 1966, entered into force 3 January 1976) 993 UNTS 3 (ICESCR)

Protocol no.11 to the Convention for the Protection of Human Rights and Fundamental Freedoms Restructuring the Control Machinery Established Thereby (adopted 11 May 1994, entered into force 1 November 1998) ETS No.155

Rome Statute of the International Criminal Court (adopted 17 July 1998, entered into force 1 July 2002) 2187 UNTS 3

European Social Charter (adopted 18 October 1961, entered into force 26 February 1965) ETS No.035

UN

Universal Declaration of Human Rights UNGA Res. 217A (III) (10 December 1948)

Declaration on the Right and Responsibility of Individuals, Groups and Organs of Society to Promote and Protect Universally Recognized Human Rights and Fundamental Freedoms UNGA A/RES/53/144 (8 March 1999)

HRC "The Guiding Principles on Business and Human Rights: guidance on ensuring respect for human rights defenders. Report of the Working Group on the issue of human rights and transnational corporations and other business enterprises" (22 June 2021) UN Doc A/HRC/47/39/Add.2 Retrieved June 7, 2022, from: https://documents-ddsny.un.org/doc/UNDOC/GEN/G21/161/49/PDF/G2116149.pdf?OpenElement

World Conference on Human Rights in Vienna. Vienna Declaration and Programme of Action (25 June 1993). Retrieved 3 June, from: www.ohchr.org/sites/default/files/vienna.pdf

EU

Charter of Fundamental Rights of the European Union [2012] OJ C 326

Council of the EU (Foreign Affairs). Ensuring protection. European Union Guidelines on human rights defenders [2008]. Retrieved 4 June, 2022, from: www.eeas.europa.eu/sites/default/files/eu_guidelines_hrd_en.pdf

Directive (EU) 2019/1937 of the European Parliament and of the Council of 23 October 2019 on the protection of persons who report breaches of Union law [2019] OJ L 305

European External Action Service. (2020). "Responses to the Questionnaire. Questionnaire on the situation of human rights defenders". Retrieved May 20, 2022, from: www.ohchr.org/sites/default/files/Documents/Issues/Defenders/GA73/IOS/EU_European_External_Action_Service.pdf

Shared Vision, Common Action a Stronger Europe. A Global Strategy on Foreign and Security Policy in 2016–2019. (June 2016). European Union Global Strategy. Retrieved May 20, 2022, from: www.eeas.europa.eu/sites/default/files/eugs_review_web_0.pdf

ProtectDefenders.eu. (2022). Retrieved May 20, 2022, from: https://protectdefenders.eu/about-us/

COE

COE Secretary General (21 December 2018). "News. Private Office procedure on Human Rights Defenders" Retrieved June 1, 2022, from: www.coe.int/en/web/secretary-general/-/private-office-procedure-on-human-rights-defenders

COE Secretary General (2019). Report by the Secretary General for the Ministerial Session in Helsinki, 16–17 May 2019, Ready for future challenges – Reinforcing the council of Europe, Council of Europe. Retrieved May 21, 2022, from: https://rm.coe.int/168093af03

COE Secretary General (2022). "Private Office procedure on human rights defenders interacting with the Council of Europe". Retrieved June 7, 2022, from: www.coe.int/en/web/secretary-general/procedure-human-rights-defenders

COE (2022). "The Collective Complaints Procedure". Retrieved June 7, 2022, from: www.coe.int/en/web/european-social-charter/collective-complaints-procedure1/-/asset_publisher/Kgl7CDHOF1Da/content/327th-session-of-the-european-committee-of-social-rights?inheritRedirect=false&redirect=https%3A%2F%2Fwww.coe.int%2Fen%2Fweb%2Feuropean-social-charter%2Fcollective-complaints-procedure1%3Fp_p_id%3D101_INSTANCE_Kgl7CDHOF1Da%26p_p_lifecycle%3D0%26p_p_state%3Dnormal%26p_p_mode%3Dview%26p_p_col_id%3Dcolumn-2%26p_p_col_pos%3D2%26p_p_col_count%3D7

COE "Declaration of the Committee of Ministers on Council of Europe action to improve the protection of human rights defenders and promote their activities" (6 February 2008). Retrieved June 7, 2022, from: www.ohchr.org/sites/default/files/Documents/Issues/Defenders/DeclarationHRDCoECommitteeMinisters.pdf

COE Commissioner for Human Rights. "Human rights defenders in the Council of Europe area: Current Challenges and Possible Solutions. Round-Table with human rights defenders organised by the Office of the Council of Europe Commissioner for Human Rights, Helsinki, 13–14 December 2018". (13–14 December 2018) CommDH (2019)10. Retrieved June 7, 2022, from: https://rm.coe.int/hr-defenders-in-the-coe-area-current-challenges-and-possible-solutions/168093aabf

COE Commissioner for Human Rights. "Human rights defenders in the Council of Europe area Round-Table organised by the Office of the Commissioner for Human

Rights of the Council of Europe, Strasbourg, 27–28 October 2011 Report". (29 March 2019) CommDH(2012)21. Retrieved June 7, 2022, from: https://rm.coe.int/ref/CommDH(2012)21

COE Commissioner for Human Rights. Third party intervention by the Council of Europe Commissioner for Human Rights under Article 36, paragraph 3, of the European Convention on Human Rights. Application No. 81553/12 *Hilal Mammadov v. Azerbaijan* (19 February 2015) CommDH(2015)5. Retrieved June 1, 2022, from: https://rm.coe.int/16806daae3

COE Commissioner for Human Rights. Third party intervention by the Council of Europe Commissioner for Human Rights under Article 36, paragraph 3, of the European Convention on Human Rights. Application No. 68762/14 *Intigam Aliyev v. Azerbaijan* (16 March 2015) CommDH(2015)6. Retrieved June 1, 2022, from: https://rm.coe.int/16806da609

COE Commissioner for Human Rights. Third party intervention by the Council of Europe Commissioner for Human Rights under Article 36, paragraph 3, of the European Convention on Human Rights. Application No. 47145/14 *Anar Mammadli v. Azerbaijan* (30 March 2015) CommDH(2015)7. Retrieved June 1, 2022, from: https://rm.coe.int/ref/CommDH(2015)7

COE Commissioner for Human Rights. Third party intervention by the Council of Europe Commissioner for Human Rights under Article 36, paragraph 3, of the European Convention on Human Rights. Application No. 69981/14 *Rasul Jafarov v. Azerbaijan* (30 March 2015) CommDH(2015)8 Retrieved June 1, 2022, from: https://rm.coe.int/ref/CommDH(2015)8

COE Commissioner for Human Rights. Third party intervention by the Council of Europe Commissioner for Human Rights under Article 36, paragraph 3, of the European Convention on Human Rights. Application No. 68817/14 *Leyla Yunusova and Arif Yunusov v. Azerbaijan* (16 April 2015) CommDH(2015)10 Retrieved June 1, 2022, from: https://rm.coe.int/ref/CommDH(2015)10

COE Commissioner for Human Rights. Third party intervention by the Council of Europe Commissioner for Human Rights under Article 36 of the European Convention on Human Rights Application No. 42705/11 *Svetlana Khusainovna Estemirova v. the Russian Federation* (14 March 2016) CommDH(2016)18. Retrieved June 1, 2022, from: https://rm.coe.int/ref/CommDH(2016)18

COE Commissioner for Human Rights. Third party intervention by the Council of Europe Commissioner for Human Rights under Article 36, paragraph 3, of the European Convention on Human Rights. Application n° 9988/13 *Ecodefence and others v. Russia and 48 other applications* (5 July 2017) CommDH(2017)22 Retrieved June 1, 2022, from: https://rm.coe.int/third-party-intervention-by-the-council-of-europe-commissioner-for-hum/1680731087

COE Commissioner for Human Rights. Third party intervention by the Council of Europe Commissioner for Human Rights under Article 36, paragraph 3, of the European Convention on Human Rights. App. No. 28749/18 *Mehmet Osman Kavala v. Turkey* (20 December 2018) CommDH(2018)30. Retrieved June 1 2022, from: https://rm.coe.int/third-party-intervention-before-the-european-court-of-human-rights-cas/1680906e27

COE Commissioner for Human Rights. Third party intervention by the Council of Europe Commissioner for Human Rights under Article 36, paragraph 3, of the European Convention on Human Rights. App. No. 1/16 *Emin Huseynov v. Azerbaijan* (28 September 2018) CommDH(2018)23. Retrieved June 7, 2022, from: https://rm.coe.int/third-party-intervention-before-the-european-court-of-human-rights-cas/16808e2966

European Commission for Democracy through Law-Venice Commission

COE European Commission for Democracy through Law-Venice Commission. "Principles on the Protection and Promotion of the Ombudsman Institution (the Venice Principles), adopted by the Venice Commission at its 118th Plenary Session (15–16 March 2019)" (3 May 2019). CDL-AD(2019)005. Retrieved June 7, 2022, from: www.venice.coe.int/webforms/documents/default.aspx?pdffile=CDL-AD(2019)005-e

ECtHR

Al-Skeini and others v. the United Kingdom App no 55721/07 (ECtHR, 7 July 2011)
Aliyev v. Azerbaijan Applications nos 68762/14 and 71200/14 (ECtHR, 20 September 2018)
Kavala v. Turkey App no 28749/18 (ECtHR, 10 December 2019)
Aliyev v. Azerbaijan Applications nos 68762/14 and 71200/14 (ECtHR, 20 September 2018)
European Court of Human Rights (2022). "Practical Guide on Admissibility Criteria (updated February 2022). Retrieved June 7 2022, from: www.echr.coe.int/documents/admissibility_guide_eng.pdf

OSCE

ODIHR (2014). Guidelines on human rights defenders. Warsaw: OSCE Office for Democratic Institutions and Human Rights (ODIHR). Retrieved May 27, 2022, from: www.osce.org/files/f/documents/c/1/119633.pdf
OSCE, CSCE "Document of the Copenhagen Meeting of the Conference on the Human Dimension of the CSCE" (29 June 1990). Retrieved May 21, 2022, from: www.osce.org/es/odihr/elections/14304 (accessed 21 May 2022)
OSCE, CSCE "Budapest document 1994 towards a genuine partnership in a new era. Budapest Summit Declaration" (21 December 1994). Retrieved May 21, 2022, from: www.osce.org/files/f/documents/5/1/39554.pdf
ODIHR (2021). "The Situation of Human Rights Defenders in Selected OSCE Participating States. The Final Report of the First Assessment Cycle (2017–2019)". Warsaw: OSCE ODIHR. Retrieved June 1, 2022, from: www.osce.org/files/f/documents/2/3/493867.pdf
OSCE "Astana commemorative declaration towards a security community" (3 December 2010) SUM.DOC/1/10/Corr.1* Retrieved June 7, 2022, from: www.osce.org/files/f/documents/b/6/74985.pdf

Germany

Basic Law for the Federal Republic of Germany, 23 May 1949. Last amended on 29 September 2020. Retrieved 29 May, 2022, from: www.btg-bestellservice.de/pdf/80201000.pdf

9 Human rights defenders and the European Union

Human rights defenders in the European Union have a twofold perspective. The *ad intra* perspective is related with the European area on freedom, security and justice (AFSJ), but there is a different EU *ad extra* policy on human rights defenders. It is closer to the European Union's external action and the framework of the Common Security and Foreign Policy (CSFP). The increasing importance of human rights defenders is not just in terms of cooperation. Under both perspectives there must be a defence of human rights as part of the EU's core values, set in article 2 of the Treaty on European Union (TEU).

After the Treaty of Lisbon, the EU reinforced external relations on human rights with the formal launch of the European External Action Service (EEAS) on 1 January 2011. In 2012, they adopted the Strategic Framework on Human Rights and Democracy, with an action plan (Lerch, 2019) to promote human rights in all areas of the EU external action, to be renewed every four years.

The EU action on human rights defenders, democracy, and human rights

In 2020, the new EU Action Plan on Human Rights and Democracy 2020–2024 was launched, proposing five lines of action, among them, "protecting and empowering human rights defenders" (Borrell, 2020). There are some new elements, that can be summarized as follows:

> New elements include: strengthening the link between human rights and the environment, leveraging the benefits of digital technologies and minimising the risks, increased action on economic, social and cultural rights, more emphasis on democracy, including shrinking civic and political space, greater focus on business and human rights, further action on the protection and empowerment of human rights defenders and greater investment in explaining what we do to promote human rights and democracy. (Gilmore, 2020).

The implementation of this new EU Action Plan 2020–2024 is undertaken by means of a coordinated EU action:

DOI: 10.4324/9780429264016-9

Effective implementation of the Action Plan requires coordinated action by the EU and Member States, while respecting the distinct institutional roles and competences: the High Representative/VicePresident (HRVP), assisted by the European External Action Service, the European Commission, the Council and the Member States. The EU Special Representative for Human Rights (EUSR) will remain a key political actor and play a central role in guiding implementation of the action plan in order to deliver sustainable progress. The European Parliament has a distinct role and importance in contributing to the promotion and protection of human rights and democracy. (EU Action Plan on Human Rights and Democracy 2020–2024)

"Protecting and empowering individuals" is at the core of the EU action on Democracy and Human Rights 2020–2024, including human rights defenders. They are at the cornerstone of the promotion and protection of human rights done by the EU with several trends to protect them and their action of defense of human rights:

- Support and protect human rights defenders (HRDs) and their legal representatives, and address the impact of their work on their families.
- Ensure assistance via the EU human rights defenders protection mechanisms.
- Take into account the particular risk that certain human rights defenders face, including women HRDs and environmental HRDs.
- Work to ensure positive recognition of the important role played by human rights defenders at all levels, including by publicly expressing support for their work.
- Ensure visibility, support activities and raise individual cases related to inter alia legitimate land tenure rights, labour rights, natural resources, environmental issues, freedom of peaceful assembly and association, indigenous peoples' rights as set out in the UN Declaration on the Rights of Indigenous Peoples, climate change, and those resulting from corporate abuses. (EU Action Plan on Human Rights and Democracy 2020–2024, para 1.1.c)

Promoting fundamental freedoms and strengthening civic and political space is key for the action of the EU to support human rights defenders. It is undertaken not merely by their physical protection but by the protection of their rights, building this way "a safe and an enabling environment for civil society as actors in their own right, including long-term strategic and flexible support to capacity building and meaningful participation of civil society at country, regional and global level" (EU Action Plan on Democracy and Human Rights 2020–2024, para. 1.3.b.). In the EU Action Plan on Human Rights and Democracy there is a synergy with article 3 DHRD on the need to have a legal framework respectful of human rights that can be harming the action of human rights defenders. The EU could "Condemn and take appropriate actions against legislation that unduly restricts the work of human rights defenders, journalists, media workers, and civil society, including arbitrary procedures or restrictions, in particular regarding foreign funding" (EU Action Plan on Democracy and Human Rights, 2020–2024, para.1.3.b).

The EU Action Plan on Democracy and Human Rights sets out several ways of helping human rights defenders at risk: "observing trials of human rights defenders and direct support to human rights defenders", ensuring "that those harassed, intimidated or threatened receive assistance via the EU human rights defenders protection mechanisms" (para.1.1.c), building "the capacities of grassroots civil society organisations, human rights defenders and civic movements to conduct regular monitoring and documentation of human rights violations and abuses, including in conflict situations"(para 2.4.b).

In the EU Action Plan on Democracy and Human Rights 2020–2024 there is a specific mention to the work of national human rights institutions and human rights defenders considering them under the open criteria of the DHRD and the criteria set by the EU Guidelines on human rights defenders, giving support long-term and strengthening long term partnerships, and "by making full use of the opportunities to fund grassroots organisations, including through the European Endowment for Democracy" (EU Action Plan for Democracy and Human Rights 2020–2024 para.3.4.d.). There is a prevision long term to deepen engagement and support plural civil society actors and key stakeholders, including:

> human rights defenders, social partners including trade unions, independent media associations and journalists, academics, legal professionals, faith-based actors, and humanitarian aid organisations, in order to defend their right to exercise their roles free from any form of intimidation, discrimination or violence. (EU Action Plan on Democracy and Human Rights 2020–2024, para.3.4.a.)

In the domain of business, the EU is concerned by human rights defenders giving support to human rights defenders' advocacy and business engagement "in decent job creation, sustainable development, and women's entrepreneurship and economic empowerment along the supply chain" (EU Action Plan on Democracy and Human Rights 2020–2024, para.3.5.d.). Finally, there is a mention to the risks online suffered by human rights defenders that require "Intensify efforts to reap the benefits of new technologies for civil society as well as with a particular focus on mitigating risks for human rights defenders and journalists" (EU Action Plan 2020–2024, para.4.2.e).

Thus, the EU action on human rights defenders is not effected just by means of the legal commitment emerging from TEU values, but also through the development of an effective system on human rights for the Common Foreign and Security Policy (CFSP) conducted by the European External Action Service (EEAS). EU core values must be promoted in the EU's relations with the wider world. Particularly, the EU shall contribute to the "eradication of poverty and the protection of human rights, in particular the rights of the child, as well as to the strict observance and the development of international law, including respect for the principles of the United Nations Charter" (article 3.5 TEU).

Human rights defenders and the European Union's external action

The EU values (art. 2 TEU) set in the TEU are undertaken a constitutional function in the EU, but there is a dual system on human rights defenders with reinforced protection in the international action of the EU:

> The Union is founded on the values of respect for human dignity, freedom, democracy, equality, the rule of law and respect for human rights, including the rights of persons belonging to minorities. These values are common to the Member States in a society in which pluralism, non-discrimination, tolerance, justice, solidarity and equality between women and men prevail. (Art. 2 TEU)

In their action on the international scene the EU shall be guided by the principles of "democracy, the rule of law, the universality and indivisibility of human rights and fundamental freedoms, respect for human dignity, the principles of equality and solidarity, and respect for the principles of the United Nations Charter and International Law" (article 21 TEU). So, the dichotomy between internal and the external action must be considered as diptych of the correlative *ad intra* and *ad extra* policies that are keys to EU legitimacy.

Hence, the support of human rights defenders is one of the "main priorities" of the EU's external action and foreign policy. The EU Guidelines on human rights defenders reinforce the framework of the EU on human rights defenders, with article one stating that: "Support for human rights defenders is already a long-established element of the European Union's human rights external relations policy" (EU Guidelines on human rights defenders, 2008).

Under the EU external action, "assistance to human rights activists is probably the most visible of the EU's human rights" (EEEAS, 2016). The guidelines were a driving force for growing common initiatives to support and protect defenders within the EU, and for recognizing HRDs and civil society as "key interlocutors of EU missions" (EEEAS, 2016).

The process of European integration has created a multilevel system for the protection of fundamental rights *ad intra*. However, there is not the same multilevel development *ad extra*, at least not yet. Foreign policy is always the area in which the EU member states are unwilling to cede sovereignty. Nonetheless, *ad intra*, the EU has created the conditions to guarantee rights that are instrumental in the application of the Declaration on human rights defenders. These instrumental rights are protected under the framework of fundamental rights and the EU area of freedom, security and justice, as well as the multilevel legal system converging with EU law: international law, EU Member States constitutional law and domestic law. The position of the ECHR is stronger, and in some states, at the regional level too, when there is a federal or quasi-federal division of powers. Still, the right to promote and protect human rights applies *erga omnes* and cannot be limited on the grounds of citizenship. Therefore, there are instrumental rights that must be guaranteed even without EU citizenship.

The right to promote and protect human rights refers international law to domestic law, and must be accommodated in the EU system, with respect to EU principles of subsidiarity, primacy and competence. It is a right, however, that should not only be guaranteed through external action focused on the protection of the legal subject: human rights defenders. According to Bilancia (2012), it is necessary to develop a strong foreign policy to make the voice of the EU heard as international actor and stakeholder for guaranteeing human rights. Therefore, the best option is not to get discouraged by the European project, but rather the opposite. The advancement of the EU is a guarantee for the protection of human rights and the respect of the right to promote and protect human rights. However, if there is increasing protection *ad extra, ad intra* there is a danger of undermining the European constitutional construction.

However, *ad extra*, there is a new trend toward human rights defenders' action in the European External Action Service. Many EU delegations worldwide have been key in the protection of human rights defenders. The EU provides important support to their activities in defence of human rights under difficult and extreme circumstances. These EU activities on human rights defenders have been carried out in coordination with civil organizations. This collaboration was consolidated by the approval of the latest EU mechanism for the protection of HRD, *protectdefenders.eu*, consisting of a consortium of 12 NGOs. This process shows the need for collaboration between civil society and EU public institutions in order to ensure the effectiveness of human rights. The EU, as a *sui generis* international organization, is aware of this. Therefore, there are human rights defenders working together with the EU for the protection of human rights, and even to protect other human rights defenders. The collaboration between institutional and civil domains can be a good perspective to keep in mind with respect to the policies of support for HRD, so that they can be effective instruments on the ground.

Nonetheless, as previously indicated, the protection and safety of HRD should not make us forget the transcendence of the right to promote and protect human rights, which is truly the fundamental aspect of the 1998 DHRD, not merely the right to be protected. Therefore, it is necessary to try to create supranational systems for the protection of rights considering the role of individuals, but not only by the superposition of multiple legal levels. It is necessary that each legal level enforces the constitutional function necessary to become a real protection of human rights, thus it will be the best guarantee for defenders' rights. It brings the principle of sovereignty into balance with the principle of human dignity—one of the EU's core values—which is also included in the Charter of Fundamental Rights.

The European Union can, at some point, be more than commercial power and "the first contributor worldwide of public subsidies for development", but "it is unquestionable that it does not play an adequate role in the international scene" (Bilancia, 2012). Events such as the refugee crisis and, later, the coronavirus crisis, emphasize the lack of consensus in international affairs when EU urgent action is needed in emergency situations. There is a lack of will in certain states who do not comply with obligations of international protection in the case of refugees. For instance, there has been a lack of implementation of the *Directive 2001/55, 20 July 2001 on minimum standards for giving temporary protection in the event of a mass* influx of displaced persons and on measures promoting a balance of efforts between Member States in receiving such persons and bearing the consequences thereof, being now necessary, and considered by the Council of the European Union to aid refugees from Ukraine under the scope of the EU Directive, applied for the first time because "there is a mass influx of displaced persons within the meaning of Directive 2001/55/EC, in order to provide temporary protection for them" in the *Council Implementing Decision (EU) 2022/382 of 4 March 2022 establishing the existence of a mass influx of displaced persons from Ukraine within the meaning of Article 5 of Directive 2001/55/EC, and having the effect of introducing temporary protection*.

The refugee system and the emerging human rights defenders' system of protection overlap with one another, but these two systems are paradoxically disconnected. According to Jones, "neither UNHCR nor any state has issued guidelines on the extent to which human rights defenders at risk may qualify for refugee protection" (Jones, 2015, p. 938). The main difference between the two systems is that the asylum system has always been separate from human rights. For human rights defenders who are at risk, it is usual to consider the international framework on human rights (Jones, 2015, p. 938). Jones reminds us that the development of a net of temporary international relocation initiatives allows defenders to come to Europe from outside the European system (Jones, 2015). Nevertheless, the EU recently adopted a specific mechanism of protection for defenders under the form of a consortium of 12 specialized NGOs.

Most of these NGOs and systems of protection are quite recent. Jones (2015) reminds us that international protection in civil society "has a long history". There are some organizations on the borderline of both systems, asylum, and human rights protection; for instance, CARA, the former Academic Assistance Council, currently Council for At-Risk Academics, because CARA helps anyone at risk even if they do not see themselves as refugees (Jones, 2015, p. 945). Created in 1933, CARA was founded to help academics flee Nazism. Many German academics were threatened and expelled from universities by the Nazis on racial and political grounds (Jones, 2015). The former director of the London School of Economics, conscious of this danger, and following the dismissal of academics, decided to create an organization to rescue intellectuals facing Nazi persecution. Thus, the Academic Assistance Council (AAC) was created. One of the most prominent academics to flee the Nazi Regime was Albert Einstein. He escaped thanks to the help of the AAC.

Intellectual freedom is the core concept for human rights defenders. However, too often academics and intellectual human rights defenders are forgotten due to the intellectual nature of their work (Quinn and Levine, 2014). It is important to recall that intellectual dissenters and academics, not only social activists or unions of workers, are part of the origin of this legal subject. This is particularly necessary to highlight because the Helsinki Act and the end of Cold War are part of the history of Europe, and thus part of the history of human rights defenders too. Consequently, the umbrella of EU protection must also consider the protection of intellectual human rights defenders. The activities of promoting and protecting human rights can be done by means of books, art, papers, articles, and lessons. History teaches us a great lesson on this, but it is a lesson often forgotten, even within the EU. Defenders are individuals who can change reality through their thoughts and intellectual works, not only through physical situations. Human rights defenders can change minds and societies; therefore, they are persecuted.

Human rights defenders are key actors in the EU's dialogue in third countries. The European External Action Service, in particular, is the balanced result of the Lisbon Treaty, even if it "has been the subject of political controversy", as explained by Poptcheva, because "In bringing together staff from the Commission and the Council, the EEAS—like the new High Representative—connects the EU's 'community' and intergovernmental elements" (Poptcheva, 2014, p. 223). The author reminds us of the development of the right to consular protection, under articles 35 TEU and article 2.c. TFEU. All this is relevant to the creation of a real multilevel citizenship in the EU (Poptcheva, 2014). What is still necessary is not only a multilevel system of rights, but also a real multilevel system of governance (Balaguer Callejón, 2013).

In the framework of the European External Action Service, the EU has developed a network of EU delegations that shall cooperate with the diplomatic and consular missions of the member states, as well as with their representations to international organizations. They must ensure that EU actions and positions on the Common Foreign and Security Policy are in good standing in terms of compliance and implementation (art. 35 TEU). But inside the EU, there is not usually any strict recognition of the right to asylum between EU countries, because it seems to be out of order under the common area of fundamental rights, justice, freedom, and security. So, the European asylum framework applies to third-country nationals and stateless asylum seekers looking for shelter in the European Union.

Each EU country must comply with EU treaty values and respect the Charter of Fundamental Rights, the traditions of constitutional members states and international law obligations of human rights without need for a secondary level of statist control by another EU Member State. This is, for instance, the same system that has followed the EU audiovisual policy and the "country of origin principle", since the development of the "Television without borders" Directive, in which the controller of the accordance with EU law of audiovisual emissions is the country of origin, without the need of a secondary check in the state/s of reception.

Hence, HRD's protection in the EU is carried out *ad intra* by means of respect for HRD fundamental rights, as well as human rights. This does not focus on their physical protection or with a Special Rapporteurship, despite necessary measures for protection, of course, such as the protection of witnesses, or precautionary intermediary measures converging and depending on different legal levels of protection.

Human rights defenders and fundamental rights: the EU areas of freedom, security, and justice

Human rights defenders' rights are protected *ad intra* in the EU by means of the protection of their instrumental rights, as are defined in the Declaration on human rights defenders, but under the framework of the EU law, the CJEU and the Charter of Fundamental Rights.

Nevertheless, in the EU there is a dual system which converges with the framework of the Council of Europe on human rights defenders. There, the case law of the European Court of Human Rights is the judiciary guarantee, while the Commissioner for Human Rights is the institutional guarantee. Both in the EU and in the COE there is not a Special Procedure or Thematic Mechanism on HRD *ad intra*. It has been developed by the UN, the Inter-American system or the African regional system on human rights, since 2000. However, recently, the Meeting Parties of the Convention on Access to Information, Public Participation in Decision-Making and Access to Justice in Environmental Matters (Aarhus Convention) created a new Special Rapporteur on Environmental Defenders, at its third extraordinary session, Geneva 23-24 June 2022.

Freedom of movement in the EU relates to the creation of an area of freedom, security, and justice. It is also relevant to understanding the rising development of social movements in the EU area. Hence, even the CJEU (12 June 2003) recognized in the famous "*Schmidberger* case" that a fundamental right, such as the freedom of assembly, can be a legitimate temporary restriction on the free movement of goods.

Hence, the HRDs' right to be protected, as established by the UN declaration is one of the main claims for defenders' action and is reciprocal to the right to liberty and security (art. 6 ECFR). Under this apparently simple statement "Everyone has the right to liberty and security of person" (art. 6 ECFR), there is a synthesis of the legal framework in the EU area, where HRDs can feel safer.

Piçarra defined security in the EU area under three areas: first, the interdiction of arbitrary detention or prison; second, as a right of public order to preserve persons and goods; and third, as the right to know what can and cannot be done (Piçarra, 2013, p. 91). Therefore, there is a connection with the interdiction of arbitrariness. Under the rule of law, in the EU Member States it is not possible to admit any kind of arbitrary detention: there is a presumption of the commitment to it and a multilevel system of guarantees for an effective remedy. The conception of security and liberty in the EU entails that violence is a monopole of state (Piçarra, 2013). State constitutional legitimacy comes from the respect of fundamental rights, democracy, and the rule of law. But, according to Piçarra, under the interpretation of the art. 6 ECFR, and in connection with the art. 53.2 ECFR, there are possible restrictions to the right to liberty and security that must not exceed the threshold of admissible restrictions under the ECHR (Piçarra, 2013). Consequently, there is a multilevel framework concerning the right to liberty and security having an impact on HRDs and their rights.

In these times of EU crisis, it is important to distinguish between the European project and some attitudes of the EU Member States. Silveira believes that "the truth is that a real space for deliberation at the European level does not exist because the Member States never wanted it to" (Silveira, 2013, p. 481). The main fault is not only with the EU institutions, but also in the reluctance of some EU Member States to go further in the EU project. Due to this reluctance, certain European Member States will lose advantages coming from the European project:

"one of them being the risk of losing a great part of what the European project has so far been able to give us" (Silveira, 2013, 2013, p. 481). To cope with this crisis, the authors suggest that it is necessary to change from the national paradigm to the supranational paradigm, and a real will and belief in the concept of solidarity: "Solidarity is a way of 'standing together'" (Silveira, 2013). The COVID-19 pandemic is unfortunate evidence of the need to reinforce EU solidarity, not only among EU members states, but also among human beings. If the EU institutional, legal, and human perspective is reinforced, solidarity can become real. The paradigm is now not just EU citizenship: it is the human condition. The paradigm on the human condition is what remains behind human rights defenders. That means that to organize EU solidarity there must be a balance between interests and a negotiation between unequal partners who have to become equal, as Silveira reminds us (Silveira, 2013, p. 488). In this sense, it would be important to decrease the asymmetry pointed out by Balaguer Callejón, between the development of a multilevel system of rights and a system of multilevel governance, that is yet to be built (Balaguer Callejón, 2013).

During the COVID-19 crisis, the EU legal framework has been overcome by a lack of competence and terms for urgent action. In this instance, the multilevel legal system's right to health failed to be protected. This is due too to the diminished framework of social rights that must be part of the EU's constitutional functionality. Under the international system there are converging legal systems, such as the WHO, international human rights regime, the funding system of the World Bank and in the UE, the ECHR as well (von Bogdandy and Villarreal, 2020). Von Bogdandy and Villarreal (2020) highlight the interdependence of civil, political, economic, social, and cultural rights as a real challenge:

> Of course, balancing between the rights of liberty, free movement and assembly, on one hand, and the right to health, on the other hand, is most difficult. It is now well accepted in contemporary human rights law that civil, political, social, economic, and cultural rights are equal. The duties to, on one hand, safeguard liberties and, on the other hand, to protect against pandemic events, are both a human rights matter. (von Bogdandy and Villarreal, 2020, p. 20)

The FRA and human rights defenders

Since its beginnings, the interdependence of human rights has been crucial for human rights defenders too. Returning to the EU's legal framework on HRDs, it is necessary to remind other actors of impact on the defenders' rights in the EU area. From this perspective, the EU Fundamental Rights Agency (FRA) contributes to the promotion and protection of human rights in the EU. The FRA becomes a mechanism for human rights defenders *ad intra* EU, due to its institutional nature. It was created in 2007 as successor from the previous European Monitoring Centre on Racism and Xenophobia. The FRA framework is based on acting within the EU's scope of application:

> The objective of the Agency shall be to provide the relevant institutions, bodies, offices and agencies of the Community and its Member States when implementing Community law with assistance and expertise relating to fundamental rights in order to support them when they take measures or formulate courses of action within their respective spheres of competence to fully respect fundamental rights. (Regulation (EC) No.168/2007 EU Agency Fundamental Rights)

The EU FRA is headquartered in Vienna, and it has undertaken several activities on fundamental rights. They are organized under three main tasks:

- Data collection, research and analysis
- Providing independent evidence-based advice to policy makers, cooperating and networking with stakeholders,
- Communicating the results of its work and raising awareness of fundamental rights. (FRA Strategy 2018–2022)

Thus, since 2007, the FRA is the EU's independent actor for protecting the ECFR. The FRA Strategy 2018–2022 set out their main five priorities. In particular, the FRA's Programming in 2020–2022 identifies one of the main risks in the FRA's action on fundamental rights and the risks suffered in the EU by HRDs, both as individuals and NHRIs:

> Recent evidence, including from FRA, shows that in a number of EU Member States, civil society organisations face growing challenges in their human rights work. Similarly, national statutory bodies with a human rights remit have expressed concerns about challenges to their independence. This, in turn, limits their ability to protect human rights and to interact with human rights defenders. A weakened human rights infrastructure ultimately means that individuals will have less support to realise their rights and lack access to effective remedies and protection when their rights are violated. It also undermines efforts to uphold the common values expressed in the EU treaty and public trust in the European Union as a human rights actor. (FRA Programming 2020–2022)

Article 10 of the FRAs 2007 Regulation states that "the Agency shall closely cooperate with non-governmental organizations and with institutions of civil society, active in the field of fundamental rights". Under this legal framework there is important activity and dialogue with civil organizations. Many of them are organizations working to defend human rights.

The FRA helps the HRDs efforts, giving independent evidence, advice, expertise, and supporting the frontline work. Under this scope, the FRA shines a light on potential risks and priority areas for defenders. Another goal for the next years is to collect objective data on women's rights defenders (FRA Programming 2020–2022, p. 74). This data collection can add knowledge about the gender dimension of HRDs in the EU.

Data protection and privacy are a particular issue to concern for human rights defenders. In this sense, Franca highlights the necessary balance among transparency and privacy in EU Law: "In other terms, when the right to access is granted, simultaneously, it becomes necessary to tackle the issue of balancing transparency and privacy. The progressive development in society and in law have made this balance still more complicated" (Franca, 2021, p. 649).

Consequently, several institutional guarantees converge under the EU's *ad intra* dimension. Of course, it is necessary to highlight the judiciary task done by the European Court of Justice that gives protection and primacy to EU law, and as a judiciary guarantee for HRDs too. All this contributes to the strength of the areas of freedom, security, and justice based on fundamental rights. There the EU judiciary CJEU can make the last decision on EU law, not EU state members, although sometimes it is challenged by constitutional court decisions that must be accurate on the primacy of EU law. The EU focus on fundamental rights, instead of on the physical protection of the subject—HRDs—gives more protection to instrumental rights, and that finally means stronger protection for them. It is important not to forget that rights are protection against abuses of power. Hence, reciprocally, reinforcing rights lessens the abuse of power and threats against HRDs.

The role of the judiciary system in the EU and the lack of a human rights defenders' special rapporteurship

There are thus several EU trends creating a presumption of compliance with the legal framework designed by the UN Declaration on human rights defenders: the Copenhagen criteria for becoming EU Member States; the effective protection of fundamental rights coming from the CJEU and the CFR; the rule of law; democracy and human rights in the interplay with the EU Member States; and domestic law and the referrals with international human rights, particularly reinforced in the case of the ECHR. Then, with the idiosyncrasies of the EU, general state patterns of persecution of HRDs cannot be present *ad intra*. This can be different when considered on a case-by-case basis.

Under EU law, primacy may be a case on HRDs that can lead to preliminary ruling proceedings in the European Court of Justice. But it is not possible to assume a pattern of general neglection of the Declaration of Human Rights Defenders in the European Union. It would be against the EU constitutional function and legitimacy.

The judiciary system in the European Union and its unique characteristics are important to understanding why it is not necessary to develop a specific Rapporteurship for human rights defenders. The focus is on the protection of fundamental rights for human rights defenders. This protection is instrumental to the main right to promote and protect human rights defenders. Hence, the respect of human rights defenders' rights does not focus on their physical protection, which is a consequence rather than the cause of the EU defenders' system, *ad intra*.

Let us examine the role of the judiciary in the EU's domestic systems of law. What is expected and respected of, and for, any individual in the EU area in the areas of freedom, security, and justice for national and EU law under the Declaration on human rights defenders in 1998, is that any individual could become "in abstract" a human rights defender.

In the domain of criminal law, legal inquiry under merely an ideological basis is not possible, because freedom of thought is part of the fundamental rights set by the ECFR. But it is true that there are certain limits to militant democracy too, and these exist due to the past of certain states. However, as with any other citizen, politicians can be persecuted in courts only with equality before the law, as is consistent and necessary for the rule of law. The criminal persecution of human rights defenders without any legal basis—as with any other citizen—is incompatible with EU law, values, the rule of law, democracy, human rights, and the Copenhagen criteria. In the case of politicians, even if they are undertaking a function in the public interest, there is equality in the law, and the judiciary guarantees of fair justice apply to them too. On a case-by-case basis, there are other judiciary instances of control at the international level, that can control or check domestic decisions. Consequently, this is evidence that there cannot be intentional persecution under the framework of fundamental rights. In any case, individual evidence must be provided, before the equality of the law. Thus, patterns of political persecution or repression under domestic criminal law are not possible, and there are apparently no grounds for a framework of *ad intra* asylum or non-refoulement. There can be, of course, unconstitutional court rulings, or rulings against fundamental rights. But the multilevel system of guarantees converges in the EU area, and it is finally accepted or inherent to EU Member States. Sometimes the domestic law that the judiciary must apply is what can make a pattern that needs to be changed, if it is not enough consistent with the European Convention of Human Rights or with the European Charter of Fundamental Rights, depending on the domain of competence. However, even under the limitation test of the ECtHR clauses, there is the exigence of previous legal provision, and in the EU, there is the possibility of the preliminary question that can become a kind of "constitutional" interpretation. In the EU, a fourfold multilevel system of protection can even apply, due to the EU multilevel legal system. Consider the expectation designed by the Declaration on Human Rights Defenders in the "constitutional clause" of article 3:

> Domestic law consistent with the Charter of the United Nations and other international obligations of the State in the field of human rights and fundamental freedoms is the juridical framework within which human rights and fundamental freedoms should be implemented and enjoyed and within which all activities referred to in the present Declaration for the promotion, protection and effective realization of those rights and freedoms should be conducted. (A/RES/53/144, 8 March 1999)

Hence, the principles of EU primacy and competence apply. According to the proceedings in article 7 TEU, there is an expectation that the constitutional compliance of article 2 values and within this system it is possible to control risk, or serious breaches against it by a state. Article 7 TEU is the last resource of EU law, and it can be applied if it can be determined that "there is a serious risk of a serious breach by a Member State of the values referred to in Article 2". The Council, after the consent of the European Parliament, can adopt this decision through the initiative of a third of the EU Member States, the European Parliament or by the European Commission. But before arriving to this last decision, the Council shall hear the Member State in question, and may address recommendations to it (article 7 TEU). The grounds for applying the article 7 proceedings must be verified regularly to determine if they continue to apply. The later stage to determine if there is a serious and persistent breach of the values of article 2 remains with the European Council by unanimity, with the consent of the Parliament. The European Council can then decide on the suspension of certain rights as sanctions, including voting rights, which would mean a *de facto* out of an EU Member State, as considered from the exclusion of their constitutional functional perspective. To sum up, the rule of law, democracy, and human rights are at the core of the EU legal framework, with a reciprocal effect for human rights defenders.

All this makes it quite sensible to presume the compliance on the DHRD framework set in article 3 for defenders *ad intra* in the European Union. It is a good example of the constitutional function under a multilevel system, as shared by different actors beyond the state. In the future it will be interesting to consider article 6 Treaty on the European Union and the consequences of the convergence of the European Union and the Council of Europe judiciary systems for the rights and protection of HRDs, after the accession of the EU to the ECHR. At the moment this is not possible, since they are under the negotiation by the Steering Committee for Human Rights *ad hoc* negotiation group on the accession of the EU to the ECHR. In present times the Committee of Ministers voted on the necessary exclusion of Russia from the Council of Europe, and at the same time, out of the negotiations. On 16 March 2022, the Committee of Ministers decided under Article 8 of the Statute of the Council of Europe that the Russian Federation would cease to be a member of the Council of Europe, adopting Resolution CM/Res (2022) 2 on the cessation of the membership of the Russian Federation to the Council of Europe. As a result, the Russian Federation will no longer participate in the work of the Steering Committee for Human Rights or any of its subordinate bodies, including the CDDH *ad hoc* negotiation group on the accession of the EU to the ECHR. This group will henceforth continue the negotiations in a 46+1 format (European Parliament, 2022).

Human rights defenders: the EU Guidelines on human rights defenders, democracy, and human rights

Since the debates in the UN Working Group on the draft of the Declaration on Human Rights Defenders (1985–1998), the EU has taken a leading role in the support of human rights defenders. In terms of EU Common Foreign policy, there was a turning point in 2004 with the adoption of the EU Guidelines on human rights defenders, which was later updated in 2008 and finally revised in 2014.

The EU guidelines are not part of the EU's primary law. The EU guidelines do not have the same value as other sources of secondary legislation. They can be considered "soft law", but with a significant impact in terms of the EU's policy in international relations. Hence, the EU guidelines are "not legally binding, but because they have all been adopted at ministerial level, the guidelines represent a strong political signal that these are priorities for the EU" (EEEAS, 2016). In this sense, the EU Guidelines on human rights defenders have an operational will to set the framework for EU action in the Foreign and Common Policy. These EU guidelines are ruled to support external action by giving operational guidelines tools. Hence, the purpose of the EU Guidelines on human rights defenders is:

> To provide practical suggestions for enhancing EU action in relation to this issue. The Guidelines can be used in contacts with third countries at all levels as well as in multilateral human rights fora, in order to support and strengthen ongoing efforts by the Union to promote and encourage respect for the right to defend human rights. The Guidelines also provide for interventions by the Union for human rights defenders at risk and suggest practical means to support and assist human rights defenders. (EU Guidelines on HRDs, 2008, para. 1)

If the EU guidelines cannot be considered binding laws, that does not mean they do not have effectiveness, because they have a leading operational rule for the EU delegations' external action on HRDs. However, this operational goal is based in a theoretical perspective, and even the European Parliament (2010) reminds us that the guidelines' implementation was not satisfactory. The EU Commission recalled that the EU Guidelines compliance must be assured, and the situation resolved.

Human rights are within the EU "external relation objectives" (Larik, 2016, p. 110). Eeckhout considers human rights as vital both for the internal and external EU, because they "are not only ever more central to the EU's internal constitutional development, they are equally vital for the EU's external action" (Eeckhout, 2011, p. 96). Human rights are named in the common values of article 2 TEU, and in the article 3.5 TEU on the EU relations with the wider world (Larik, 2016, p. 111). Beforehand, in article 21 (1), the TEU states that there must be a reciprocal commitment in external relations with the core principles of the EU, such as the universality and indivisibility of human rights. In practical terms, there have been several ways for promoting human rights from diplomatic action by means of démarches and dialogues. There are economic measures, such as trade benefits and sanctions, and specifically, "inserting human rights related 'essential clauses' into agreements with third countries" (Larik, 2016, p. 110). In the case of human rights defenders, we are undergoing a deployment of the multilevel legal system of protection for third countries and external relations. The participation of civil society organizations is under the umbrella of the EU. It does not mean, however, that this system is perfect. Even the European Parliament complains about it. In 2010, the European Parliament recalled that after the Lisbon Treaty, the EU delegations could use these new opportunities for action. But in terms of the implementation of EU guidelines on human rights defenders, the EP considered it unsatisfactory. Therefore, the EP suggested the creation of Focal Points on human rights defenders in the European External Action Service. All this reminds us again for the need to integrate the EU guidelines on human rights defenders into the EU's human rights practices. This is why the European Parliament made this decision in the Resolution of 17 June 2010 on EU policies in favour of human rights defenders, where the EP:

> reiterates therefore its call to systematically appoint to each country a highly qualified political official with a specific responsibility on human rights and democracy, and to integrate guidelines and develop best practices on human rights and their implementation in EU mission staff training programmes, job descriptions and appraisal processes. (EP resolution of 17 June 2010 on EU policies in favour of human rights defenders)

It is necessary to remember that in the EU framework on human rights defenders, Regulation No. 235/2014 established a financing instrument for democracy and human rights worldwide (2014–2020), no longer in force. Under this funding instrument, there was a specific mention of human rights defenders:

> Under this Regulation, the Union is to provide assistance to address global, regional, national and local human rights and democratisation issues in partnership with civil society. In this regard, civil society is to be understood as spanning all types of social actions by individuals or groups that are independent from the state and whose activities help to promote human rights and democracy, including human rights defenders as defined by the UN Declaration on the Right and Responsibility of Individuals, Groups and Organs of Society to Promote and Protect Universally Recognized Human Rights and Fundamental Freedoms ('Declaration on Human Rights Defenders'). In the implementation of this Regulation, due consideration should be given to the Union's local human rights country strategies. (EIDHR, 2014, para. 115)

The EIDHR paid particular attention to the human rights defenders' measures of protection, with the goal to

> address urgent protection needs of human rights defenders and democracy activists, the Union should be able to respond in a flexible and timely manner, through the use of faster and more flexible administrative procedures and by means of a range of funding mechanisms. (EIDHR, 2014, para. 18).

Under this framework and the goals set up by Regulation 235/2014 Preamble, article 1.b considered how the EU's assistance, objectives, and the subject matter of the EIDHR shall focus especially on human rights defenders:

> enhancing respect for and observance of human rights and fundamental freedoms, as proclaimed in the UN Universal Declaration of Human Rights and other international and regional human rights instruments, and strengthening their protection, promotion, implementation and monitoring, mainly through support to relevant civil society organisations, human rights defenders and victims of repression and abuse. (EIDHR, 2014, art. 1.b)

Under the Thematic Programme on Human Rights and Democracy Multi-Annual Indicative Programming 2021–2027, human rights defenders are considered a priority, as well as in the EU Action Plan on Human Rights and Democracy 2020–2024. This challenge it has been present during past years:

> It has contributed to achieving significant progress in countries and regions where human rights were under strain, through innovative engagement and investment in economic and social rights, and strong political and financial support to protect and empower human rights defenders, civil society and media actors. (EU Action Plan on Human Rights and Democracy 2020–2024).

However, one of the patterns to cope with in next years is the "increasing violence and intimidation of human rights defenders (over 2600 reported attacks in the past 3 years)". This is due to the

> retreat of some of the EU's traditional partners from the active promotion and defence of human rights and democratic values. Thus, there is a strong impact of 'systemic efforts to undermine the rule of law, restrict civic and political space and weaken the multilateral rules-based order'. (EU Action Plan on Human Rights and Democracy 2020–2024).

The Action Plan 2020–2024 highlights the key role against climate change being done by environmental human rights defenders to face challenges posed:

> Civil society and environmental human rights defenders are playing a key role in calling out human rights violations and demanding action to protect the planet and its climate. Building a sustainable environmental future is a key goal, cutting across traditional lines between the economy and security, and between internal and external policy dimensions. The negative impacts of environmental degradation and climate change threaten and can multiply the challenges to a range of rights—to health, food, water, universal education and even life itself. (EU Action Plan on Human Rights and Democracy 2020–2024)

Since the origins of the EU support human rights defenders, the concept of human rights defenders is understood under the EU Guidelines and the article 1 of the UN DHRD, where they "are considered not only as natural persons but also as groups of natural persons without a legal personality and civil society organisations" (European Instrument for Democracy and Human Rights

(EIDHR) Strategy Paper 2007–2010). The EIDHR (2014–2020), under the scope of EU action on democracy and human rights worldwide, considered specifically the support to human rights defenders, meaning:

> Support for, protection of, and assistance to human rights defenders, including addressing their urgent protection needs, in accordance with Article 1 of the UN Declaration on Human Rights Defenders; these objectives, including longer-term assistance and access to shelter, could be covered by a human rights defenders mechanism. (EU EIDHR 2014–2020, art. 2.1.b.iii)

There was also the possibility of giving "small grants" to help human rights defenders. These grants were ruled by *Regulation (EU) no 236/2014 of the European Parliament and of the Council of 11 March 2014 laying down common rules and procedures for the implementation of the Union's instruments for financing external action,* no longer in force.

The new EU Action Plan 2020–2024 aims to respond to challenges of the global world. It particularly remarks on "the crackdown of human rights defenders" as a problem that the plan aims to tackle:

> In recent years, the global political landscape has changed, conflicts have deepened and new risks have emerged. Human rights and democracy have never been more challenged. The shrinking space for civil society, the crackdown of human rights defenders, widespread impunity for human rights violations, attacks against the International Criminal Court, intimidation of journalists, illustrate the current dynamics. These trends have had tangible negative consequences including declining public confidence in democratic institutions and increased polarisation. In this context, the development of new technologies, and Artificial Intelligence in particular, need to be carefully analysed weighting its positive impact also against its possible use to limit and undermine human rights and democracies. The Action Plan 2020–2024 aims to respond to these challenges. (EU Action Plan on Human Rights and Democracy 2020–2024)

This action on human rights defenders is a strategic part of the EU's interests. However, to achieve it is not an easy task. Under the basis of the previous EU Action Plans, the new Action Plan 2020–2024 considers the support and protection of human rights defenders a priority, with actions such as observing trials on human rights defenders, dialogue with them, and ensuring assistance via the EU human rights protection mechanism, with particular attention to the problems environmental human rights defenders and women HRDs they face. The relevance of domestic law not restricting human rights defenders legitimate activities and is highlighted by the EU Action Plan 2020–2024 and it wants "grassroots civil society organisations, human rights defenders and civic movements to conduct regular monitoring and documentation of human rights violations and abuses, including in conflict situations" (EU Action Plan 2020–2024).

To conclude, the path to arrive at this multilevel EU legal framework, with different actors taking on constitutional functions *ad intra*, and even *ad extra*, came to a turning point with the adoption of the EU guidelines, in 2004, and then in their revision in 2008. The Annual Reports of the EU on human rights and democracy in the world are a useful tool for research and to create knowledge on human rights defenders. Returning to the context of the EU Guidelines on human rights defenders, the (2008) EU Annual report on human rights and democracy in the world highlighted the first expectations of the EU support for human rights defenders:

> Human rights defenders look at the EU to support them in their relentless efforts to promote human rights. This report shows that the European Union is endeavoring to fulfil these expectations through constantly renewed efforts and making use of the large number of instruments available to it. (EU Annual report on human rights, 2008)

These expectations, however, are far from being achieved, and the need to reinforce the EU support to human rights defenders is present in the EU Action Plan 2020–2024.

Now more than ever it is necessary to reinforce the EU's role as an international actor in protecting human rights defenders. Yet they must not just provide them with physical protection. The EU must give support to human rights and instrumental rights under the Declaration on Human Rights Defenders. Only by making real the right to promote and protect human rights, can the right to be protected be truly understood as an instrumental right for defenders, and not as their main right. Human rights defenders live under threats and risks, even against their lives. In tackling this, the EU is experiencing difficulties, such as the lack of confidence in the public opinion on EU democratic institutions, populism, and the increasing polarization *ad intra* of the EU–which must reinforce their policy *ad extra* despite the reluctance of certain states. The EU is undertaking a constitutional function of article 2 that values not just physical protection of defenders, *ad intra*, but *ad extra* too. The right to promote and protect human rights is the main right of human rights defenders; the right to be protected should remain another instrumental right, but global threats require immediate EU action. The EU must focus on urgent protection of at risk HRDs across the world.

Furthermore, human rights defenders are a new legal subject based on the human condition. Thus, the protection of human rights defenders' rights is the protection of not only the EU's interests—it protects humankind and fosters respect for human beings. Aristotle's concept of the human being is interrelated with their political nature as active citizens of the *polis*. This is at the core of the human condition. This active universal citizenship, to paraphrase Arendt, demands respect and recognition for the right to promote and protect human rights, both inside and outside the EU.

References

Balaguer Callejón, F. (2013). "Una interpretación constitucional de la crisis económica". *ReDCE*, 19.

Bilancia, P. (2012). *The Dynamics of the EU Integration and the Impact on the National Constitutional Law: The European Union After the Lisbon Treaties*. Milan: Giuffrè Editore .

Bilancia, P. and Pizzetti, F. (2004). *Aspetti e problema del costituzionalismo multilivell*. Milan: Giuffrè Editore.

Eeckhout, P. (2011). *EU External Relations Law*. Oxford: Oxford University Press.

EU High Representative of the Union for Foreign Affairs and Security Policy (2016). *EU Annual Report on Human Rights and Democracy in the World in 2016*.

Franca, S. (2021) "Balancing transparency and privacy in Italian administrative litigations: General remarks and some considerations on locus standi in the light of the GDPR". In Saura-Freixes, N. (Ed.), *Derechos Humanos, Derecho Constitucional y Derecho Internacional: Sinergias Contemporáneas. Human Rights, Constitutional Law and International Law: Contemporary Synergies*. Madrid: Centro de Estudios Políticos y Constitucionales.

Jones, M. (2015). "Protecting human rights defenders at risk: Asylum and temporary international relocation". *International Journal of Human Rights*, 19(7), 935–960. https://doi.org/10.1080/13642987.2015.1075304.

Larik, J. (2016). *Foreign Policy Objectives in European Constitutional Law*. Oxford: Oxford University Press.

Lerch, M. (2021). "Human rights". Fact Sheets on the European Union European Parliament. Retrieved 30 October 2022 from: www.europarl.europa.eu/factsheets/en/sheet/165/human-rights

Piçarra, N. (2013). "Direito à liberdade e à segurança". In A. Silveira and M. Canotilho (Eds), *Carta dos Direitos Fundamentales da Uniao Europeia Comentada*. Coimbra: Almedina.

Poptcheva, E. (2014). *Multilevel Citizenship. The Right to Consular Protection of EU Citizens Abroad*. Brussels: Peter Lang.

Quinn, R. and Levine, J. (2014). "Intellectual-HRDs and claims for academic freedom under human rights law". *The International Journal of Human Rights*, 18(7–8), 898–920.

Saura-Freixes, N. (2016) *Human Rights Defenders. El derecho a promover y proteger los derechos humanos*. Madrid: UNED

Silveira, A. (2013). "Artigo 52 Ambito e interpretaçao dos direitos e dos principios". In A. Silveira and M. Canotilho (Eds), *Carta dos Direitos Fundamientais da Uniao Europeia Comentada*. Coimbra: Almedina.

von Bogdandy, A. and Villarreal, P. (2020). "International law on pandemic response: A first stocktaking in light of the coronavirus crisis". *Max Planck Institute for Comparative Public Law and International Law Research Paper*, 07. https://papers.ssrn.com/sol3/papers.cfm?abstract_id=3561650

Documents

Treaties

Charter of the United Nations, (adopted 24 October 1945) 1 UNTS XVI
Consolidated Version of the Treaty on European Union [2012] OJ C 326/13

Convention for the Protection of Human Rights and Fundamental Freedoms, as amended, (adopted 4 November 1950, *entered into force 3 September 1953) ETS No.* 005 (ECHR)

International Covenant on Civil and Political Rights (adopted 16 December 1966, entered into force 23 March 1976) 999 UNTS 171 (ICCR)

Consolidated version of the Treaty on the Functioning of the European Union [2012] OJ C 326

UN

Universal Declaration of Human Rights UNGA Res. 217A (III) (10 December 1948)

Declaration on the Right and Responsibility of Individuals, Groups and Organs of Society to Promote and Protect UniversallyRecognized HumanRights and Fundamental Freedoms UNGA A/RES/53/144 (8 March 1999)

World Conference on Human Rights in Vienna. Vienna Declaration and Programme of Action (25 June 1993). *Retrieved 3 June,* from: www.ohchr.org/sites/default/files/vienna.pdf

UNECE, Decision VII/9 (18-20 October 2021), ECE/MP.PP/2021/2/Add.1, 2.

EU

Charter of Fundamental Rights of the European Union [2012] OJ C 326

Council Directive 2001/55, 20 July 2001on minimum standards for giving temporary protection in the event of a mass influx of displaced persons and on measures promoting a balance of efforts between Member States in receiving such persons and bearing the consequences thereof [2001] OJ L 212/12

Council Directive 89/552/EEC of 3 October 1989*on the coordination of certain provisions laid down by law,* regulation or administrative action in Member States concerning the pursuit of television broadcasting activities [1989] OJL 298/23

Directive (EU) 2018/1808*of the European Parliament and of the Council of 14 November 2018 amending Directive 2010/13/EU on the coordination of certain provisions laid down by law,* regulation or administrative action in Member States concerning the provision of audiovisual media services (Audiovisual Media Services Directive) in view of changing market realities [2018] L 303/69

Directive (EU) 2019/1937 of the European Parliament and of the Council of 23 October 2019 on the protection of persons who report breaches of Union law [2019] OJ L 305

Regulation (EU) No 235/2014 of the European Parliament and of the Council of 11 March 2014*establishing a financing instrument for democracy and human rights worldwide.* [2014] OJ L 77/85

European Council. European Council in Copenhagen 21–22 June 1993, *Conclusions of the Presidency.* SN 180/1/93 REV 1

European Parliament, Lecerf, M. (2022). *"Completion of EU accession to the European Convention on Human Rights In "A New Push for European Democracy"".* Legislative Train Schedule European Parliament. Retrieved 2 June, 2022, from: www.europarl.europa.eu/legislative-train/theme-area-of-justice-and-fundamental-rights/file-completion-of-eu-accession-to-the-echr

European Parliament resolution of 17 June 2010*on EU policies in favour of human rights defenders,* Thursday, 17 June 2010. (2009/2199(INI)) [2011] OJ C236 E/69. Retrieved 2 June, 2022, from: https://eur-lex.europa.eu/legal-content/EN/TXT/HTML/?uri=CELEX:52010IP0226&rid=7

European Parliament. (2022). "*Completion of EU accession to the European Convention on Human Rights In "A New Push for European Democracy"*". Legislative Train Schedule European Parliament. Retrieved 2 June, 2022, from: www.europarl.europa.eu/legislative-train/theme-area-of-justice-and-fundamental-rights/file-completion-of-eu-accession-to-the-echr

Borrell Centelles, J. (2020). "Foreword by Josep Borrell Centelles, High Representative of the European Union for Foreign Affairs and Security Policy", p. 4. In: EEEAS (2020) *EU Action Plan on Human Rights and Democracy 2020–2024*. Retrieved 7 June, 2022, from: www.eeas.europa.eu/sites/default/files/eu_action_plan_on_human_rights_and_democracy_2020-2024.pdf

Gilmore, E. (2020). "Introduction". In: EEEAS (2020) *EU Action Plan on Human Rights and Democracy 2020–2024*. Retrieved 22 May, 2022, from: www.eeas.europa.eu/sites/default/files/eu_action_plan_on_human_rights_and_democracy_2020-2024.pdf

EEEAS (2016). "*EU Guidelines on human rights defenders*" Retrieved 22 May, 2022, from: www.eeas.europa.eu/eeas/eu-guidelines-human-rights-defenders_en

EEEAS (2020). "*Responses to the Questionnaire. Questionnaire on the situation of human rights defenders*". Retrieved 20 May, 2022, from: www.ohchr.org/sites/default/files/Documents/Issues/Defenders/GA73/IOS/EU_European_External_Action_Service.pdf

Council of the European Union "2012 Strategic Framework on Human Rights and Democracy, Luxembourg", *Press* (25 June 2012) 11855/12. Retrieved 7 June, 2022, from: www.consilium.europa.eu/uedocs/cms_data/docs/pressdata/en/foraff/131181.pdf

Council of the European Union. Brussels, 29 October 2008, *EU Annual Report on Human Rights* [2008] 14146/1/08

European Union (2020). *EU Action Plan on Human Rights and Democracy 2020–2024*. Retrieved 2 June, 2022, from: www.eeas.europa.eu/sites/default/files/eu_action_plan_on_human_rights_and_democracy_2020-2024.pdf

European Instrument for Democracy and Human Rights (EIDHR) Strategy Paper 2007–2010. DG RELEX/B/1 JVK 70618. Retrieved 7 June, 2022, from: www.ituc-csi.org/IMG/pdf/EIDHR_Strategy_paper_2007_-_2010.pdf

Thematic Programme on Human Rights and Democracy Multi-Annual Indicative Programming 2021–2027 https://ec.europa.eu/international-partnerships/system/files/mip-2021-c2021-9620-human-rights-democracy-annex_en.pdf

FRA

Council Regulation (EC) No 168/2007 of 15 February 2007 establishing a European Union Agency for Fundamental Rights [2008] OJ L 53/1

European Union Agency for Fundamental Rights. "*FRA Strategy 2018–2022*". Retrieved 7 June, 2022, from: https://fra.europa.eu/sites/default/files/fra_uploads/fra-2018-fra-strategy-2018-2022_en.pdf

European Union Agency for Fundamental Rights. "*FRA Programming Document 2020–2022*". Retrieved 7 June, 2022, from: https://fra.europa.eu/sites/default/files/fra_uploads/fra-2020-programming-document-2020-2022_en.pdf

COE

Resolution CM/Res(2022)2 on the cessation of the membership of the Russian Federation to the Council of Europe (16 March 2022). *Retrieved 7 June*, 2022, from: https://search.coe.int/cm/Pages/result_details.aspx?ObjectID=0900001680a5da51

CJEU

Case C-112/00 *Eugen Schmidberger, Internationale Transporte und Planzüge v Republik Österreich. Reference for a preliminary ruling: Oberlandesgericht Innsbruck – Austria.* [2003] EU:C:2003:333

OSCE

OSCE "*Conference on Security and Co-operation in Europe (CSCE): Final Act of Helsinki*" (CSCE Helsinki 1 August 1975). Retrieved 26 May, 2022, from: www.osce.org/es/mc/39506

NGOs and other

Cara a lifeline to academics at risk. Available at: www.cara.ngo (accessed 22 May 2022)
Cara. (2022) "*Our history*", www.cara.ngo/who-we-are/our-history/
Protectdefenders.eu. Retrieved 2 June, 2022, from: https://protectdefenders.eu/

Index

abuse of rights 59–63, 127, 150, 156, 169
Academic Assistance Council (AAC) 105, 204
academic freedom 171
academics 101–106
ad extra, on HRDs 1, 40, 128, 133, 181, 192, 199, 202, 216
ad hoc negotiation group 211
ad intra, on HRDs 1, 40, 128, 143, 181, 182, 192, 202, 205, 209, 211, 216
Adorno, Theodor 82
African Commission on Human Rights 31, 39
African Union's system 7, 141
Agamben, G. 49
Alapini-Gansou, Reine 15
Alexeyeva, L. 99
Alfredsson, G. 30
allegation letters 34–38
Alston, P. 26
Alvarez, J. E. 24
American Convention on Human Rights 31
Amnesty International 11, 27, 99
Andre Lawrence Shepherd v Bundesrepublik Deutschland (2015) 104
Angelus Novus (Klee) 80
area on freedom, security and justice (AFSJ) 199
Arendt, H. 2, 6, 49, 59, 62, 80, 85, 127, 130, 132, 163, 167, 170, 216
Aristotle 1, 2, 6, 49, 120, 127, 216
Association of Southeast Asian Nations (ASEAN) 12
asylum: European Union 4; human rights defenders 4; and refugees' protection 104–105
asymmetric enforcement 140–143
Austin, J. L. 61

Balaguer Callejón, F. 189, 207
Banjul Charter (1981) 31
Barayagwiza, Jean-Bosco 61
¡BASTA YA! movement 114
Benjamin, Walter 80
Bennett, K. 3, 16, 38, 74, 96, 180
Beveridge, William 105
Beyond Human Rights (2016) 41
Biden, Joe 78
Bilancia, P. 203
binomial theory of law 127
Bobbio, N. 52, 71, 116, 127, 132, 158
Boyle, K. 152
Brandt, Willy 81, 82
Brecht, Bertolt 82
Breitenmoser, S. 84
Breton, André 105
Brotat, R. 160
Brunnée, J. 85

Canetti, E. 65, 81, 88
Canton, Santiago A. 16
Capa, Robert 81
Carrillo Salcedo, J. A. 49, 50, 180
Chagall, Marc 105
Chang, W. H. 41, 180
Chronicle of Current Events, The (Horvath) 99
citizenry, concept of 41
citizenship 185; European Union (EU) 4; notion of 41
civil and political rights (CPR) 7, 9, 182, 188; constitutionalization 189; defence 188; domain of 187
civil movement 98
civil populations 159
Civil Rights Movement 110
civil society organizations 152, 159, 212
Clapham, A. 84

classic democratic theory 129
COE Commissioner of Human Rights 191–192
collective action 114
Collective Complaints Procedure 188
collective entities 110
collective rights/individual rights 109–116
command-and-control principle 81
Commission on Human Rights 24, 25, 54; *ad hoc* by 25; disappearance 25; thematic mechanism 26
Committee on the Elimination of Racial Discrimination (CERD) 190
Common Foreign and Security Policy (CFSP) 199, 201, 205
communal law 112
communications 35; with civil society's organizations 159; with international bodies 158–160
Compensatory Constitutionalism 10
Conference on Security and Cooperation in Europe (CSCE) 100
"conscientious objection" 104
constitutional continental theory 129
constitutional democracy 130
constitutional function 2, 30–34, 36, 60, 65; privatization 65, 127, 189; of state 187
constitutionalization/constitutionalism 1, 2, 116, 139, 167; core concepts 86; cosmopolitan paradigm of 85; of international law 29, 36, 53, 77, 180; multilevel 2; principles of 76, 86
constitutional law 40–43, 77–79, 126; function 54; influence on 43; internationalization 180; international law and 42, 51, 52, 87, 140; paradigm of 110, 127–131; possible internationalization 41; progressive internationalization of 41; reciprocal challenge in 117
constitutional safeguards 139
Constitution of Greece (2008) 60
"constructive dialogue" 31–33, 190
contemporary constitutions 167
"content-based test" 168, 173
conventional system 31
Copenhagen Criteria (1993) 181
"cosmopolitan status," Kantian concept of 2
Council for Assisting Refugee Academics (CARA) 105
Council of Europe 183–192
Court of Justice of the European Union (CJEU) 29, 63, 104

criminal responsibility 62
Crowds 88

data protection 209
De Carreras, F. 187
Decaux, E. 116
decentralized power 65
Declaration on human rights defenders (DHRD) 3, 6, 9, 51; adoption 13, 54; architecture 42; backbone 51; constitutional function under 63–65; framework and draft 114, 132, 150; for instrumental rights 27, 147; in international arena 42; key rights articulated in 135; legal and social effects 137; legal framework by 11, 40, 109; legal recognition in 138; main focus 132; multilevel legal framework 42; principles in 86; right to protection *see* human rights protection; schematic analysis 147; UN Commentary of 155; UN Working Group on 8–17, 130; *see also* human rights defenders (HRDs)
de Miguel Bárcena, J. 163
democracy 60, 77–79, 130, 156; constitutional 130; EU action on 199–201; and human rights 211–216; and individuals 88; instrumental rights 163–174; and rule of law 65, 165
Der Himmel über Berlin 81
Diagne, S. B. 7
dictatorship 12, 60, 79, 98, 110, 111, 153
digital attacks 103
dissent: instrumental rights 163–174; intellectual dimensions 99; movement 98; notion of 101; protest and 170; rule of law and 170
domestic law 16, 56, 59, 162, 163; and human rights treaties 154; regional systems of 51; UN Charter and human rights treaties in 63–65
Dominguez Redondo, E. 25
Donnelly, J. 52
Duchamp, Marcel 105
Dupuy, P.-M. 5

ECJ 104, 128, 143
Economic Commission for Europe 75
Economic Commission for Latin America and the Caribbean (ECLAC) 55, 75
economic, social, and cultural rights (ESCR) 7
ECOSOC: Commission on Human Rights 25; Resolution 1235 25; subsidiary body 24

Eco, U. 55
Eguren Fernández, L. E. 96, 164, 165
Eide, A. 30
Einstein Albert 105, 204
Enrich, M. 185
"environmental human rights defenders" 75
environmental rights 5; protection of 77
environmental rule of law 76
Erica-Irene Daes 8, 9
Escazú Agreement 55, 75–77
Estatuto de autonomía 79
EU Action Plan on Human Rights and Democracy 2020–2024 199–201, 214, 215
EU Fundamental Rights Agency (FRA) 207–209
European Charter of Fundamental Rights (ECFR) 104, 129, 142, 143, 149, 150, 169, 181, 185
European Committee of Social Rights (ECtSR) 188
European Convention on Human Rights (ECHR) 7, 12, 29, 30, 126, 129, 143, 150, 167, 180, 185, 186, 189; civil and political rights 188; extraterritorial application 186; and human rights defenders (HRDs) 184–191
European Court of Human Rights (ECtHR) 30, 40, 52, 56, 62, 81, 82, 172, 187, 190, 191; case law of 52, 86, 117, 156, 158; Charter on Fundamental Rights 104; freedom of expression 112; and institutional guarantees 30; judiciary case law of 40; protection 154; Special Procedures and 40
European External Action Service (EEAS) 55, 199, 201, 205, 213
European Instrument Democracy and Human Rights (EIDHR) 213, 215
European Social Charter 188
European Trade Union Confederation (ETUC) 188
European Union (EU): *ad extra* protection 133, 199; *ad intra* protection 143, 181, 209, 211; asylum system 4; citizenship 4, 166, 207; crucial aspect in 143; delegations 181; on democracy 199–201; "Equality Directives" 108; external action 202–205; foreign policy 128; framework 29; freedom, security, and justice 205–211; guidelines on HRDs 74, 211–216; of HRDs 1; integration process 202; internal legal framework 73; international action 202; judiciary system in 209–211; merits 40; policy on defenders 181; public institutions 203; social movements 143
European Union External Action 4
exercising instrumental human rights 131–136

Fabre-Alibert, V. 172
federal/quasi-federal states 65
female human rights defenders 155
"fighting words" 61, 168–169
Final Helsinki Act 97, 98, 193
Forst, Michel 26, 71, 75
FRA 106–107, and human rights defenders 207–208
freedom of assembly 112–113, 150–152
freedom of association 114–116, 152–153
freedom of expression 7, 11, 86, 111, 112, 170
freedom of movement 143, 206
freedom of speech 61
freedom of thought 102–106
fundamental rights guarantees 41, 85
Future of Mankind, The (Jaspers) 62

Gardbaum, S. 50
Gavara de Cara, J. C. 3, 49, 57, 137, 189
genocide 78; in Rwanda 61
Genovés, Juan 111
German academics 105
German Basic Law (1949) 118, 129
Gillion, D. Q. 113
Global Alliance for National Human Rights Institutions (GANHRI) 106
global constitutionalism 54, 130, 139, 180; concept of 1; despite trends 88; function 53; parameters in 2; Peters' theory on 60; process 16
globalization 5
Gómez Sánchez, Y. 5, 13, 49, 112, 137
González Domínguez, M. 112
Goodman, R. 26
Gorbachev, Mikhail 82
groups, as human rights defenders 109–116; and right to freedom of assembly 112–113; and right to freedom of association 114–116
Guillen, F. 149
Guterres, Antonio 75
Gutter, J. 25

Habermas, J. 2, 130, 132, 166
Hammarberg, Thomas 16

hate speech, criteria and limits on 59–63
Haubrich, Josef 82
Helsinki Final Act (1975) 12, 97–101
Higgins, John 83
Hodgson, D. 8, 13
homogeneous legal system 42
Homo Sacer 49
Horvath, R. 99
human condition 40–43, 131, 132; principle of 126
Human Condition, The (Arendt) 6
human dignity 41, 126, 138, 183; overcomes sovereignty 50; principle 36, 163, 203; and sovereignty 117
human rights: activism 43; defence of 158–159; democracy and 211–216; domain of 62; EU action on 199–201; fundamental rights and 53; Inter-American system of 7, 29; internationalization 49; multilevel system of 155; NGOs working in 99; non-conventional system 25; protection and promotion 182; regional systems of 156; right to promote and protect *see* human rights protection; Second World War 138; strive for 116–120, 163; struggle for 134; universality 150; violations 25, 52, 78, 109, 133; weakened or failed states for 53; *see also* human rights protection
Human Rights Act (1998) 77
Human Rights Committee 31
human rights defenders (HRDs): Amnesty International 27; asylum or protection for 4; binomial convergence in 6; COE Commissioner of Human Rights 191–192; concept of 60, 96, 109; and Council of Europe 183–192; criminal persecution 210; definition 74; DHRD 50; emergence 3, 13, 53, 117, 127–131; and environmental defenders 75; in environmental matters 75–77; EU guidelines on 74, 170, 181; and European Court of Human Rights 184–191; European Union *see* European Union (EU); female 155; FRA and 207–209; framework 3; freedom and security for 149; and fundamental rights 205; global framework and human condition 40–43; groups and 109–116; guarantees of 138, 140; and individual responsibility 59–63; intellectual 101–106; journalists and 155; legal framework 57, 60; legal recognition of 179; levels 1; LGBT 182; limitations 72; limits and challenges 77–79; multilevel framework on 27; multilevel system for 87, 136, 180; national human rights institutions and 106–108, 201; OAS Rapporteurship on 39; OSCE Guidelines on 192–194; *per se* 71, 73; physical protection of 14; precedent for 97–101; protection and promotion *see* human rights protection; public officers 72–73; in regional human rights systems 179–183; rights' guarantees 136; Secretary General on 26; security and protection 134, 136; self-identification as 3; Special Procedure on *see* UN Special Procedure; Special Rapporteur on *see* Special Rapporteurship; status of 60; thematic mechanism on 27; UN Special Representative of 28, 74; work 142; *see also* Declaration on human rights defenders (DHRD); human rights
human rights protection 24, 117; abuse of rights 59–63; asymmetric enforcement 140–143; exercising instrumental 131–136; hate speech, criteria and limits on 59–63; individual responsibility 59–63; individuals and 54–59; instrumental rights *see* instrumental rights; international humanitarian law 59–63; internationalization 49; legal recognition of 140; multilevel guarantees 136–140; negative dimension 56; positive dimension 56; and promotion 5–6, 10, 15, 28; responsible for 50
human rights treaties 2; in domestic law 63–65, 154; limitative clauses in 153

individual-centered international community 41
individualization, of international law 5, 13, 40, 49, 50, 77, 110, 117, 126, 128, 130, 131, 164, 183, 184
individual rights 109–116; social function of 154
individuals/individualism 97–101; concept of 62; democracy and 88; dissolution 88; exercise 42; and legal pluralism 126; and privatization 65; right for protection 137
Ingleton, D. 16, 38
innovative constitutional function 60
instrumental rights 140–143; communicate with international bodies 158–160; democracy 163–174; DHRD for 27, 147; discussion of new ideas 157–158;

dissent 163–174; right to access 158–160; right to access funding 161–163; right to an effective remedy 160–161; right to be protected 148–150; right to freedom of assembly 150–152; right to freedom of association 152–153; right to freedom of opinion and expression 153–155; right to protest 155–157
intellectual freedom 105, 106, 204
intellectual human rights defenders 101–106
intent 61, 62
Interamerican Court of Human Rights 112
Inter-American system 141, 142, 148; of human rights 7, 29
internal legal system 42
international civil society 5, 24
International Commission of Jurists 99–101
international community 4, 14; individual-centered 41; individuals and duties for 65; state-centered 41
International Covenant on Civil and Political Rights (ICCPR) 151, 152, 154, 161, 190
International Criminal Court Statute 126
international humanitarian law (IHL) 36, 37, 41, 54, 59–63, 137
international individualism 131
international institutional guarantee 27–28, 30, 32, 33, 40, 87, 138
internationalization: of constitutional law 41, 180; of fundamental rights guarantees 85; of human rights 49; possible 41; process 42; progressive 41
international law 36, 126; constitutionalization 29, 36, 77, 180; and constitutional law 42, 51, 52, 77–79, 87, 140; domain 3; domestic and 29; humanization of 41, 54; individualization 5, 13, 40, 49, 50, 77, 110, 126, 128, 130, 131, 164, 183, 184; paradigm 41, 127–131; philosophy 5; principles of 142; sovereign state in 49; subject in 84
international NGOs 10, 161
ius puniendi 77

Janowiec and Others v. Russia (2013) 81
Jaspers, K. 62, 80, 81
Jilani, Hina 26, 28, 38, 58, 135
Jones, M. 4, 104, 105, 204
Joo, H. 99

judicial functions 186
judiciary case law 40
judiciary system, in European Union 209–211
Juliana v. the United States (2020) 52
jurisdiction 2, 51, 168

Kennedy, John Fitzgerald 83
Kiai, Maina 156
Kirchheimer, Otto 82
Kononov v. Latvia 62
Kumm, M. 41, 85, 86, 166, 180

language 61
Lauren, Gordon 158
Lawlor, Mary 26, 27
Lawson, Mary 135
Lee, J. H. 41
"legal force" 13
legal pluralism 119, 126
legitimacy 53; of state power 118
Levine, J. 101, 102, 171
lex generalis 173
lex specialis 173, 174

majoritarian principles 65
The Manden Charter 7
Marcuse, Herbert 82
Marrani, D. 5, 119, 140, 141
Martin-Ortega, O. 65
Masse un Macht (Canetti) 88
McCarthy, Joseph 83
McChesney, A. 12, 57, 97, 100, 101
McCorquodale, R. 84
Moeckli, D. 114
Mosser, C. 194
Mukwege, Denis 43
multilateral international law 1
multilevel constitutionalism 2, 5, 87
multilevel governance 3
multilevel guarantees 136–140
multilevel legal framework 4, 5, 17, 42, 111; on human rights defenders 27; state and the cosmopolitan society 50; UN Special Procedure 38–40
multilevel system 179; of human rights 155; for human rights defenders (HRDs) 87, 136, 180
Murray, R. 107

Nah, M. A. 16, 38
national human rights institutions (NHRI) 106–108, 128, 188; composition 107;

goal 106; Human Rights Council 108; members and staff 107; NGOs and 106
National Preventive Mechanisms (NPM) 107–108
nation-state law 132–133
Nazi persecution 105
negative state obligations 179
non-binding method 35
non-conventional system 25
non-governmental organizations (NGOs) 10, 11, 13, 109–116; in law-making 24; and NHRIs 106; working in human rights 99
non-intervention policy 25
non-state actors 24, 27, 56, 65, 77, 83–84, 115, 133, 134, 138, 140; negative aspects 182
non-violent action 111, 152
"No Power to Act" 1946-1966 25
Nuremberg Trials 80, 164

Oetheimer, M. 154–168–169–172
Office for Democratic Institutions and Human Rights (ODIHR) 193
Organization of American States (OAS) 38–39
Orwell, George 62
OSCE Guidelines, on human rights defenders 192–194
Owen, N. 53

Parekh, S. 170
Paris Agreement 78
Paris Principles 72, 106–107, 116
Parra Cortés, R. 56
participation, notion of 83
Patel, C. 96, 164, 165
people, concept of 129
Pérez Luño, A. E. 141
Pérez-Reverte, A. 81
Peters, A. 2, 10, 13, 16, 41, 60, 117, 130, 138, 164, 166, 167, 169, 180, 183, 194
Piçarra, N. 143, 149, 150, 206
Pizarro Sotomayor, A. 30, 190
"plural deliberation" 13
Policastro, P. 3
positive state obligations 179
"possession paradox" 52
possible internationalization, of constitutional law 41
privatization: of constitutional functions 65, 127, 189; individualism and 65
progressive internationalization, of constitutional law 41

pro-human rights groups 98
protectdefenders.eu 133, 181, 203
"protoconstitution" 2
public institutions 36, 72
public officers 72–73

quasi-federal states 65
quasi-jurisdictional guarantees 142
Quinn, R. 101, 102, 171

racial discrimination 6
raison d'être 36, 110
refugee system 204
Regional Agreement 55
regional human rights systems 7, 41, 74; in Europe 179–183
Reparation for Injuries Suffered in the Service of the United Nations 83–85
Resolution 60/251 26
Reuter, Walter 82
right to access 158–160
right to access funding 161–163
right to be protected 148–150
right to freedom of assembly 112–113, 150–152
right to freedom of association 152–153
right to freedom of expression 7, 11
right to freedom of opinion and expression 153–155
"right to have rights" 2, 119–120, 163
right to promote and protect *see* human rights protection
right to protest 155–157
Rodley, N. 11, 12, 57, 97, 158
Roskis, Edgar 61
Rovira Viñas, A. 41, 87, 128, 169
rule of law 76, 86, 165, 207

Sakharov, Andrei 98
Samizdat 98–99
Savage, J. 16, 38
School of Frankfurt 82
Sekaggya, M. 15, 26, 106, 135
self-identity 3
Shaw, M. N. 24
Silveira, A. 206, 207
social and economic rights 143, 182, 189
social movements 98, 110, 151
solidarity, concept of 207
sovereignty 85, 117, 185; principle of 126, 203
Soviet dissent 97–101
Spanish Constitution (1978) 79, 110, 128
Spanish constitutional system 77

Special Rapporteurship 24, 25, 29, 30–34, 59, 71, 75, 103, 114, 134, 139, 140, 147, 152, 153, 157, 161, 164, 166, 180, 190, 209–211
Special Representative, on HRDs 28
state actors 27, 134, 138
state-based legal framework 53
state-centered international community 41
state constitutional legitimacy 206
state-nation, framework 1
state obligation 148; positive and negative 179
Steinbrück Platise, M. 194
Steiner, H. 26
Steinerte, E. 107
strive for human rights 116–120, 163
sui generis 203
supranational legal systems 149

tabula rasa 80
Tajadura, J. 163
Taro, Gerda 82
Tenorio Sánchez, P. J. 42, 155
thematic mechanisms: creation of 24; Human Rights Council 26; and regional human rights systems 41; Special Procedures as 31
Tiananmen Square in China (1989) 12
Tilly, C. 113, 151
Tomuschat, C. 183
Toope, S. 85
Torres del Moral, A. 128
totalitarianism 98, 153
Treaty on European Union (TEU) 5, 142, 199
Trump, Donald 78

Ubuntu 7–8
UN Charter 2, 59; constitutional nature 63; in domestic law 60, 63–65; and human rights treaties 60, 63–65, 165; limits or violations of 63
UN Declaration on human rights defenders 13–17
"under national law" 149
UN Environment Programme (UNEP) 76
UN Environment Rule of Law 56
UNESCO Intangible Cultural Heritage 7
UN General Assembly 8, 9, 25
UN Human Rights Commission on Human Rights 8

UN Human Rights Council (HRC) 26, 28
United Nations Vienna Declaration of 1993 188
Universal Declaration of Human Rights (UDHR) 117, 126, 128
universality 42, 154
universal personhood 6
UN Special Procedure 24, 190; action in response 25; allegations 34–38; challenging questions 29; Code of Conduct 33; constitutional function 30–34; creation of 24; dealing with communication 35; DHRD and practice 55; duplication of procedures 30–34; framework 26; function 31; Human Rights Council 26; international and constitutional law 40–43; multilevel legal framework 38–40; principal functions 32; situation 27–38; as thematic mechanisms 31
UN Working Group 9, 54, 57, 100; debates 96, 101, 211; on Declaration on human rights defenders 8–17; International Commission of Jurists in 99–101; mandate 11; "urgent action" procedure 190
urgent appeals 34–38

Venzke, I. 29, 166
Vienna Conference (1993) 12
Vienna Convention on the Law of Treaties 13
Vienna Declaration (1993) 64
"Vigilant citizenry," notion of 170
Villarreal, P. 207
violations, of human rights 25, 35, 52, 78, 133
violence 60, 151; in criminal law 61; by non-direct physical 62
violent action 111
Vogelfanger, A. D. 115
von Bogdandy, A. 29, 166, 207
vulnerable groups, of defenders 182

Wapner, P. 24
whistleblowers 73
Wildhaber, L. 158, 184
Wood, L. J. 113, 151
World Conference on Human Rights 9

Yeh, J. R. 41, 180

zoón politikón 6, 49

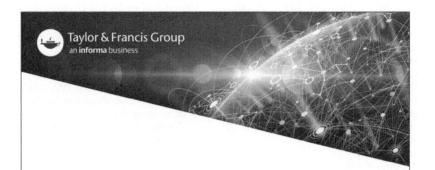